"Stephen Hawley Martin makes a bold claim that this enlightening book could save the world. It certainly could change your life, if you put the ideas into practice for yourself. And if you believe that one person's changes can impact others, bringing about a bigger shift, then maybe the author is right."

Alice Berger
Bergers Book Reviews

"Excellent book . . . As one who believes that the universe and my role in it are part of something both magic and collective, this book was akin to getting a spiritual GPS loaded with the latest satellite maps. It is well worth rereading and sharing with fellow travelers."

John R. Clark, M.ED, MLIS-Librarian, Hartland, Maine
for TCM Reviews

"This is not a book of magic in the medieval sense, but it is a book of attainable MAGIC for the growth of the individual fortunate enough to come upon this wise, immensely readable book."

Grady Harp,
Art & Literary Critic

"Very Highly Recommended . . . a good read that will educate the inquisitive mind and help readers shift to higher consciousness before 2012. It is a highly interesting book that will make readers 'think' about important issues in life."

Liana Metal
Midwest Book Review

"Martin delivers a real eye opener that will definitely give you something to think about. It is an engaging read that is well explained for complete understanding. Topics are explained through illustrations and substantial evidence in science and real life experiences. *The Truth* has all the right tips to bring about a great change in our universe and a greater change in ourselves."

Tempestt Patterson
Book Reviewer

"Martin's book puts life into perspective! Thank you Mr. Martin!"

Eva Herr,
Author, *Agape: The Intent of the Soul*
and Host of BBS Radio's "Infinite Consciousness"

"This book is filled with spiritual truth and techniques in a clear, simple fashion without any kooky stuff thrown in. I recommend it for people on a true spiritual journey and those who are questioning the reality they find themselves in."

Meria Heller
Producer/Host, the Meria Show

"What differentiates [this] book from many other new-agey, self-help type volumes is his extensive use of current scientific study to substantiate his ideas. His bibliography at the end of the book includes citations of Stephen Jay Gould, Elizabeth Kübler-Ross, and Henry P. Strapp. [The author] has clearly done his research, and it shows in his thoughtful, approachable work. His engaging writing style takes difficult scientific and philosophical ideas and makes them accessible to the everyday reader."

Elizabeth Schulenburg,
BookLoons Reviews

"5 Stars . . . I found *The Truth* to be intelligently written and inspiring. It brought me to a higher level of understanding . . . "

Paige Lovitt,
ReaderViews.com

"Through case studies and a worthy summary of current scientific discovery, Martin helps to prove that the fearful mythical god is no less than you and I. The world is of our making and as the old paradigms begin to crumble under their own absurdity, read *THE TRUTH* and discover that it is not 'out there,' it is within."

Philip F. Harris
Award winning author and
nationally syndicated writer

The Truth

What You Must Know Before December 21, 2012

Also by
Stephen Hawley Martin

IN MY FATHER'S HOUSE
A Metaphysical Thriller

DEATH IN ADVERTISING
A Whodunit

SUCCESS! Through Auto Hypnosis
(An Audio CD)

30 DAYS TO PURPOSE AND PROSPERITY
(A Workbook and Audio CD)

LEAN ENTERPRISE LEADER
How to Get Things Done without Doing It All Yourself

LEAN ADVERTISING
How to Get Breakthough Work Faster and Cheaper

A WITCH IN THE FAMILY
An Award-Winning Author Investigates His Ancestor's
Trial and Execution

The Truth

What You Must Know Before December 21, 2012

by

Stephen Hawley Martin

RICHMOND, VIRGINIA

ISBN 10: 1-892538-21-0
ISBN 13: 978-1-892538-21-5

If your bookseller does not have this book in stock,
it can be ordered directly from the publisher.
More information can be found at the
Web site shown below,
or call our toll-free number.

The Oaklea Press
6912-B Three Chopt Road
Richmond, Virginia 23226

Voice: 1-800-295-4066
Facsimile: 1-804-281-5686
Email: Orders@OakleaPress.com

Web site: http://www.OakleaPress.com

Publisher's Note:

Earlier versions of parts of this book were published in 2002
under the title *Keys to the Kingdom and the Life You Want*

For the delights of my life,
Hawley, Hannah Grace, and Hans

CONTENTS

Preface: The Value of This Book to You

Down through the ages only a tiny percentage of the world's population has known The Truth. A few mystics in every age have known intuitively. At different times a sizable number of people have caught a glimpse, such as the followers of "The Way" in the first century of the common era known as Gnostics. But The Truth has rarely if ever been put into easily comprehensible words as will be done in this book. Most who have known The Truth have guarded it out of the fear of what might happen if the uneducated masses got a hold of it. This is the reason for and the origin of some secret societies, which have kept The Truth alive in their inner circles. The Rosicrucians is one of which I have been a member. The history of that order maintains it was passed down from one generation to the next from the time of ancient Egypt.

It is now possible for all to know. The world is ready. This has come to pass in the nick of time because the life of our planet and the human race has reached a critical stage and may depend on it. Signs are everywhere. The ancient Mayans, for example, believed the world would end in the year 2012. Some calculate the exact day as December 21. The I CHING, written 5,000 years ago in China, points to the very same date — December 21, 2012. A computer program called the Web Bot, developed in the late 1990s to predict which stocks and industries were emerging as good investments — the computer program that accurately predicted the 9/11 attacks — indicates that an earth shattering, catastrophic event will take place in 2012. Some believe a meteor such as killed the dinosaurs will hit the earth, others that nuclear war or a plague will strike. Some say the seas will rise from melting polar ice and flood the world's great cities along seacoasts. Others believe the earth will slip on its axis and the poles will slide into new positions. This has apparently happened before in the geological history of the earth. Evidence

11

indicates Alaska once was traversed by the equator.

Many in the New Consciousness movement say this sort of physical catastrophe may or may not happen, but that the real change will be a shift in humanity's consciousness to a new and higher level — that this is what will mark the end of the world as we know it, and the beginning of the new.

Let's hope this view is correct.

Others say that the passageway through 2012 will be a time of tribulation and that many will perish, or as they say, "Pass into another dimension." Those who do survive will be the ones who make the shift to higher consciousness. Not all will make this shift, however, because they will be either unwilling or unable.

But no one really knows.

The good news is that you can take part in this consciousness shift right now, today, in the relatively short time it takes to read this book. The shift is one you will want to have made whether or not disaster strikes, and doing so will not be difficult. This book will tell you The Truth about life, and if you will keep an open mind, it will convince you of the veracity of The Truth.

Consider the reward. At the conclusion of this book — when you have finished and digested what it has to say — you will know The Truth and its major ramifications.

And you know what? The Truth will set you free.

And that's no lie.

STEPHEN HAWLEY MARTIN
July, 2008

Chapter One: The Truth Is Revealed

A few days before writing this, on July 16, 2008, I interviewed a man named Stephen Braude for my weekly radio show, *The Truth About Life*. Dr. Braude is a tenured professor of philosophy at the University of Maryland Baltimore County, who investigates cases of the paranormal. I'd read his latest book, *The Gold Leaf Lady and Other Parapsychological Investigations* (The University of Chicago Press, 2007), and wanted to talk with him about it.

The interview did not disappoint. Dr. Braude related several well documented and amazing stories of mind over matter, but perhaps the most fantastic, as well as the one that supports the thesis of this book most directly, had to do with Katie, a woman born in Tennessee, the tenth of twelve children. Katie is apparently a simple woman. Illiterate, she lives in Florida with her husband and works as a domestic. She is also a psychic who has had documented successes helping the police solve crimes. In one instance she was able to describe the details of the case so thoroughly and accurately, the police regarded her as a suspect until those actually responsible were apprehended. She apparently also apports objects — in other words, she somehow causes them to disappear in one place and reappear in another. And that's not all. Seeds reportedly germinate rapidly in her cupped hands. Observers have claimed to have seen her bend metal, and she is both a healer and a medium or channel. Being illiterate, she cannot read or write in her native English, but she has been video taped writing quatrains in medieval French similar both in style and content to the actual quatrains of Nostradamus. But most amazing, perhaps, is what appears spontaneously on her skin — on her hands, face, arms, legs, back — apparently out of thin air. It looks like gold leaf, a thin version of the wrapping on a Hersey's Kiss.

Katie cannot control when this happens, but Dr. Braude and other witnesses have seen the foil materialize firsthand. He has even video taped it appearing on her skin and taken the foil to be analyzed. It turns out not to be gold at all, but brass — approximately 80 percent copper and 20 percent zinc.

Dr. Braude thinks there's a reason she produces brass and not gold. I'll explain shortly, but first let me say that eyewitness reports even by credible witnesses such as Dr. Braude and other researchers who have studied Katie are not going to convince ardent skeptics. Even the video tape Dr. Braude took won't convince them because only one camera was used. A person viewing the tape cannot be sure what Katie might be doing with her hands, which are out of the frame. Nevertheless, Dr. Braude assured me he has seen the foil take form, and Katie is, in his words, "the real deal." Even so, I have no doubt some skeptics would say they don't believe Katie produces brass foil on her skin even if they, themselves, saw it happen. I know this because I have interviewed such people on my show.

There is a reason. Much of science today is based on an erroneous assumption, and for some this erroneous assumption has become dogma engraved in stone. Many scientific beliefs today are built on this tenet. Showing it to be in error will mean they will have to be discarded. Nevertheless, my intention is for this book to dispel this erroneous assumption and to make it socially acceptable for scientists to believe The Truth no matter how hard those who remain in denial may fight against it. This can and will happen, I believe, because according to studies that have been conducted recently on this subject, most scientists are open minded and willing to review the facts about paranormal phenomena. If the facts are there, they say they are willing to adjust their thinking. But at present, it appears newly enlightened scientists often keep quiet about their beliefs. This is because a small minority of skeptics in the scientific community are very vocal and ready to lash out at anyone who gets out of line and questions sacred dogma. I once interviewed a fellow on my radio show who fell into this category. I laid out the facts for him and my audience. He huffed and he puffed and refused to listen. He put forth silly and stupid arguments. I felt sorry for him.

He was an older gentleman, and had spend his life believing a falsehood. No wonder it was practically impossible for him to accept The Truth. No wonder he made a fool of himself.

This is not difficult to understand. If a person has spent his life writing books and teaching several generations of students information that turns out to have been wrong, what is true would be hard to accept. The first reaction would naturally be denial. Even if that person was open-minded, he or she would have to pass through the five classic stages on the way to acceptance of a major loss or change: Denial, anger, bargaining, depression, and acceptance. One of my recent radio show guests, Oxford University graduate Chris Carter, author of the book *PARAPSYCHOLOGY AND THE SKEPTICS: A Scientific Argument for the Existence of ESP*, thinks many of these ardent skeptics will *never* change. He said he believes that it will take a generation for The Truth to be widely known. We will simply have to wait for the diehards to die off.

It has always been this way down through history. There is nothing new about those in authority stonewalling against the dissemination of new information that would upset their cherished world view — a world view that keeps them in power. Nicolaus Copernicus (February 19, 1473 – May 24, 1543), for example, was able to determine that the sun was at the center of the solar system. The Church — which was the authority back then as science is today — pretty much ignored this concept because it did not go along with accepted canon that held the earth was the center of everything. Hey, if God made it, why would he put it out there hurling around the sun?

Then along came Galileo Galilei (15 February 1564 – 8 January 1642) a century later. Galileo — among other things an astronomer — championed Copernicus's assertion as proven fact. Then Galileo started having to watch his back because this was heresy. At that time people were being burned at the stake for less. Indeed, the leaders of the Church told Galileo he'd better recant, and Galileo did. As a result, he got off easy by spending the final years of his life under house arrest on orders of the Inquisition.

So, Dr. Braude and others have actually seen Katie brass foil appear on Katie's skin, and Dr. Braude has video taped it. Why would anyone say it must be done by trickery?

Here's the problem: It has to be her mind that makes it happen. There is no other plausible explanation. In fact Dr. Braude believes she produces brass rather than gold for a reason. Katie has a very difficult and tense relationship with her husband. Once she apported a carving set. It just appeared. And her husband — apparently nonplussed — said, "So what? It's not *worth* anything." Soon afterward, gold colored foil began appearing on Katie's skin. But it wasn't gold, it was *fool's* gold — brass. Dr. Braude thinks this is how she gets back at her husband.

Katie generates brass foil with her mind. This may be amazing. It may land her in *Ripley's Believe It or Not*. But what would science possibly have against that?

A lot. You see, the erroneous tenet of establishment science is that intelligence and awareness came about as a result of evolution. Through a series of accidents and lucky breaks that defy the odds and the second law of thermal dynamics,[1] humans through natural selection have evolved such complex assemblies such as eyes, kidneys, ears, livers and so forth, and ultimately the most complex assembly of all, a brain. No matter that this has not been demonstrated or proven, and that Darwin's theory is about plant and animal species adapting to different environments — which, by the way, they clearly do. According to the erroneous tenet, before the brain there was no intelligence — no awareness. But the brain, with its billions of neurons — and electrons jumping across synapses — creates the rainbow-like "illusion" we call awareness.

Thought and awareness are supposed to be the result of

---

[1] The second law of thermodynamics is an expression of the universal law of increasing entropy, which says that things in a closed system will break down over time. In other words, your old car will not repair itself by itself. It's just going to get worse and fall apart as time goes by if someone doesn't do something about it. This being a universal law, how did DNA form in the first place? How did DNA become one celled animals? How did one celled animals develop into complex organisms, et cetera?

processes going on inside the brain. Mental activity is supposed to be completely inside our heads. The mind is thought to be like a computer without the Internet — isolated. It can't go outside and link up with other minds to cause ESP and other psychic phenomena, and it certainly cannot spontaneously generate brass foil on Katie's skin.

But it can and it does because the assumption that the brain creates mind and awareness is wrong. The evidence clearly indicates mind is the primal stuff of the universe. This can be seen simply by observing nature. Consider a sunflower. It has no brain. According to the erroneous tenet, it can have no awareness. But it does have awareness. It turns its face to the sun and it follows the sun across the sky from sunrise to dusk. That has to require some form of awareness.

There's no doubt about it. Living plants are aware. Scientifically constructed, double blind experiments by researchers, including theoretical biophysicist of the University of Marburg in Germany, Fritz-Albert Popp, have demonstrated this.[2] And this isn't news. About 40 years ago a fellow named Cleve Backster demonstrated plants are aware using polygraph machines. In Backster's most famous experiment, he hooked up plants in his office suite to polygraph machines and then set up a device to randomly dump a cup of living brine shrimp into a pot of boiling water. The needles on the polygraph machines would go wild each time the shrimp hit the water and went to their deaths.

But what led Cleve Backster to construct and carry out this experiment may be even more of an eye-opener. Lynne McTaggart, author of *The Field: The Quest for the Secret Force of the Universe,* told the following story on my show early in 2008.

Backster was and is an expert on polygraph machines and their operation — in other words, lie detectors. One evening about 40 years ago when Backster was a young man, he was sitting in his

---

[2] *Integrative Biophysics: Biophotonics* by Fritz-Albert Popp (Editor), L.V. Beloussov (Editor), Springer, February 2003.

office with nothing much to do. His eyes fell on an office plant and he had an idea. He decided to hook up one of his machines to the plant and see if he could get it to react. He hooked up the machine and poured a glass of water into the soil around it. Nothing happened. The polygraph registered boredom.

Backster started thinking about what he might do to get a reaction out of the plant, and he had an idea.

"I think I'll *burn* one of its leaves."

At that moment, the polygraph machine went wild. The plant had reacted to his thought! The more Backster thought about burning the plant, the more the needle on the polygraph machine went ballistic.

Cleve Backster conducted many experiments along these lines which are described in his book, *Primary Perception: Bio Communication with Plants, Living Foods, and Human Cells* (White Rose Millennium Press, 2003).

People who have what's called green thumbs may think it is because they send kind thoughts to their plants. It may be true that kind thoughts help make happy plants, but research demonstrates thoughts are not sent and received. Thoughts just are. They are non local — part of the mind we and everything and everyone share. This was demonstrated by a lifelong paranormal researcher named Stephan A. Schwartz, author of the book *OPENING TO THE INFINITE: The Art and Science of Nonlocal Awareness* (Nemoseen Media, 2007). His research proves telepathy does not work by electromagnetic waves being sent and received like a walky-talky or radio and TV, but rather, that mind and thought are ubiquitous. In one experiment Schwartz lowered researchers in a submarine to a water depth below which electromagnetic waves — regardless of their frequency or strength — simply cannot penetrate. ESP between researchers in the sub and those on the surface was shown to be at the same high level as and in no way diminished from what had been the case when all were located on the surface.

That plants read our minds is not the most dramatic proof the tenet that mind exists only inside the head is erroneous. What's coming up next demonstrates mind can change physical reality.

You may be aware that light behaves as though it consists of waves and of particles (photons). In 1803, a gentleman named Thomas Young demonstrated that light is waves by means of a simple experiment wherein he placed a screen with two parallel slits between a source of light — sunlight coming through a hole in a screen — and a wall. Each slit could be covered with a piece of material. These slits were razor thin, not as wide as the wavelength of the light. When waves of any kind pass through an opening that is not as wide as they are, the waves diffract. This was the case with one slit open. A fuzzy circle of light appeared on the wall.

When both slits were uncovered, alternating bands of light and darkness were seen, the center band being the brightest. You might call this a zebra pattern. The areas of light and dark resulted from what is known in wave mechanics as interference. Waves overlap and reinforce each other in some places and in others they cancel each other out. The bands of light on the wall were where one wave crest overlapped another crest. The dark areas were where a crest and a trough met and canceled each other out.

In 1905, Albert Einstein published a paper that proved light also behaves like particles, and he did so by using the photoelectric effect. When light hits the surface of a metal, it jars electrons loose from the atoms in the metal and sends them flying off as though they had been struck by tiny billiard balls. Light is both a wave and it is particles. This sort of paradox led scientists to develop quantum mechanics.

Now let's take a look at an experiment in which what the person conducting the experiment knows or doesn't know — what he thinks — changes the outcome. We set up the double slit experiment this time using a photon gun that fires only one photon at a time. This case is summarized, by the way, from an article entitled, "Faster Than What?" that can be found in the June 19, 1995 issue of *Newsweek*, which reported on a paper to be published by a well-known quantum physicist, Raymond Chiao, then teaching at the University of California at Berkeley. In July 2008 I reviewed the recap of the facts of this experiment as they are presented here with one of my radio show guests, the noted quantum physicist Henry P. Stapp, author of the book, *MINDFUL UNIVERSE: Quantum Mechanics and the Participating Observer* (Springer, 2007). He indicated I had captured them correctly.

Both slits were open and a detector was used to determined which slit a photon passed through. A record was made of where each hit. Only one photon was shot at a time, so one would suppose there could be and would be no interference. This was the case. The photons did not make the zebra pattern.

Now comes the twilight zone part. When the detector was turned off, and it was not known which slit a photon passed through, the zebra pattern appeared.

In the *Newsweek* article reporting on this, Noble-winning physicist Richard Feynman was quoted as saying this is the "central mystery" quantum mechanics, that something as intangible as knowledge — in this case, which slit a photon went through — changes something as concrete as a pattern on a screen. The erroneous scientific tenet certainly doesn't allow for this. It would seem ludicrous to even suggest that thought that remains inside a person's head would be capable of having an effect. Yet thought in the form of the certainty of having knowledge of which slit a proton passed through and where it hit does have a profound effect. When the researcher can access this knowledge, the zebra pattern simply does not occur. If he cannot, the zebra pattern appears. This was verified by setting up the experiment in several different ways. In the first, the detectors were in front of the two slits. In the second, researchers placed detectors between the screen and the two slits, i.e., after the photons had passed through the slits. As in the original experiment, knowing about a photon's behavior at the two slits made the zebra pattern vanish. When the detectors were switched off, the zebra stripes returned.

In a third variation, a detector was placed before the slits and a mechanism erased the knowledge after the photon had passed through. The same thing happened. The zebra pattern returned. No matter which way the experiment was set up — before the slits, after the slits, or before the slits and then erased — whether or not the researcher was able to know where each photon hit determined the presence of the zebra pattern, or the lack of it.

Versions of the experiment were carried out at the University of Munich and at the University of Maryland. The behavior of the photons, the researchers report, "is changed by how we are going to look at them."

The question is, how?

I think I know the answer. This was given in part by Gary Zukav in his book, *The Dancing Wu Li Masters: An Overview of the New Physics* (HarperOne, 2001):

". . . the philosophical implication of quantum mechanics is that all of the things in our universe (including us) that appear to exist independently are actually parts of one all-encompassing organic pattern, and that no parts of that pattern are ever really separate from it or from each other."

To this I would add that underlying this seamless organic pattern is mind and that mind is the ground of being of all that is. It seems to me everything in the physical universe comes from it. Quantum physicists have developed what they call "String Theory" to try to explain how subatomic particles form out of vibrations, but they don't say what exactly is vibrating, according to what I have read including *The Fabric of the Cosmos: Space, Time, and the Texture of Reality* (Alfred A. Knoph, 2004) by Rhodes Scholar and physicist, Brian Greene. I say it is mind. This One Mind is the medium of thought and, as is characteristic of mind, it is aware.

As mentioned above, in July 2008 the well-known quantum physicist, Dr. Henry Stapp was on my radio show and confirmed the facts of the double slit experiment as presented here. After laying out these facts, I told him of my theory that mind is the primal stuff of the universe, the ground of being. He said that what I proposed was possible — a plausible explanation that some physicists lean toward and by implication are pursuing — but more evidence was needed before it could be said to definitely be the case.

It seems to me Katie the Gold Leaf Lady is the smoking gun. Unless the eyewitnesses are lying and Dr. Braude's video is faked, through some subconscious process Katie produces a substance that is 80 percent copper and 20 percent zinc. In other words, copper and zinc are produced by her mind.

And why not? The physical universe had to come from something. One thing quantum physicists agree on is that the physical universe isn't really physical. It is vibrations. Subatomic particles are not particles at all. They are vibrations. They arise out of something that forms string-like vibrations and these string-like vibrations form atoms that in turn form molecules that in turn form matter. Why shouldn't this something be mind? It would make sense.

If this is the case, there is only one mind. My mind, your mind. The Universal Mind. All of it is connected and all is one. It follows that there is only one awareness — although we each appear to have our own separate and unique awareness. This is an illusion created by our brain and our senses. In the East they call this "Maya." More will be said about this later, but in brief our brains and our bodies are a way for awareness, or mind, to enter into and experience physical reality. Because we experience awareness through a focal point — our brain — via the medium of our eyes, ears, sense of smell, taste and touch, it seems to us that this is where our awareness is located. And it is. We are focal points of awareness within the a larger awareness often called the Universal Mind.

Mystics have been saying "All Is One" for millennia. I have had a number of people describe the experience of this on my radio show. For some it was brought about spontaneously when they were out in nature and experienced a sunrise or sunset. For others it happened as a result of a near death experience.

In his book, *The Rebirth of Nature, The Greening of Science and God*, Oxford educated bio chemist, Rupert Sheldrake, quotes a woman, an art teacher, who recounted an experience she had while walking on the Pangbourne Moors at the age of five. She puts into words what I believe many of us have felt at one time or another but perhaps later dismissed when our "rational" minds again got the upper hand:

> *Suddenly I seemed to see the mist as a shimmering gossamer tissue and the harebells, appearing here and there, seemed to shine with a brilliant fire. Somehow I understood that this was the living tissue of life itself, in which all that we call consciousness is embedded, appearing here and there as a shining focus of energy in the more diffused whole. In that moment I knew that I had my special place, as had all other things, animate and so-called inanimate, and that we were all part of this universal tissue which was both fragile yet immensely strong, and utterly good and beneficent.*

In early 2008 I interviewed, Timothy Freke, an English philosopher who has written more than twenty books on religion and spirituality. Tim says the experience of oneness is a perennial philosophy of most religious traditions. He explained on the air what he calls "Lucid Living," which he says is what one experiences when one wakes up to this reality. Tim has written a short book with that title in which he attempts to explain it. Essentially, he said that life on earth in a human body can be compared to a dream we might have. When we're dreaming, we are both a character within the dream and we are the one who is doing the dreaming. Of course, while we are having the dream, we may not realize it. But when we have a dream and realize we're dreaming while it's going on, we have what is called a lucid dream.

If you've ever had a lucid dream, you know that once you realize you're having it, you can direct the action. I have lucid dreams from time to time and when I do, I like to fly. I say to myself, hey, I'm having a dream. That's cool, let's have some fun. I start running, spread my wings, and take off like a B-29 of the end of a runway in southern England during World War Two.

Now, can life be like a dream that we can — as Tim Freke says — make lucid? Can we direct our lives as we can in a lucid dream? There are certainly accounts of people levitating and even flying — though mostly in the distant past. In general people no longer take these accounts seriously. But who knows? I suspect one reason Katie is able to produce brass foil, apport objects and do all the psychic things she can do is that she thinks she can. She doesn't know the tenets of modern science. She is illiterate. She didn't go to school. No one ever told her she couldn't do what she can clearly do, which is a reason she can. The same was true with people in days gone by.

One thing I do know is that once we make the shift in consciousness I've been talking about, which entails understanding who we really are, we can take control of our lives because we realize we control our own destiny and are not — as many believe — controlled by outside forces. The reason is simple. As mystics have said down through the ages, *All Is One.* A single intelligence underlies everything. We come from that intelligence and you might say, we *are* that intelligence. That is who you are. So is your neighbor and so is your enemy. All of us are connected. All of us are one.

Knowing that has got to change how you look at the world.

And that's The Truth.

In the next chapter we will begin to explore the ramifications. There are many and you may find some mind boggling. During the course of this book, we will also review an abundance of additional evidence that indicates The Truth is true.

Chapter Two: The Power of Belief

A startling realization came to me one evening some time ago after a local radio interview about one of my novels. It was evening. I was beat, having just spent an intense hour trying my best to be entertaining and witty. On my way home, I stopped at my local Seven Eleven for a bottle of beer. A sign caught my eye as I approached the register.

"We I.D. under 27 years of age."

I took my place in line behind a couple of teenagers with Slurpies. An acquaintance from college took the spot behind me, and we exchanged pleasantries. My turn came. I put the bottle on the counter and reached for my wallet.

The clerk eyed me. "Sorry, I'll have to see your I.D.," she said.

"Excuse me?" I said.

"I'm going to need to see your I.D.," she repeated.

"You're kidding," I said.

She let out an exasperated sigh. "No, I need to see your I.D. before I can sell you that beer."

I placed my driver's license it in her hand, turned to my friend, and gave a little shrug. Her mouth gaped. "It's true," she said, shaking her head. "You really do look young."

On the way home, I sipped, kept an eye out for police, and pondered the fact that I'd been asked to prove I was old enough to buy alcohol. You see, I was 55 years old at the time—more than twice what the clerk was required to I.D.

It's definitely true that I *feel* much younger. I can detect no difference in how I feel now and how I felt when I really was twenty-seven. I started wondering why, and after a while, a possibility surfaced in my mind. Thirty years before, when I was 25, I'd read an article about a study of people who'd been consuming large doses of vitamin E for ten years. The article said that no measurable signs of aging had occurred among them. So I went out and bought a bottle, and I'd been taking it since.

For years, I believed I wouldn't age. And for years, it seemed I didn't age.

Much later, I read that researchers had concluded that vitamin E in pill form cannot be *proven* to retard aging. As has often been the case, newer studies refute older ones. But I kept taking it anyway.

According to recent articles, we've come almost full circle. No researcher is ready to say vitamin E stops aging altogether, but new research indicates that taking the vitamin results in lower incidence of heart disease and cancer, while helping mitigate all sorts of health problems. Even so, I've come to believe that it may have worked for me in large measure due to the placebo effect. But it worked. Thirty years ago I read an article that said I wouldn't age if I took it. I expected it to work, so it did. If the following week I'd read another article that said the anti-aging qualities of vitamin E were hogwash, I probably would not have experienced the same result.

Belief is extremely potent. That, I believe, is a key factor in Katie's case. She wasn't "educated" enough to think was she was capable of was impossible.

The effectiveness of placebos, for example, has been demonstrated time and again in double-blind scientific tests. The placebo effect — the phenomenon of patients feeling better after taking dud pills — is seen throughout the field of medicine. One report says that after thousands of studies, hundreds of millions of prescriptions and tens of billions of dollars in sales, sugar pills are as effective at treating depression as antidepressants such as Prozac, Paxil and Zoloft. What's more, placebos cause profound changes in the same areas of the brain affected by these medicines, according to this research. For anyone who may still be in doubt, this adds evidence to that generated by the double slit experiment. Thoughts and beliefs can and do produce physical changes — in this case in our bodies.

The same research reports that placebos often outperform the medicines they're up against. For example, in a trial conducted in April, 2002, comparing the herbal remedy St. John's wort to Zoloft, St. John's wort fully cured 24 percent of the depressed people who received it. Zoloft cured 25 percent. But the placebo fully cured 32 percent.[3]

Taking what one believes to be real medicine sets up the expectation of results, and what a person expects to happen usually does happen. This book will explain why. It's been confirmed, for example, that in cultures where belief exists in voodoo or magic, people will actually die after being cursed by a shaman. It appears such a curse has no power on an outsider who doesn't believe. The expectation causes the result. If you've read my novel, *IN MY FATHER'S HOUSE,* you know I used this phenomenon as a factor in the plot. In my book, *A Witch in the Family,* I cited this phemonenon as part of what was behind the Salem witch hysteria of 1692.

Let me relate a real-life example of spontaneous healing that concerned a woman I've known for a dozen years.

Nancy is a minister's wife. She's a devout Christian — as firm a believer in her religion as a bushman who'd drop dead from a witch doctor's curse is in his. Some years ago, a lump more than half an inch in diameter was discovered in one of her breasts. Her doctor scheduled a biopsy.

A prayer group gathered at her home the night before this procedure was to take place. They prayed not that the lump would be benign, but rather, that it would disappear entirely.

Nancy is a member of a denomination that takes the Bible literally. In Matthew 18:19-20, Jesus is reported to have said, "Again, I tell you that if two of you on earth agree about anything you ask for, it will be done for you by my Father in heaven. For where two or three come together in my name, there am I with them."

As you can imagine, it was more than two or three. It was a

---

[3] "Against Depression, a Sugar Pill Is Hard to Beat," by Shankar Vedantam, *The Washington Post,* May 7, 2002.

living room full. As in my case and vitamin E, Nancy quite naturally expected the prayers to work.

Jesus also said, "Therefore I tell you, whatever you ask for in prayer, *believe* that you have received it, and it will be yours." (Mark 11:24) Notice the tense change in this verse. Jesus is saying to believe that you *already* have what you ask for and it will be given to you *in the future.* Jesus apparently knew that thoughts are things and that what we believe already exists — as in the case of the researchers in the double slit experiment — does indeed already exist in the nonphysical realm of spirit. It exists as a thought form. Thoughts are things, as we will see, ready to materialize on the physical plane.

A study carried out on the Discovery TV Channel gives an indication of what happens when someone believes and when someone does not believe. In this case, two researchers conducted the same ESP experiment in the same laboratory using the same equipment. They went to great pains to keep everything identical except for one thing. One researcher believed ESP was valid and the other did not. Both tests were supervised by impartial observers, including the Discovery Channel TV crew.

The experiment that employed the researcher who believed in ESP had a statistically significant number of correct scores, which meant that the experiment was a success. ESP was demonstrated scientifically to be real. But the number of correct hits in the experiment that had employed the doubting Thomas researcher fell within parameters that could be accounted for by chance. So this time the experiment failed to demonstrate the validity of ESP. Apparently, the one and only variable — belief — made the difference. The first researcher believed and the second didn't. Each got the result he expected. It has also been reported by researchers into the paranormal that even the presence of skeptics can lower or nullify positive results. Could their negative thoughts be be self-fulfilling? I suspect so.

The same phenomenon is at work in prayer by believers. Prayer works. Prayer is thought released into the subconscious. Prayers shape mind in a way that bolsters its natural tendency to organize matter in a way that is beneficial to life. Soon it will be clear to you precisely how this works, and in Chapter Nine we will cover in some depth the effects of prayer as demonstrated in scientifically-constructed, double-blind experiments.

But first, let's get back to Nancy. The next morning, upon self examination, the lump in her breast appeared to have vanished. But nonetheless Nancy kept her appointment at the hospital where her doctor conducted a thorough examination.

The lump indeed was gone. Not a trace could be found, and the bewildered doctor sent her home.

How could a solid lump of tissue disappear? Nancy's mind did it, the same way Katie's mind produced brass foil — through belief unfettered by doubt. We indeed create our own reality. What I believe to be a plausible explanation was given in lectures I came across given by a man named Thomas Troward. He first delivered them at Queens Gate at Edinburgh University in Scotland in 1904. Called *The Edinburgh Lectures on Mental Science,* they provide a rationale that fits perfectly with the two findings of research studies on prayer — that distance between those praying and the one being prayed for is not a factor, and that the one being prayed for does not have to know about the prayers on his or her behalf. How prayer works is simple, but let me lay some groundwork before I place the explanation before you.

It helps to begin by considering the difference that appears to exist between what we think of as "dead" matter and something we recognize as alive. A plant, such as the sunflower I mentioned in Chapter One, has a quality that sets it apart from a piece of steel. The sunflower will turn toward the sun under its own power. When first picked, it possesses a kind of glow. Thomas Troward called this quality the Life Force, or spirit. On the other hand, the piece of steel appears totally inert. Yet, we know now that at the quantum level, the steel is alive with motion. Quantum physicists tell us that motion or energy is what comprises all matter. Atoms and molecules are are energy. Vibrations. Many believe the universe is alive — a living thing. When the physicist, Henry P. Stapp, was on my radio show, I asked him about this. He confirmed the widely-held view by quantum physicists that the universe resembles a giant thinker.

I have come to picture it as the thought of an infinitely vast mind of organizing intelligence.

Back to the sunflower. By outward appearances it is alive and the steel is not. Few would argue this. But one might argue that a plant's state of "aliveness" is not the same as an animal's. Consider the difference in aliveness between a sunflower, an earthworm, and a goldfish. Each appears to be progressively more alive.

Now, let's add a dog, a three year old child, and a stand up comedian on the Tonight Show. Each has a progressively higher level of intelligence. So, to some extent, what we call the degree of "aliveness" can be measured by the amount of awareness or intelligence displayed — in other words, by the power of thought.

As was written above, mind — which consists of intelligence and is the medium of thought — underlies and creates the entire universe. But it becomes more evident to us — we can see it more clearly — as this intelligence becomes more *self-aware*. From Troward's point of view, "mind," "spirit" and "life" — or the Life Force — are one and the same, the distinctive quality of which is thought. He argued that the distinctive quality of matter, as in the piece of steel, is form.

Consider for a moment form versus thought. Form implies the occupation of space and also limitation within certain boundaries. Thought (or life) implies neither. When we think of thought or life as existing in any particular form we associate it with the idea of occupying space, so that an elephant may be said to consist of a vastly larger amount of living substance than a mouse. But if we think of life as the fact of "aliveness," or animating spirit, we do not associate it with occupying space. The mouse is quite as much alive as the elephant, notwithstanding the difference in size. For Troward this was an important point. If we can conceive of anything as not occupying space, or as having no form, it must be present in its totality anywhere and everywhere — that is to say, at every point of space simultaneously.

Life/thought/mind not only does not occupy space, it transcends time. The scientific definition of time is the period occupied by a body in passing from one point in space to another. So when there is no space there can be no time. That life/thought/mind is devoid of space must also mean it is devoid of time. The bottom line is that all life, or thought, must exist everywhere at once in a universal here and an everlasting now.

How does this help us understand how Katie creates brass and how we create our own reality — as well as how prayer works?

First, Troward would point out that it is implicit in the discussion above there are two kinds of thought. We might call them lower and higher, or subjective and objective because what differentiates the higher from the lower is the recognition of self. The plant, the worm, and perhaps the goldfish possess the lower kind only. They are unaware of self. Perhaps the dog, and certainly the boy and the comedian possess both. The higher variety of self-aware thought is possessed in progressively larger amounts as if ascending a scale.

The lower mode of thought, the subjective, is the subconscious intelligence or mind present everywhere that, among other things, supports and controls the mechanics of life in every species and in every individual. It causes the plant to grow toward the sun and to push its roots into the soil. It causes hearts to beat and lungs to take in air. It controls all of the so-called involuntary functions of the body. And, as we will see, it controls a lot more.

That this lower kind of thought is everywhere at once coincides with the theory of Carl Jung who maintained that we humans share a Universal Mind. Moreover, we each have our own portion, our individual subconscious mind that blends into the collective mind. We also have a conscious mind, the producer of higher thought that makes us self-aware. The two types of mind are inextricably linked in that our conscious mind arises out of the subconscious. The gradual emergence of self-aware thought out of the subconscious is implicit in our consideration of the plant, earthworm, goldfish, dog, boy, comedian and so forth up the scale.

Now let us consider an important point made in the *Lectures*. The conscious mind has a power over our subconscious mind that creates our reality. I discovered the truth of this firsthand in college when I learned to hypnotize others. I would put a willing classmate into a trance and tell him he was a chicken or a dog. Much to the amusement of my audience, he would then act accordingly.

Hypnotism works because the hypnotist bypasses his subject's conscious mind and speaks directly to his subject's subconscious. A subconscious mind has no choice but to bring into reality that which is communicated directly to it as fact by a conscious mind.

Being totally subjective, the subconscious mind cannot step outside of itself and take an objective look. As such, it is capable only of deductive reasoning, which is the kind that progresses from a cause — the conscious mind's directive — forward to its ultimate end. It does not stop to question or analyze. This is the reasoning that a criminal might use in committing a crime. He may walk into a room, see a man counting his money, and think: "I need money, so I will take his. Since the man is protecting the money, I will get rid of him. I'll shoot him. He'll drop to the floor. I will then take the money and run. I'll leave by the window."

On the other hand, the conscious mind, being objective and self-aware, *can* step outside. It can reason both deductively and inductively. To reason inductively is to move backward from result to cause. A police detective, for example, would arrive at the crime scene and begin reasoning backward in an attempt to tell how the crime was committed and who might have done it.

The result is that the subconscious (subjective) mind is entirely under the control of the conscious (objective) mind. With utmost fidelity, the subconscious will work diligently to support or to bring into reality whatever the conscious mind believes to be true. Since the individual subconscious blends with the collective subconscious and is present everywhere, it is able to influence circumstances and events so that whatever the conscious mind believes to be true will indeed become true. So, for example, if I believe I am a sickly person, I will be a sickly person. If I believe that by sitting in a draft I will catch cold, I will catch cold when I sit in a draft. Conversely, if I believe that I am rich, that I deserve to be so because it is my birthright, I will become rich even if this is not already the case. If I think I am unlucky, I am unlucky.

This also explains how, why and when prayer works. When people who pray sincerely believe their prayers will have a positive effect, their prayers most certainly will. The belief they hold is impressed upon their own subconscious minds. Their subconscious minds blend into the collective subconscious. The more people praying and believing, the greater the effect. The subconscious mind of the person for whom they are praying is also part of the collective subconscious. This goes to work to bring about positive results.

It does not make any difference whether the person praying is at someone's bedside or halfway around the world. As noted above, thought, and therefore prayer, is present everywhere at once. It is non-local. This explains why prayer is not hindered by distance.

Most people go through life hypnotized into thinking that they have little or no control over their circumstances. The fact is that to a large extent they create their circumstances with their thoughts and beliefs. The message of the *Edinburgh Lectures* is simple. Change your beliefs and your circumstances will change. Of course, things do happen that are totally out of our control, including so called "acts of God" and the results of actions by others exercising their free will. A "call to adventure," which we will discuss shortly, can also result in circumstances we would never consciously have choosen — as you soon will see.

By the way, I still take vitamin E, and will continue to do so regardless of what the next study to be published might say. I've come to realize that science and the medical profession do not have a corner on knowledge. Far from it.

Speaking of vitamin E, as the days went by after that episode in the Seven Eleven, something else occurred to me. Starting a new life can have the result of deducting decades from a person's chronological age. Some years before, I realized I'd gone stale in my career. I began having a recurring vision of myself coming around the track again and again. You might call it daily deja vu. I'd excelled in my career — was president of my own advertising agency. I was pulling down a salary well into six figures, was listed in *Who's Who in the Media and Communications*. I'd done what our society and our educational system seem to indicate should be the primary goal of life and the one true way to happiness and fulfillment. I'd picked a profession and risen to the top. And as many who reach such rarefied air also have found, it wasn't all it had been cracked up to be.

Don't get me wrong. I love the creative process, and being creative is what advertising is all about. But when you are successful, and this is true in many other lines of work, often after a certain point you no longer do what made you successful. You end up supervising others who get to have all the fun, while *you* get the headaches. Plus there was something else I'd always wanted to do, and it started calling to me.

I since have found that when you want something, and remain attentive, an opportunity will appear. Joseph Campbell (March 26, 1904 – October 30, 1987) labeled this opportunity "The call to adventure." This call will come whether the desire you hold is known to you on a conscious level, or whether it's hidden in the subconscious. You'll be presented with a choice. You can follow your adventure and gain from it. Or you can refuse the call, in which case you will stagnate and eventually die — figuratively, or perhaps even literally. This points to a cause of much ill health that's hidden beneath our noses. Here is an important truth: *To accept the call to adventure is to choose life over old age and death.*

Myths of all cultures recount the same tale repeatedly, each in its own cultural guise. This is not surprising since the call to adventure is something each of us receive, often a number of times during a lifetime. We are compelled to leave the safety and security of our home base and venture forward into the unknown where inevitable dragons and demons of one kind or other must be faced and overcome. Supported by unseen or supernatural powers, the hero who pushes forward will invariably succeed, later to return to familiar territory more highly evolved than when he or she left, and in possession of a new level of understanding. You see, the goal of the life is evolution.

Our society by and large ignores this entire phenomenon, even though the call comes whenever the time is at hand to move to a higher plane of understanding. This denial of such a basic component of life is particularly tragic in that dire consequences always result from our refusal to accept the call.

You need not take my word for this. Warnings can be found in myths throughout the ages. Refusal converts what otherwise would be positive and constructive into negative form. The would-be hero loses the power of action and becomes instead a victim bound by boredom, hard work, or even imprisonment. King Minos refused the call to sacrifice the bull, for example, which would have signified his submission to the divine. Of course, he didn't know that this would have resulted in his elevation to a higher state. So instead, like a modern day business executive or professional, he became trapped by conventional thinking and attempted to overcome the situation through hard work and determination. Indeed, he was able to build a palace for himself, just as many executives and professionals today build their mansions in the suburbs. But it turned out to be a wasteland, a house of death, a labyrinth in which to hide, and thus escape from the horrible Minotaur.

And look at what happened to Daphne, the beautiful maiden pursued by the handsome Greek god, Apollo. He wished only to be her lover, and called to her, "I who pursue you am no enemy. You know not from whom you flee. It is only for this reason that you run." All Daphne had to do was submit, to accept the call, and beautiful and bountiful love would have been hers. She, too, would have had a relationship with the divine. But as you probably know, she did not submit. She kept running, and as a result turned into a laurel tree, and that was the end of her.

Let me relate one more story. It is the same one as the two above, and conveys the same warning. This time it comes from Jesus. It can be found in all three synoptic gospels. This account is from Mark 10:17-23, the New International Version (NIV) translation:

As Jesus started on his way, a man ran up to him and fell on his knees before him. "Good teacher," he asked, "what must I do to inherit Eternal Life?"

"Why do you call me good?" Jesus answered. "No one is good—except God alone. You know the commandments: 'Do not murder, do not commit adultery, do not steal, do not give false testimony, do not defraud, honor your father and mother.'"

"Teacher," he declared, "all these I have kept since I was a boy."

Jesus looked at him and loved him. "One thing you lack,"[4] he said. "Go, sell everything you have and give to the poor, and you will have treasure in heaven. Then come, follow me."

At this the man's face fell. He went away sad, because he had great wealth.

Jesus looked around and said to his disciples, "How hard it is for the rich to enter the Kingdom of God!"

The disciples were amazed at his words. But Jesus said again, "Children, how hard it is to enter the Kingdom of God! It is easier for a camel to go through the eye of a needle than for a rich man to enter the Kingdom of God."

Well, there you are. If ever a person received the call to adventure, it was this rich man. If he answers the call, he will be on the road to Eternal Life. As with Minos and Daphne, the promise is

---

[4] The first law is "to put no other gods before Me." The rich man had done this by making money his number one god, i.e., it was the "one thing he lacked."

that he will develop and eventually experience the ecstasy of a relationship with the divine. But first, as was the case with them, he must give up his earthly treasure[5]. As those two before him and many of us today, he was much too attached to his earthly wealth to do so.

So, returning to my personal story, there I was, tired of the ad game and ready for my consciousness to move up to a higher plane, but I was held in place by golden handcuffs like the man in the story. I was ripe for the call, and naturally it came. It was not easy to turn away from that earthly treasure, but I did. I started writing. And I loved it.

Like any hero's adventure, it was frightening to take that first step, to answer the call, and the adventure became even more frightening as it continued. Soon more money was going out than coming in. Then a lot more. I won't bore you with a detailed account of sleepless nights. Let it be sufficient to say I had to fight my own dragons and demons and to confront the fears that told me I ought to get my nose pressed back against the grindstone of the workaday world. But, as in any hero's adventure, when the going got really tough, unseen hands, the support of the divine, stepped in.

I have not yet arrived back at the beginning. I'm still emerging from the dark night as I write this. But I do know that now, today, I'm already on a higher plane of understanding, mentally and spiritually. I'm not yet better off financially, but I *feel* more alive than I was before I answered the call. I know I'm on purpose, that I've achieved the state of lucide living, which is what I believe Jesus meant when he talked about "Eternal Life" or "Entering the Kingdom." I am no longer afraid of poverty or death. I expect those mysterious helping hands to be there when I need them, and I have yet to be disappointed.

Does this have anything to do with staying young?

Before I had reasons to stay in bed. Now I have reasons to get up in the morning. I'm aware of unseen hands constantly at work on my

---

[5] Minos would have to give up his prized bull; Daphne her maidenhood.

behalf. I'm following my bliss. I'm doing it in my own way, with talents I was given, making a contribution I hope, and perhaps most important, I'm doing what my subconscious mind or soul would have me do. I'm evolving and helping others do so.

This keeps me full of life or spirit.

W*hat* is spirit?

Life Force or spirit is the energy that heals a wound, the same energy that animates the body — makes it alive. When this energy is at its optimum, we feel good. Wounds heal faster. We are more resistant to disease. What fills us is the force behind all creation — the force that is also mind, the medium of our thoughts. It underlies everything and is present everywhere. To become truly aware of its presence and that we come from it and are linked to it — that we *are* it, as is everyone and everything — is to step into a lucid life where we are both the dreamer and a character within the dream. We emerge from mind when we are born, and we slip back into it when we die.

Contemplate this. Think of the universe as a mother. Think of humankind as a developing fetus. And think of Earth as a womb. Implicit in our discussion up to now, there is only one life, one organism of which you and I are parts. We each might be compared to cells that make up the whole, but our individual perspectives — our ego minds and the illusion created by our brains as the nexus of our five senses — keep us from recognizing this. We are fooled into thinking we are separate because our conscious awareness is centered in one location, and this location is not where the real action of this larger organism takes place.

Let us hypothesize for a moment that the goal of life is evolution and that our ultimate purpose is to serve the whole. First, we must continue to evolve, or we become a drag on the greater whole. Second, we must perform a service that directly or indirectly enables others who do grow. When we stop — when our growth becomes arrested and we no longer assist others — then as cells in the developing fetus of humankind, we no longer serve a purpose, and it is natural for us to die. Our ego minds are unaware of this, but our subconscious mind, the part that connects us to the universal subconscious, knows precisely what's happening. The time has come to check out — to return to the place from which we came, perhaps to have another go at it.

How can we save ourselves?

The first step is to answer the call when it comes. We must learn to be attentive and we must get in touch with the subconscious mind that resides within each of us. By getting in touch with this intelligence, which some people call our soul, we can determine what way it would have us go. Then we must set aside our fears and move ahead.

One intent of this book is to lead you to begin a dialog with this intelligence and to help you develop the confidence to put into practice what you learn. Sooner or later this will lead to a shift in your consciousness, and once this happens, your ego mind and your subconscious mind will begin to form a partnership. As they start to work in harmony, your life will continually change for the better and your sense of fulfillment will grow. It won't be long before doors will swing open simply because you approach them, and you'll be on the way to your birthright, which is Eternal Life.

Mind is the master power that molds and makes. And man is mind, and ever more he takes the tool of thought, and shaping what he wills, brings forth a thousand joys, a thousand ills. He thinks in secret, and it comes to pass. Environment is but his looking glass.

—James Allen
(1864-1912)

Chapter Three: The Mind and How It Works

The great twentieth century prophet, Edgar Cayce[6], often said, "Spirit is the life, mind is the builder, and the physical is the result." These few words describe the formula behind the existence of the physical world and all its trappings, you and me included. Spirit is the life. It is the force that animates living creatures. It is mind imbued with a raw organizing intelligence that formed the stars and the planets out of nebulae. It organized atoms into RNA, and later DNA, molecules. Mind is the builder. The mind is the medium of thought. Thoughts are things that exist in spirit, and what exists in spirit will in time exist on the physical plane.

We humans, and everything else in the universe evolved out of the organizing intelligence that is spirit. In the beginning, spirit created an almost infinite number of variations of living things. Those that were most suited to the environment survived. These living things reproduced by the millions, each offspring slightly different from its siblings. Again, those best suited to the environment survived and reproduced. And so on and so on. As evolution progressed, living organisms themselves developed intelligence. This intelligence impressed itself upon the organizing intelligence of spirit, and the organizing intelligence of spirit went to work to create ever more sophisticated and evolved adaptations. The result of this process can be seen in ever-increasing levels of intelligence displayed by ever more evolved life forms. As intelligence evolves it becomes and more more self aware. Flowers and earthworms possess only subjective or subconscious minds, their own small portions of underlying organizing intelligence. Their "minds" are subjective because they cannot think about themselves. They can only react in a programmed way to the input or stimuli

---

[6] So much has been written about Edgar Cayce (1877-1945) that I will not take the space to do so here. Amazon.com, for example, lists 265 books that have to do with Cayce and his work.

42

they receive. A dog and to a much greater extent, a human, have both a subjective mind and an objective mind. Their subjective minds keep them breathing and their bodies functioning while their objective minds think about and analyze situations. Unlike the subjective mind, an objective mind can worry and be afraid. This is both a blessing and a curse. It is a blessing in that we can plan ahead in order to avoid trouble and thereby eliminate the uncomfortable sensation of worry. It is a curse because a fear is a kind of belief — a belief charged with emotion. Since it does not analyze or judge, the subjective mind works hard to bring about what the objective mind believes. A fear is almost certain, therefore, to manifest if it is allowed to continue unchecked — whether or not that particular fear was originally grounded in reality.

As has been said, there is only one mind, and this mind is constantly evolving. Like the vast majority of water on earth that is connected but divided into oceans, seas, and rivers, we can think of the one mind as being connected but divided into three levels: a Universal Mind, individual subconscious minds, and last but not least the part of each person's mind of which he or she is aware, the conscious mind. Each of our conscious minds are in turn divided into a conscious portion and an unconscious portion.

We're all familiar with the conscious mind — the place where our attention remains most of the time when we're awake. It is here that we're aware of what is happening around us. We touch, taste or see something. Impulses travel along nerves such as the optic nerve from the eye to the brain. An event takes place. Let's say we take a bite of a chocolate bar. We immediately recognize the flavor. That's the conscious mind at work. To identify the flavor, the conscious mind calls upon the memory of the taste of chocolate that's stored in its unconscious part.

What other functions does the unconscious part of the conscious mind perform? Let's say you get into your car to go somewhere. You turn the key, you release the brake, you drive. You don't have to think much about what you're doing. If you're like me, you may drive along thinking about something else and take a turn that you would normally take even though today you're going somewhere else and shouldn't have taken it. After a few blocks you realize you're on the wrong road. You were led astray by the unconscious, programmed part of you.

The unconscious part of your conscious mind becomes programmed very much like a computer. Remember the first time you got behind the wheel? When you turned the key and released the brake you had to pay close attention to every detail in order to make the automobile operate smoothly. You had to watch all the buttons, people, stoplights and so on. Over the months and years that you've been driving, however, your conscious mind made all those details a part of you. They slipped into the unconscious part of your conscious mind as surely as a computer program is loaded onto a hard drive.

The truth is, all the bits of information you've come in contact with in this particular life are stored in the unconscious part of your conscious mind, including information that in a practical sense you've forgotten or never fully understood. Erroneous information is there. For example, as a child perhaps your parents said, "People in our family are cursed with a tendency to be overweight. All you have to do is look at food and it goes straight to your hips. There's nothing you can do about it." Or maybe they said, "Nobody in this family ever got rich. It's just not meant to be. So you might as well resign yourself to a life of being poor." So, contained within the unconscious part of your conscious mind today are the beliefs that because you're a Jones or a Johnson or a Smith, you are destined to have a weight problem, or to struggle when it comes to money. You didn't question the information when it was programmed in because it came from someone in authority. But it is still there, and it's keeping you from a life of joy because as long as those beliefs are in the unconscious part of your conscious mind they are being impressed upon your individual subconscious; it and the shared subconscious, in turn, are duty bound to make them into reality.

In Chapter Seven, we'll discuss techniques you can use to deprogram yourself, but in the meantime let's take a minute and make sure there's no confusion between a person's subconscious mind and the unconscious mind that contains this life's programming and memories. The subconscious mind is that part of you that has been built up over many lifetimes and contains the truth and knowledge of all lessons learned during those lifetimes. It is at one with the universal subconscious, a cup of water within the ocean in which all knowledge resides. Your unconscious mind is part of your conscious or ego mind and contains the memories and the programming of this life only.

Your personal subconscious contains your personal evolutionary history. Some call this the soul. A goal of this book will be to help you gain access to your subconscious mind, ultimately to begin the process of a merger, or at least a partnership, between it and your conscious or ego mind. Whether or not you realize it, your current situation — whether you are a prince or a pauper, the CEO of your company or an assembly line worker — is determined by how well your subconscious and conscious minds work together. A good working arrangement is crucial to achieving the life you want.

Baloney, you say? Others have decided what your lot in life will be. Neither your conscious mind nor your subconscious had anything to do with it.

If this is true, it is because you have, unconsciously, allowed others to misdirect you. You haven't been paying attention to your subconscious mind or soul, the part of you that's been around since the incarnation in which you first achieved self-awareness. If you are intelligent enough and interested enough to have read this far in this book, your soul had a plan for you in this incarnation. This part of you — your soul or individual subconscious mind — has been trying, apparently unsuccessfully, to nudge you in the right direction. If you are not where you want to be and intuitively know you are not where you *ought* to be, it is because unconscious thought patterns have brought you here. This being the case, you have some programming issues to deal with.

Let me attempt to throw some light on how this works in many cases. Feelings of frustration, discontent, and dissatisfaction, for example, are ways of solving problems that we all "learned" as infants. If a baby is hungry he expresses discontent by crying. A warm, tender hand then appears magically out of nowhere and brings milk. If a baby is uncomfortable, let's say he has a poopie diaper, he again expresses dissatisfaction with the status quo, and the same warm hands appear magically and solve the problem by removing the yucky diaper and putting on a fresh one.

Many children continue to get their way, and have their problems solved by indulgent parents, by merely expressing their feelings of frustration. All they have to do is feel frustrated and dissatisfied, and the problem is solved.

This way of life "works" for the infant, and for some children. But it does not work in adult life. Yet many of us continue to try it, by feeling discontented and expressing our grievances against life, apparently in the hope that life itself will take pity, rush in and solve our problems for us — if only we feel bad enough. Yet, the subconscious mind in us knows this isn't so. It learned this in other incarnations. The conscious mind ought to be able to figure this out, but the feelings are buried in its unconscious part and simply have never been brought into the light for critical examination. As a result, our unconscious programming just keeps on trucking, and in doing so keeps on tripping us up.

Imagine, for example, you are a management trainee in a corporation. With you in training are several other bright young men and women fresh out of business school. Imagine that the way things work in the company is often not to your liking. Management trainees, for example, are relegated to cubicles with five-foot-high walls affording little or no privacy, while the senior staff have corner offices with large windows and spectacular views of the East River. You spend a good deal of time grumbling to yourself and to others about this injustice, unconsciously believing this will get you out of that cubicle and into a corner suite. Your fellow trainees, on the other hand, spend their time making positive suggestions and anticipating and providing for the needs of customers as well as those fellow workers higher on the corporate ladder. Whom do you suppose is most likely to be first to break out of his or her cubicle?

Don't you feel a twinge inside that intuitively "knows" the positive attitude, the attitude of service to others, will eventually win the day? That "twinge" is a message from your subconscious mind. If you have been ignoring this feeling when it comes, now is the time for you to begin recognizing such messages. They have a light and airy feeling to them, even though they may seem to run counter to egocentric notions, such as, "The first order of business is to look out for number one." That egocentric notion may work in the short term, but in the long, it is bad advice. Jesus said, for example, "The first among you will be the servant of all," as well as, "Whoever wants to become great among you must be your servant."[7] Verses such as these have been much puzzled over because humans are basically selfish. The thought of being someone else's servant is an anathema to the ego mind. Nonetheless, Jesus's words make perfect sense to the subconscious mind to which he was so well attuned.

Let's consider for a moment why some people may spend their valuable time on earth grumbling and complaining away opportunities to get ahead. It is probably because they have practiced feeling frustrated and defeated so much — ever since they were babies in a crib, and then while growing up with indulgent parents — that feelings of defeat have become habitual. Their minds are in a kind of holding pattern, and they've never taken a step outside of themselves to get in touch with their subconscious minds which would tell them, if they would only listen, that grumbling and complaining are counterproductive and accomplish nothing. Until they wise up, they will continue to project those feelings into the future and will expect to fail. As discussed, more often than not, people get what they believe and expect they will get.

---

[7] Matthew 20:26.

Thoughts and feelings are intertwined. You might say that feelings are the soil in which thoughts and ideas grow. This is why, when a person begins an endeavor, he or she would be well advised to imagine how she would feel if she succeeded — and then *feel* that way. This feeling of accomplishment will help generate the belief that she has or will achieve what she set out to. The feeling creates the belief, and the belief creates the feeling. A mental form of success has been created and now exists in the realm of spirit. Soon this will appear on the physical plane, provided what is desired is in line with the Life Force's push toward growth and evolution. No wonder "Everything is possible for him who believes."[8]

A positive attitude may be not all that's needed to lead a consistently successful life. Belief is the key, and this is where many self-help books fall short of their intended purpose. I can be as positive as Santa Claus about achieving the sales goal that will bring me a brand new Mercedes Benz. But if I still have worry and doubt in spite of my positive attitude, I'm constantly throwing a monkey wrench in the workings of the subconscious mind. And there's something else. The Universal Mind may only reason deductively, but it has an overall goal for you and me. That goal is the evolution of our consciousness because the Universal Mind wants you to realize who you are — you are the universe experiencing itself — and it wants you to be a conscious co-creator rather than an unconscious co-creator. That's what it's working toward. If a new Mercedes Benz in some way will help further your personal evolution or even someone else's, get ready for one to materialize in your driveway. On the other hand, if a new Mercedes would be in some way counterproductive, don't hold your breath.

Why in the world does what we fear often come about? Because getting what we fear may actually help us grow. Like it or not, sometimes difficult experiences result in much more growth than good. Ask for the virtue of patience to come to you and you can expect to encounter an experience in which patience is required. The

---

[8] Mark 9:23.

hard way is the only way to learn, or perhaps I should say, *earn* it.

Sometimes we get what we ask for and later wish we hadn't. No doubt many lottery winners have had their lives turned upside down and found out that all that money was in reality a burden they wished they didn't have to carry. But think how much they grew as a result of the experience. They became more conscious or self aware and this serves the long-range goal of the Universal Mind.

The lesson is that what will virtually guarantee success is to bring the egocentric, conscious mind into alignment with the subconscious mind. When the two are working in concert, Katie bar the door.

Remember Edgar Cayce's saying, "Spirit is the life, mind is the builder, the physical is the result." Once a symbiotic relationship between spirit and your conscious mind is formed, you will automatically create the life you want. This cannot help but happen. Until then, however, things will be hit or miss. They will seem to work for you one day, and against you the next because you're sending out mixed signals. The conscious part of you might be saying, "I want to win this big contract so my boss will think I'm really on the ball and give me a big bonus," and another part of you might be saying just as forcefully, though unconsciously, "Please don't let me land this contract because I can't possibly handle all the work it will generate, and even if I could, it's not the way I want to spend my time." Your egocentric mind may want to win and even believe it can. Your unconscious mind selfishly may not want the baggage that will go along with it. And perhaps your subconscious would rather you lose because then there may be a chance you'll wake up and begin to follow the destiny you came to earth to pursue. So the different parts of you are at odds. When this is the case, things will not turn out the way you consciously think you want them to. In fact, your subconscious may very likely put a stop to all the nonsense by thrusting you into a crisis in an effort to get your attention. This could take the form of an illness, an accident, the loss of a job, or whatever. But whatever form it takes, you will be forced to reevaluate your life.

People often have accidents, or develop major illnesses, when they are not on track and refuse to heed the call of their subconscious minds to change direction. In this way, the subconscious mind forces a hero's adventure on them. If it is accepted as such, if the individual involved recognizes that fate has stepped in, goes along, does what must be done but also surrenders to the divine, the illness or accident will likely turn out to be a side trip. It will have been a hero's adventure that has resulted in spiritual growth. The hero or heroine will return to the place where she began with a higher level of understanding. Her life will have been changed. She will be more fully prepared to step into the larger adventure that awaits.

On the other hand, if a person fights it, if she refuses to give herself over to the hands of grace, if she develops no intention of altering the situation that led to the illness — in other words, if no growth comes or appears forthcoming — then illness may indeed result in the termination of this incarnation.

All crises are potential hero's journeys. They are opportunities for rebirth. Once you understand this and accept it, you are in a much better position to deal with them. It is essential to understand that fear and doubt can stifle or derail the process. Conversely, facing a crisis in a positive attitude of expectancy can help immensely and can speed you along, sometimes almost painlessly, to rebirth at a new level.

Here are the steps to keep in mind the next time you are confronted with what appears to be a dire situation:

Step One: Accept your condition. Whether your problem is physical, mental or spiritual — if it is a health problem, it is likely a combination of all three — the first requisite is to accept it. As the famous psychiatrist Carl Jung said, "Nothing can be changed until it is accepted." Acceptance does not mean giving up. It means looking the situation in the eye, and seeing that it is real. What percentage of alcoholics, or people who continue to be addicted to something, do you suppose have taken this step? Once they have reached this point, however, they are ready to take action.

Step Two: Take responsibility for your situation.

I realize this may be easy for me to say but difficult for you to do. Let's say a hurricane comes along and knocks down your house and your business. You might have a hard time taking responsibility for that. Nevertheless, it is a necessary step. To do otherwise is to cling to a "victim consciousness" that will get you absolutely no where at all. In winter the heating grates in major cities throughout the United States are occupied by people who consider themselves helpless victims of circumstances. Rightly or wrongly, they will never get off those heating grates permanently and into a warm bed with a roof over it until they take responsibility for their situation.

Most who think of themselves as "New Age" have bought into the idea that nothing happens by accident, and that everything is always happening just as it should — as part of a big plan. They would say that the hurricane happened for a reason. At the other end of the spectrum, Scientific Materialists tend to believe that everything is a big accident. If I were forced to choose between these extremes, I'd have to go with the New Age folks. I feel they're slightly closer to the truth. But the fact is, I think accidents do happen, and that everything is *not* always just as it should be. If it were, then the people on steam grates *belong* there, and I don't think so.

In either case, the best course of action is to take responsibility. If you are an alcoholic, stop blaming your mother or your father. If you are hit by a hurricane, you may have to rationalize how you got yourself into the situation. For example, some part of you knew when you bought a house and set up a business in Florida or the Outer Banks that someday a hurricane might come along and knock it down. Your subconscious mind may even have agreed to this because it knew that out of this adversity would come needed spiritual growth. You and the universe are one. So you as the universe have sent yourself this problem for a reason, and that reason is to grow. Whether or not that is the real truth, you will be much better off to look at it this way.

Step Three: Identify the quality you need in order to deal with the situation effectively.

Try to determine what exactly is being demanded of you. This is at the heart of the "lesson" that the universe is out to teach. One crisis may call for assertiveness, another gentleness, another creativity, and still another, courage, another frugality. Another could call for a high degree of tenaciousness. Still another could require that you achieve a balance between giving and receiving. By recognizing the quality or trait you need in order to handle the crisis, you begin to usher in the breakthrough. As you strive actively to develop that, you are no longer a victim of circumstance, but a hero or heroine on a transformative journey.

Step Four: Stay hopeful.

Without hope and an underlying expectation that the situation will turn around, you may give up too easily. I once read, for example, that in World War II the Royal Air Force conducted a study of victims and survivors among flyers who were forced to ditch in the English Channel. Officials were surprised to learn that the survival rate actually increased along with the age of the flyers, which was the opposite of what they'd expected. The youngest men, who also were in the best physical condition, were more likely to die of hypothermia.

A survey was conducted to determine why. It was found that the older men, having lived longer and through more adversity, were less likely to give up hope than the young men. Hope like fear is a form of belief — a belief in possibilities. Hope, rather than physical condition, was judged to be the more important indicator of survival.

Some people seem to attract more crises into their lives than others. For whatever reason, they are being handed more opportunities for growing and evolving than their peers. Once they understand this and begin to follow the steps outlined above, they should find that life may not be as difficult as they once believed. As has been said, spirit is always pushing in the direction of evolution.

An important idea to grasp is that all of you — your conscious mind and your subconscious mind together — need to join with spirit in order to produce the desired (physical) result. When all the pieces work in harmony, not only have you begun to follow the path of least resistance, you are now on the road to fulfillment and happiness.

Traveling this road is likely to require serious self-examination, which can be painful. It may require some spiritual evolution on your part, which could take time, study and meditation. But take heart. Whether or not you were aware of it before today, *all humanity* is on a spiritual journey. This journey is the heart of the reason for life on earth: the evolution of individual human souls, and the evolution of the combined soul of all humans. W. E. Butler, the founder of Ibis, an organization dedicated to the teaching of metaphysics, likened the spiritual evolution of humankind to a great crowd making its way along a road that winds up a hill. The crowd plods forward as a flock of sheep might, kicking up dust but moving slowly, stopping now and then, scrapping and biting each other; now and then getting panicky and shifting one way or the other; often hardly moving ahead at all.

We humans are like sheep, highly susceptible to peer pressure. With this in mind, you may want to share this book with others. Perhaps, after a quick read through, you may wish to study it along with another seeker or group of seekers. It can be lonely when you possess a level of understanding much higher than those around you, and this is what this book will give. Moreover, the knowledge here is difficult to share because it cannot be summed up in 30 seconds. Moreover, it may sound like heresy to those who cling tightly to the dogma of a particular religion.

So, how did I come by it?

Looking back, I realize that I started on this journey as a confirmed atheist at the age of twenty-seven. It began the day I had a brief "experience of mystery," as Joseph Campbell called a glimpse of the Eternal. The pace of my progress shifted into overdrive, however, at the age of 44 when I made the conscious decision to seek "mastery of life." I've made progress toward this goal, but I still have quite a way to go. Writing this book has helped me consolidate, digest and gain deeper understanding of what I've learned. This by itself would be worth the effort. But, in the process, I also hope I will save others some time and a number of trips down blind alleys I have taken along the way.

Speaking of the evolution of the soul, several theories have been put forth in recent years concerning the various stages one passes through as he or she grows spiritually. One such theory that I believe to be accurate can be found in a book by Scott Peck (May 22, 1936 - September 25, 2005), *Further Along The Road Less Traveled.* As you read ahead, perhaps you'll see some of your co-workers, your boss — perhaps even your Uncle Charlie.

Stage One is the Chaotic/Antisocial. People at this level are unprincipled and antisocial. In effect, Stage One is a condition totally absent of spirituality. While they may pretend to be loving, all of their relationships are self-serving and manipulative. Truly, they are looking out for number one. Being unprincipled, they have nothing to govern themselves except their own wills, which is why people in this stage are often found in trouble or difficulty, in jail, in hospitals, or whatever. It is possible for them to be self-disciplined from time to time and in the service of their ambition to rise to positions of prestige and power. Some evangelistic preachers and politicians may fit into this category. I was once acquainted with someone I now recognize as a Stage One individual who headed a successful company. Under his direction the firm became one of the fastest growing in its field. The man was a brilliant speaker and strategist. He had a photographic memory. But he was totally without principles or anything close to what might be called a conscience. Even though he was married, he took pride in himself as a master of seduction of members of the opposite sex. Figuratively speaking, he left the landscape strewn with the bodies of his lovers and adversaries, and to my knowledge, he never felt an inkling of remorse. This man was extremely successful for a time and made millions before the age of forty. But in the end, his closest colleagues turned on him. They ejected him from the firm he'd helped to build, perhaps because they feared they too would someday become victims of his egocentric nature. This was the principle of cause and effect at work. What goes around indeed comes around — though one can never be sure how long it will sometimes take to come back around.

The Stage One person can have a difficult time of it if he ever happens to get in touch with himself and realizes the chaos within and the hurt he has caused others. It seems possible that such anguish may be the root cause of some unexplained suicides. A happier possibility is that the Stage One personality may suddenly and dramatically convert to Stage Two, which Peck has labeled the Formal/Institutional. Those at this place in evolution depend on an institution to keep them on the straight and narrow. This may be a prison, the military, or a rigidly organized corporation. For many in our society it is the Church.

Stage Two individuals tend to be attached to ritual and dogma and become very upset if someone challenges this or tries to institute change. We all know of those who take the Bible literally, who believe the world was created in six twenty-four hour days and that man was brought into being as a fully-evolved *homo sapiens* known as Adam. Rather than viewing the story as a myth about the ascent of man from a primate ruled by instinct into a human with free will, they believe that God literally banished the very first man — whose name was Adam — and the very first woman — whose name was Eve — from an actual idyllic spot known as the Garden of Eden.

Stage Two people think of God as an external being and almost always envision him as up there on a cloud looking down, making a list and checking it twice. More than likely they picture a man who looks remarkably like Michelangelo's depiction on the ceiling of the Sistine Chapel, and they ascribe to him the power and the will to make them extremely sorry for their transgressions. God is seen as a giant benevolent cop in the sky.

I know for a fact, however, that many Christians and followers of other religions are by no means stuck in Stage Two. I attend church regularly and personally know many who are well into Stage Four and even Five. A characteristic of more advanced believers is an image of God as immanent in all of creation and a belief that much of what is presented in the Bible is figurative or metaphorical.

Let's move on and consider the characteristics of Stage Three. It's not surprising that members of this group are likely to have been raised in a family headed by Stage Two parents (whether Christian, Buddhist, or Jewish) and as a result internalized their parents' religious and moral principles. By the time they reached adolescence, however, they were questioning the dogma. ("I looked at Playboy and God didn't strike me blind. Who needs these silly myths and superstitions?") To the horror of their parents they eventually fell away from the Church and became doubters, or agnostics, or perhaps even atheists. This is the Skeptic/Individual stage. Its members are not religious, but neither are they antisocial. They are often deeply involved in social or ecological causes. Often they are scientists and almost always are scientific-minded. To my way of thinking, they comprise a plurality of the educated middle and upper middle class in America. They can be found in large numbers teaching our children and young adults in schools and universities. The media are chock full of them. They are reporters, columnists and commentators. Because they frequently rigidly adhere to mechanistic views of reality, and to secular humanist philosophy, they often strike Stage Two and Four/Five individuals as misguided. They are usually unwilling to consider the existence of anything they cannot see or touch. Many, however, do tend to be truth seekers, and if they seek truth deeply enough and widely enough and get enough bits and pieces to catch glimpses of the big picture, they will come to an understanding that the truth curiously resembles the primitive myths and superstitions held so dear by their Stage Two parents. It is at the point of catching these glimpses that Stage Three individuals begin to convert to Stage Four, which has been called the Mystical/Communal.

Stage Four individuals are referred to as mystical because they see a kind of cohesion behind physical reality. As Scott Peck put it, "Seeing that kind of inter-connectedness beneath the surface, mystics of all cultures and religions have always spoken in terms of unity and community." In reality, what they have experienced is that the universe is a single organism and that each one of us — along with every animal, tree, rock or celestial sphere — is a facet of this organism. Each seemingly separate part is a component of the whole, just as a nose, or a foot, is a facet of one's physical body.

Peck observed that we tend to be threatened by those in the stages of spiritual development ahead of us and by what they believe. For example, while people in Stage One may seem as though nothing bothers them, underneath they are terrified of virtually everyone, which explains why my Stage One acquaintance left so many bloody bodies in his path. Far from being frightened of them, Stage Two folks see Stage One folks as fertile ground for conversion, recognizing them to be sinners who need to be shown the light. Conversely, Stage Two people tend to be threatened by Stage Three skeptics. They are even more put off by Stage Four mystical types who seem to believe the same things they do, but with a kind of freedom they find terrifying. They usually hate to be reminded, for example, that it was their savior, Jesus Christ, who turned water into wine at the wedding when the host had run out of the joy juice. They prefer to think of Jesus as serious and pious, even though the most casual reading of the gospels will reveal that he enjoyed a good time perhaps more than anyone else around him. He compared his ministry to a wedding feast in that it was a time for joy and celebration. There can be little doubt he advocated love as much or more than duty or discipline.

Let's consider how the various stages view one another. Stage Threes certainly aren't threatened by Stage Ones, except when they find themselves facing one wielding a gun or a knife. They see Stage

Twos as mostly idiotic zealots — harmless except for their efforts to legislate morals or to ban certain books or the teaching of evolution in the public schools. But Stage Threes are threatened by Stage Fours, who seem to be scientifically minded but also inexplicably believe in this crazy God thing. As Scott Peck says, "If you mentioned the word 'conversion' to a Stage Three individual, he or she would see a vision of a missionary arm-twisting a heathen and would go through the roof."

Regardless of the skepticism of Stage Three individuals, mystics and spiritual thinkers throughout the centuries and in all societies have believed in the connectedness sensed by Stage Four individuals. In her best-selling book, *A History of God*, Karen Armstrong writes, "One of the reasons why religion seems irrelevant today is that many of us no longer have the sense that we are surrounded by the unseen. Our scientific culture educates us to focus our attention on the physical and material world in front of us. This method of looking at the world has achieved great results. One of its consequences, however, is that we have, as it were, edited out the sense of the 'spiritual' or the 'holy' which pervades the lives of people in more traditional societies at every level and which was once an essential component of our human experience of the world." Indeed, in the television series *Power of Myth*, Joseph Campbell said that the theme of all mythology throughout all history and in every culture is the existence of an invisible plane that supports and informs the visible.

Scott Peck didn't go beyond Stage Four in his theory of the levels of spiritual growth, but I believe that at least one more stage exists. Stage Five, as I call it, might be called the Spiritual/Transient. These are folks who are so attuned to the spiritual side of reality that they are able to slip back and forth between the physical and nonphysical. Mystics, from Buddha to Jesus, to the current Dalai Lama, would qualify. Edgar Cayce was able to tap into the Universal Mind at will, simply by lying back and closing his eyes. He did this every day for forty years or more in, correctly diagnosing and offering effective cures to thousands of afflicted persons who

wrote to him for help. I've witnessed this sort of thing done n.
on the occasions I've had to visit the School of Metaphysic:
Windyville, Missouri. At the gentle urging of a "conductor," trained
readers slip easily into a trance and access the Akashic records[9] at
will. Want to know about a past life of yours that may be having an
effect on you today? Look up the School on the web at
www.SOM.org and click on past life readings.

In my own striving for life mastery, there are times when I can
feel or sense that all life is connected in one uninterrupted pattern
that, in a metaphor created by my mind, takes the form of an
enormous spider web. The trick is to learn how to manipulate that
web. Apparently, some masters can do so as if the strands were the
strings of a harp that they "play" using the power of their minds. A
tug here, a thump there, and the predictable takes place.

Although it wouldn't surprise me if charlatans outnumber
authentic psychics, some people indeed seem to have a gift of
second sight or hearing that connects them with the unseen world.
Others appear to be adept at out-of-body travel. Robert Monroe
(October 30, 1915 – March 17, 1995), for whom the Monroe Institute
is named and the author of several books on this topic, is an
example. I know people who believe that at some point in the future,
man may be able to transport himself to far corners of the universe
by tapping into the flow of energy that Robert Monroe described in
his books. This is the energy I call spirit, mind, or Life Force.
Someday, this energy will be the subject of scientific study, but the
majority of people living in the western world today are oblivious to
it. Nevertheless, it is the glue that binds us — the common ground of
being all of us share.

As has been mentioned, spirit or Life Force came first and we
evolved out of it. Since our individual subconscious mind or soul
remains always in the medium of spirit, each time we are born, our
personal evolution unfolds again as our fetus grows in our mother's

---

[9] The Akashic records are thought to be the memory of all thoughts and actions from the
beginning of time that exist as a sort of mental libary or data base in the Universal Mind.

womb and passes through the stages from single-celled animal to fish to aquatic animal with webbed fingers and toes, to a reptilian form with tail, and so on up the ladder. The memory of the construction of all those previous bodies is eternally present and is unfolding once again. Our minds are not products of our bodies and our brains. Our brains and bodies are products of our minds and a way to bring our minds back into physical reality. This being the case, you might think of our brains as radio receivers adjusted to our frequency that help us turn thoughts into action by allowing us to manipulate our physical bodies. Our subconscious mind also works through the brain to keep our lungs breathing and the mechanics of our bodies functioning. And our nervous systems and brains keep us in touch with the physical world. Input reaches us through sense organs that relay messages to the brain. Here they are unscrambled and presented to our minds for consumption and consideration. In the process, our brains create the illusion that we are separate entities, islands in the stream, rather than pieces of the continent of humankind. The result is that each one of us experiences his individual dream within the larger dream of reality.

We are spirit playing hide and seek with itself and only appear to be separate. In truth, we each are a spark of the energy of spirit, just as a cup of water submerged in the ocean is fully part of the whole. This is why the number of true accidents are few, why synchronicities happen constantly — which you will begin to realize once you begin looking for them — how prayer and grace are able to work, and the reason psychic phenomena are real. As we shall see, without the unseen world of spirit, that common ground of being, the physical dimension, would and could not exist.

In order to facilitate the shift of consciousness I hope you will achieve, another goal of this book is to provide a rational framework of the invisible that you can hang onto. But let me state clearly that I do not pretend to have all the answers. I fully expect that scientists of a future age will correct or modify much of what I will cover here. My intention is to at least point in the right direction and in many cases to outline the answers in broad strokes. Eventually, the scientific community will reverse their currently held premise that matter gives rise to awareness, consciousness and intelligence and will turn that assumption on its head where it belongs. The blinders cannot stay on much longer. When they come off, scientists will be in position to determine how things work in far greater detail and with more accuracy than is possible now. In medical research, for example, most of the effort is now being spent in finding ways to eliminate or ease symptoms, rather the actual underlying causes of illness. Many doctors realize what truly ails us is almost always psychic or spiritual in nature, but at present they'd put their reputations at risk if they said so publicly. Yet, whether the treatment given is medicine in the form of a chemical compound, or nonmaterial in the form of prayer, treating symptoms rather than causes is likely to produce only temporary results. Almost inevitably, problems will pop up again since root causes remain. For example, remember the case history of Nancy in Chapter Two who had a lump in her breast? A group gathered at her home, prayed for her, and the lump disappeared. What I didn't tell you is that two years later a new lump formed. This indicates that Nancy had an unresolved issue that kept manifesting as a lump in her breast. Maybe it was simply fear of cancer. Maybe it was a wake up call for her to grow. Whatever the case may be, once researchers understand and take to heart Edgar Cayce's assertion that "Spirit is the life, mind is the builder, and the physical is the result," the way will be cleared for all kinds of scientific and medical discoveries.

In the meantime, I will attempt to draw what I'll admit is probably a rough map. Time may reveal it's no more accurate than the first crude maps of North America drawn by the first European explorers. Nevertheless, those maps served their purpose. They got the explorers who came later pretty close to where they wanted to go, just as I believe this book will be helpful for those who come after me. My map has gotten me fairly far, and it can help bring you to the same place. Read ahead, and allow yourself to suspend disbelief.

Every man is a creature of the age in which he lives. Very few are able to raise themselves above the ideas of the time.

—Voltaire (1694-1778)

Chapter Four: A New View of Life

Most Baby Boomers probably were born into Stage Two families and taught by Stage Three teachers, certainly at the college level, which may be one reason why they rebelled against their parents and what they came to view as corny ideas about the wrath of God, the virtues of celibacy before marriage, and the like. My parents, on the other hand, already were firmly entrenched in Stage Three when I arrived on the scene. This didn't mean I got to skip stages One, Two, or Three. We have to pass through all the stages of growth in the womb each time, and once we exit the womb we have to do so as well. So we don't skip stages. But the higher up the ladder of spiritual evolution our teachers, mentors and parents are, the faster we tend to move through the lower rungs.

No matter where a person may be on the ladder, however, he or she is likely to think he's pretty near the top. It's not surprising, then, that skeptics like my parents are susceptible to their own brand of dogma: Scientific Materialism. This is what I had to rebel against. Other Boomers had to become skeptical about the beliefs of their Stage Two parents before moving to Stage Three. I had to become skeptical about the beliefs of Stage Three Skeptics before I could move to Stage Four.

How did someone in my situation get past the idea held from childhood that the universe is constructed of separate, distinct, unconnected pieces? How does one do that if one was brought up as I was by parents who told me that if I wanted to fool around with my girlfriend, then by all means be sure to take the necessary precautions? As a teenager, a guy had to respect parents who thought like that.

Don't get me wrong. They weren't immoral or amoral. It was simply that my mother and father had been a generation or two ahead of their time. My mother had been a flapper in the Roaring Twenties, the equivalent in her era to a roach-toting flower child of the Sixties. I'm certain she and Pop made out in the rumble seat of a Model T between sips of bootleg whiskey from a sterling silver flask. She'd done it all and so had my father. They simply expected nothing more or less from me. And since people almost always get what they expect, I didn't disappoint.

Looking back, I realize my parents did have a solid moral underpinning. As I dredge up memories of early childhood, I now suspect my father actually wondered about the existence of a dimension he couldn't experience with his senses. I'll never know for sure because it was not something he ever talked about. Not to me, anyway. He died when I was seven. I believe he did wonder, though, because of comments my mother and aunt made about him from time to time, and because I once found a Rosicrucians recruiting pamphlet among his papers. In my own case, I'd like my children to have a clear understanding of what I believe. I tell them whenever the opportunity arises and, hopefully, they will read read this book when they are ready.

One can never know what someone else thinks until that person says what is on his or her mind. A case in point is my mother, who remained staunchly anti-Christian Church until her death at the age of 90. She did not care at all for those she considered Bible thumpers. Once, she yanked me out of a church-run kindergarten after I told her that the teacher had read the story about Moses coming down from the mountain and tossing the stone tablets at his wayward followers who'd constructed a golden calf.

Yet, three years before she died, I found out to my surprise that she believed in an afterlife.

"When I die," she said one day, "I want my body donated to science."

I looked at her with furrowed brow, realizing she was talking about becoming a cadaver.

"My father was a doctor," she continued. "They might learn

something from examining the lungs of an old woman who smoked for 50 years, and then stopped. It will be my part for science." She'd quit smoking twenty years earlier at 67. "Besides," she said. A faraway look came over her. "They say that when you die, you simply leave your body. You can see it lying there as you float away. It's not like I'll feel anything."

I was too stunned to ask where she believed she'd go when she floated away. But I did think, "Fine time to tell me this." Until well into my twenties, I'd believed there was no afterlife — that when you died, everything came to a halt. I'm pretty sure I believed so because that's what I thought she believed.

Actually, we did go to church sometimes. It was one I might enjoy nowadays, a Unitarian Church in Richmond that had been founded by Thomas Jefferson, or so the story went. Unitarians bring people together into one congregation in an attempt at unification, regardless of their specific beliefs, so you won't find a Unitarian Church where the preacher or anyone else comes at you waving some dogma or other. I'm certain this appealed to my parents. In those days, the Sunday sermons were thinly veiled lectures on psychology or philosophy.

Looking back, and thinking hard, I realize my Mom and Dad were probably Deists. In my household the universe was viewed as a giant clock constructed by the Creator. The unalterable laws of physics were built into the mechanism. This clock had been set loose and required and received no further help or interference from God. That's what my parents apparently believed.

When I went to high school, and later to college, Newton's mechanical view of things was not only reinforced, but taught as unquestioned fact. Quantum physics hadn't quite made it into the curriculum. Instead of a clock, however, it was a giant billiard game. Instead of God creating and building the laws into it, the universe just happened. It was caused by a Big Bang. The laws were laws, nothing more; fundamental to the basic structure. We students were supposed to buy the idea that it was all a giant accident, I guess. No one ever asked who caused the big bang or how it happened.

Somehow this lack of a prime mover didn't sit well with me. What was there before God or the bang or the laws? What was behind it? How had life come about? Was it really possible for something as complex as a DNA molecule to form by accident? And what then? The accidentally formed double helix became a writhing mass of protoplasm when lightning struck? Another freak accident? Then, by random chance, tiny one-celled animals formed and evolved into all the elaborate forms of life on the planet today? This was totally in opposition to the second law of thermodynamics, which in part states that "in a closed system, entropy (disorder) always increases." In other words, things don't just organize themselves. This being the case, how had the first kidney evolved? The first liver? The eye? Gills? Lungs?

Physical attributes such as the long neck of the giraffe, or the coloration of birds or insects, I was able to understand. Let's say the environment was getting drier over time, causing what once was forest to gradually change into savanna. Giraffes' main source of food, the leaves of trees, would over the years become higher from the ground. Giraffes who happened to be born with longer necks would have an advantage over short-necked siblings. They'd get more food, and as a result, live longer and be healthier, in which case, they'd be more likely to reproduce. Just as two champion race horses are more likely to produce a champion offspring than two nags, two long-necks would create offspring with even longer necks and so it would go. But whether it had been short or long, a neck is something the giraffe had all along, from the time the species was no taller than a goat. A change in the environment favored giraffes with longer necks. This made perfect sense to me, but it in no way explained how one celled animals evolved into something more complex. How did a central nervous system evolve? Could this have been accidental? A heart and liver and lungs came about by accident, too? Was it actually possible that enough monkeys with enough typewriters would eventually write *War and Peace?*

With no typos?

This defied logic. The odds were simply much too great. I was forced to the conclusion that a lot of people had been kidding themselves and others.

What I didn't understand, then, was that a new religion had grown up from the time of Newton and Descartes called Science. Science as it was practiced in the time of my parents was concerned solely with what could be measured. Only what existed in the material world fell into this category. If something could not be measured, it either didn't exist or wasn't important. As is often the case with religions, denial took hold and dogma developed. Everyone had to go along. Anyone who pointed to the holes in thinking, no matter how obvious they might be to the casual observer, was in danger of being kicked out for heresy. This religion had as its primary tenet that only matter is real. Supposedly, even human consciousness could be explained in terms of matter. What the professors and everyone else turned a blind eye to is how much exists that cannot be explained within the confines of the religion of Scientific Materialism. For starters, what animates the body? Nowhere in any of my college textbooks, including the one on biology, is there any reference to the Life Force — by this name or any other. Nothing even alludes to it.

How does consciousness spring from inert matter? Where in the brain is memory stored? Within the science of materialism, how can psychic phenomena — which have been scientifically demonstrated — be explained? If only matter exists, how does thought travel from one brain to another? Why and how does prayer work? How can the number of times heads or tails comes up be affected by thought? These phenomena have been demonstrated in laboratories. The standard answer of scientific materialists is to dismiss them as anomalies, but this explains nothing. They continue to exist.

The genes may account for hair color and eye color, but how do different cells know their role is to become a kidney or a foot or a brain when an animal or human embryo grows in the womb? My professor of biology said this information is also encoded in the genes. But this has never been demonstrated. The genes dictate the primary structure of proteins, not the individual parts of the body. Given the right genes and hence the right proteins, and the right systems by which protein synthesis is controlled, an organism is supposed to assemble itself. But how? As the Cambridge-educated biochemist Rupert Sheldrake wrote, "This is rather like delivering the right materials to a building site at the right times and expecting a house to grow spontaneously."

We will return to this. The point is, believing dogmatically in Scientific Materialism takes as much faith as believing Adam literally was created by God out of dirt, and that he came into the world as a fully-evolved *homo sapiens*.

I don't recall precisely when I first began to doubt the religion practiced in my home. Perhaps it began with my penchant for waking up before the alarm clock went off. On a day when I had an important meeting, or a plane to catch at say 6:30 in the morning, I'd wake up seconds before the alarm. My eyes would pop open and my hand would go out and push down the plunger an instant before the second hand reached twelve and the buzzer sounded. Not so extraordinary, perhaps, and easily explained from a scientific point of view. My body, like everyone else's body is equipped with its own biological clock. At least that's the explanation I received. No one could say where the clock was located, but it must have been there. Otherwise how could this happen?

I found this impossible to accept. Now I know the answer. But at the time I wondered how my biological clock could adjust so quickly to different time zones, or to a clock in a hotel room that was a few minutes fast or slow. It also struck me as odd when the phenomenon continued in Europe, where I was six time zones away from home.

Another thing that troubled me was a feeling I often get when I walk into a room or step onto an elevator and someone is watching me. I turn. They look away.

How could I know?

Then one day I went to a luncheon given by a television station. A door prize was to be given away, a new Sony TV. When the time came for the drawing, I pulled my ticket from my pocket, looked at it, and experienced a sensation that said, *You've won.*

The numbers were read. Each one matched.

Nowadays I wonder whether the belief and feeling that I'd won produced the fact that I won, or whether precognition is possible and somehow my intuition looked into the future and saw what was about to happen. Now I realize it could have been either, but back then *coincidence* was the only acceptable explanation — although this didn't seem at all adequate and certainly wasn't satisfying.

I remained a faithful Scientific Materialist to the outside world because I didn't want to be excommunicated. But on the sly, I was now on the lookout for more inexplicable incidents. The next one came at the end of a vacation in Corsica where my wife and I, and our then three-year-old daughter, had spent a week at the summer home of one of my wife's childhood friends.

Both my wife and her friend were French. Or, more accurately, the friend was half French and half Corsican. No matter what this mixture might be called, this young woman was most definitely not a Scientific Materialist. I suspect this is often the case among those who feel particularly close to a place as Corsicans do to their "Isle of Beauty." I found myself amused by what I considered to be her fantasies of spooks and fairies lurking here and there — in wildflowers called four-o'clocks, in mountain glades and the maquis. She even believed she could tell fortunes by reading tea leaves and tarot cards.

I resisted her attempts to tell me my fortune until the last night of our visit. Even then, I limited my participation to only two cards, which I pulled from the deck and handed to her.

She studied them. "You will soon be going on a journey," she said, folding them together and handing them back. "On this journey you will meet a young man. You will know him because he is blond. He will be in need of your help. Whether you come to his assistance is your decision."

She was half right, I thought. I was going on a journey. We were leaving the next morning, as she well knew. That didn't prove a thing.

Before I returned the cards to the deck, I looked at them. One pictured a young man — blond as a Nordic god. He did look in need of help.

I forgot about this until something happened after we landed at the airport in Marseille. We had to catch a cab. I was afraid I didn't have enough cash, so I took a place in line at an airport bank to change some dollars into francs.

The man directly ahead of me reached the teller window, unfolded an enormous bill, and slipped it through. The teller looked at it, and turned it over. "Ooh, la, la," he muttered.

He looked up, shook his head, and handed back the bill.

The man's face fell as he took it. "What's wrong?" he said with a Norwegian accent.

The bank teller spoke in rapid French. He gestured with his hands, his head, his eyes. My glance shifted to the man with the big bill. He was young and blond.

"I've just arrived from Oslo," he said in English. "I have no French money. What will I do?"

The teller waved his hands as if to dismiss the subject. Then he leaned forward and spoke slowly and loudly in French.

"What? I do not understand." The young man shook his head. "Please repeat. Oh, no, what am I to do?"

"Excuse me," I said. "Maybe I can help." I leaned forward to hear the teller, who explained in French that the bill was too large. He didn't have authority to change that many kroner. The man would have to go to the main branch of the bank in downtown Marseille and change the bill there.

I turned to the blond young man, and translated. "You don't have something smaller?" I said.

He shook his head. "I'll take a taxi. The driver will have to wait to be paid until I've changed this." He looked me in the eye. "Thank you, thank you very much. You've been most helpful."

I'd assisted him all right, a blond young man, as my wife's friend had predicted.

This "coincidence" got me thinking again and it wasn't long, only a matter of hours, before I had another incident to chew on.

It happened that same night.

Marseille is not a stop I'd recommend if you have the choice of going elsewhere in the south of France but even this filthy port city has at least one neighborhood with charm — the one where Joel, another of my first wife's childhood friends, lived. That day's final destination was her home, which was situated on a steep, curved lane where walls hid quiet gardens, on the southern side of the hill below the statue of Notre Dame.

This icon of the mother of Jesus looks down from atop the highest point in Marseille. She has a magnificent view of the burning bright, azure harbor and the island fortress of Count of Monte Cristo fame. Joel's house could be found a hundred feet or so directly below Mary's statue, behind an iron gate, recessed into the side of the hill. The stucco covered stone house had three levels, the bottom of which was an English basement at grade with a terrace in front. Joel lived there with her widowed mother. Neither of them worked outside the home, and I imagine money was short. Perhaps as a result, they had turned the ground floor into a separate apartment and had rented it out. The first tenant had turned out to be a dashing young man who worked with Jacques Cousteau (11 June 1910 – 25 June 1997). This young Frenchman named Philippe gallivanted around the world on a converted minesweeper called the Calypso along with Cousteau and his motley ban of adventurers and marine biologists. The apartment in the quiet Marseille neighborhood was where he lived when he wasn't gallivanting. As luck and love would have it, he and Joel fell for each other and got engaged. The four of us had chummed around before my wife and I were married, and when we two tied the knot, Philippe had been the French equivalent of my best man and she had been the maid of honor.

That had been in happier times. The mood was somber when we arrived at the house in Marseille that year. Only a few months prior, the dashing young man had died a tragic death.

Philippe had been possessed of a fascination with death. He sincerely believed that it did not represent the end. Rather, he hypothesized that we enter another dimension, that we "cross over" into what I now realize is the mental world of spirit that in many respects mirrors the physical side of existence. Looking back with the perspective that time and increased knowledge give, I believe his preoccupation, his burning curiosity, may have led him to harbor an unconscious death wish. I recall vividly how he would barrel down a narrow Marseille city street on a 750 cc Triumph motorcycle at 120 miles an hour. He did this once with me hanging on in back, praying as no Scientific Materialist had ever prayed before. He also flew small planes, once taking a Piper Cub to Corsica across open water at night with no instruments. Skydiving was another hobby, and deep sea diving was part of his job. You can still catch sight of him in reruns of Cousteau, playing ring around the rosy with a bunch of hungry sharks.

In the year or two leading up to our visit to Marseille that year, Philippe had fallen into despair, and his death was thought to have been the result of suicide.

Several things had gone wrong for him. First, by that time — the mid 1970s — Cousteau and the Calypso were no longer taking voyages to exotic locations. Replacing a job as a seafaring adventurer isn't easy. But he needed one, and he'd taken a position as captain of a boat that tended offshore oil rigs. The result was that he was bored to death, perhaps almost literally. Second, his romance with Joel was on the rocks. From what I could determine, they'd broken up after a couple of silly arguments. She was still mad about him, but was playing a game some people play — hard to get. She refused to see him, no matter how he tried. Who knows what else had gone wrong. Other factors may have come into play that I cannot recall or of which I was unaware. But the bottom line was, he was found dead one day in his cabin at sea.

On several occasions Philippe had told friends, his ex-fiancee included, that he would communicate with them after he died if it were possible. The fiancee was all aflutter when we arrived. She was bursting to unload a lot of pent up stuff on my wife. For starters, her wristwatch had stopped when his funeral had begun, and had not resumed until the moment the funeral ended. I didn't see that this actually proved anything, but it did make me wonder. Anyway, I didn't have much opportunity to think because Joel was jabbering on and on about black cats and bumps in the night.

We all had a late dinner that evening, and I decided to turn in. My head was starting to ache from trying to keep up with the conversation, which was in French. It looked as though Joel and my wife were well on the way to staying up all night talking, so I suggested that I put our daughter Sophie to bed and then turn in myself.

Sophie was in another room, playing with her dolls. We said good night to her mom and Joel, descended a dark, circular staircase, and walked hand in hand through a dimly lit storage room. As in past years, we'd be sleeping in Philippe's old apartment. My hand closed around the knob and I pushed the door open.

Nothing had changed. Every piece of furniture, every wall hanging was exactly as he'd left it.

The most bizarre sensation overwhelmed me. I felt that Philippe was here in the room, present among his belongings: the American Indian throw on the bed, the primitive masks and spears on the walls, the little statues and knickknacks from all over the world, including local deities and fertility gods. His presence was palpable, and it grew more so each second, seeming to close in on me, as if he had moved close to examine my face. I could almost feel his breath.

I did not want to upset my daughter, so I helped her into her pajamas, and went through the usual bedtime routine of a story. At last, I put her down in a child's bed, which had been positioned at the foot of Philippe's and turned out the lights, except for one by the bed I'd use to read by. Then I crawled under the covers.

All was silent. I opened a book but could not concentrate. Philippe's presence was strong, particularly when I looked at the primitive wall hanging of a sunburst. The handwoven image reminded me of the rising sun of Japan. My eyes were drawn to the center until the circle filled my vision.

What seemed a disembodied voice said, "Don't think about ghosts. It doesn't do any good to think about ghosts."

It was Sophie. I'd thought she was asleep but along with every hair on my body, she was sitting up.

I had no idea she even knew what a ghost was, or rather what a ghost was supposed to be. We'd never talked about them. At that point, I still wasn't sure they even existed. Nothing except matter did, right? I certainly hoped so.

In retrospect I should have asked, "Why do you say that, dear?" But I wasn't thinking clearly. Instead, I said, "That's correct, dear. It doesn't do any good to think about ghosts." She laid down, and I didn't hear from her again that night.

What do you suppose caused her to sit up and make that rather interesting observation? I believe that three possibilities exist. First, although I don't recall that we'd ever talked about it and neither did my wife when I told her about it later, Sophie may have been aware that Philippe was dead and that we were spending the night in a dead man's apartment. This unsettling idea may have played on her mind, as it obviously played on mine. She simply may have been reassuring herself—"There's no need to be afraid of the dark. There aren't really any goblins under the bed." Only, my experience as a father of four is that young children believe there are goblins under the bed no matter how emphatically one assures them that they're not. Anyway, she didn't say that ghosts aren't real. She said I ought not to think about them.

Second, she may have picked up on my thoughts through mental telepathy. People who believe in such things think those who are closely related such as a mother and son or father and daughter or sister and brother are particularly susceptible to this sort of telepathy. I was indeed thinking about a ghost. Maybe she tuned in on this and decided to give me a piece of worldly, three-year-old daughter advice. I must say, however, that she refrained from dishing it out again until she was approximately nineteen. As every parent of a nineteen-year-old can verify, at that age the child knows everything and the parent knows nothing, encumbered as parents are by the stupidity that comes from having reached one's forties.

The third possibility is that Philippe was using Sophie's three-year-old, half-asleep mind to communicate as he'd promised he would. If so, the message he chose is particularly significant in light of his former preoccupation with death and his reported suicide. "Don't think about ghosts. It doesn't do any good." I've taken that to mean, live life while you can. Death will come soon enough.

Maybe you can think of another explanation. If so, write to me in care of the publisher of this book because I'd be interested in hearing it. Otherwise, take your pick from the possibilities listed above. Be advised, though, that the second two require something to have happened that my parents and other Scientific Materialists would say cannot: Either unspoken thoughts passing between Sophie and me, or unspoken thoughts passing from Philippe's ghost to Sophie and then aloud to me. My intuition—which Scientific Materialists would say doesn't exist—tells me it was the latter. Why? Because of the extremely strong sense of Philippe's presence in the room.

It was much stronger than eyes on my back.

And so we have the question before us, after the flesh and blood body roams Earth, does a spiritual body continue? If this experience was more than a coincidence and hallucination, it may well be the case. In fact, anyone who doubts the possibility should read Dr. Stephen Braude's book, *Immortal Remains: The Evidence for Life After Death*, Rowman & Littlefield Publishers, Inc., 2003. Dr. Braude was on my show in August 2008. A university professor and meticulous researcher, he has taken a close look a number of cases suggesting survival after death and concludes that we definitely have good reason to believe that it is so. This would also seem to be supported by the near death experiences (NDEs), which have been reported and written about ad infinitum since Raymond Moody's book, *Life After Life*, was first published in 1975.

Scientific Materialists have tried to explain NDEs by telling us people were experiencing some sort of process that takes place in the brain when we die caused by a lack of oxygen. But not all scientists agree. Consider what one medical doctor wrote:

> *The Light is the one element of the near-death experience that brain researchers can't even come close to explaining. The testimony of children is clear on this point: The Light is the key element of the NDE.*
>
> *How can we scientifically explain this light after death? I do not know of any biochemical or psychological explanation for why we would experience a bright light as the final stage of bodily death.*[10]

We have spoken of the unity of all things — that we are all connected by the ground of being that is spirit. It's interesting that this sense of unity often is reinforced by an NDE. Raymond Moody tells us in his book, *The Light Beyond*, that NDEers come back to life with a sense that everything in the universe is connected. They don't always find this concept easy to define but most have new respect for nature and the world around them. To illustrate, Dr. Moody quotes a man he described as a hard-driving, no-nonsense businessman who had an NDE during a cardiac arrest at the age of sixty-two:

> *The first thing I saw when I awoke in the hospital was a flower, and I cried. Believe it or not, I had never really seen a flower until I came back from death. One big thing I learned when I died was that we are all part of one big, living universe. If we*

---

[10] Morse (with Paul Perry), page 133.

think we can hurt another person or another living thing without hurting ourselves, we are sadly mistaken. I look at a forest or a flower or a bird now, and say, "That is me, part of me." We are connected with all things and if we send love along those connections, then we are happy.

Five steps seem to be common to NDEs:

1. A sense of being dead; sudden awareness of a fatal accident or of not surviving an operation.

2. An out-of-body experience; the sensation of peering down on one's body. NDEers often report back the scene of their near-death with uncanny accuracy, quoting doctors and witnesses verbatim.

3. Some kind of tunnel experience, a sense of moving upward or through a narrow passage.

4. Light; light "beings"; God or a God-like entity. For those having a "hell-like" experience, the opposite may be true — darkness or a lack of light.

5. Life review; being shown one's life, sometimes highlighting one's mistakes or omissions.

An argument can be made that the NDE adheres fairly closely to the Christian idea of heaven and hell. Heaven is generally supposed to be a place or a state of being where one is with God or Christ. This corresponds to the Light and the beings of light described in step four above.

Hell is often thought of as being separated from God, or lost in the darkness so to speak. In her bestseller, *Embraced by the Light*, Betty Eadie writes, "Some who die as atheists, or those who have bonded to the world through greed, bodily appetites, or other earthly commitments find it difficult to move on, and they become earth-bound. They often lack the faith and power to reach for, or in some cases even to recognize, the energy and light that pulls us toward God. These spirits stay on Earth until they learn to accept the greater power around them and to let go of the world. When I was in the black mass (of the tunnel) before moving towards the light, I felt the presence of such lingering spirits."

The review that takes place could be the judgment spoken of in the Bible, although it is not what most Christians are expecting since in NDEs judgment is made not by God or the Being of Light but by the very individual whose life is in review. Dr. Moody wrote of this:

When the life review occurs, there are no more physical surroundings. In their place is a full color, three-dimensional, panoramic review of every single thing the NDEers have done in their lives.

This usually takes place in a third-person perspective and doesn't occur in time as we know it. The closest description I've heard of it is that the person's whole life is there at once.

In this situation, you not only see every action that you have ever done, but you also perceive immediately the effect of every single one of your actions upon the people in your life.

So for instance, if I see myself doing an unloving act, then immediately I am in the consciousness of the person I did that act to, so that I feel their sadness, hurt, and regret.

On the other hand, if I do a loving act to someone, then I am immediately in their place and I can feel the kind and happy feelings.

Through all of this, the Being is with those people, asking them what good they have done with their lives. He helps them through this review and helps them put all the events of their life in perspective.

All of the people who go through this come away believing that the most important thing in their life is love.

For most of them, the second most important thing in life is knowledge. As they see life scenes in which they are learning things, the Being points out that one of the things they can take with them at death is knowledge. The other is love.

This emphasis on the importance of love brings to mind the teachings of Jesus and is echoed in the words of Betty Eadie, "With all of this understanding, I understood again that love is supreme. Love must govern. Love always governs the spirit, and the spirit must be strengthened to rule the mind and flesh." She also wrote, "Whatever we become here in mortality is meaningless unless it is done for the benefit of others. Our gifts and talents are given to us to help us serve. And in serving others, we grow spiritually."

I find this message from Betty Eadie to be quite profound. It certainly dovetails with my personal experience. But beyond this, reports of NDEs, as well as out of body experiences, have become routine. According to one Gallup poll, some 13 million people in the United States claim to have gone through the dark tunnel toward the light.

And certainly the idea of ghosts is far from new. I had an uncle, for example, who told me that his best friend dropped in to see him just after having died. My uncle didn't know his friend was a ghost until the next morning, when he found out the friend had passed away an hour before the visit. During that visit the friend explained several aspects of his will and told my uncle where the key was hidden to the safe deposit box in which the will was kept.

Usually, however, we don't see ghosts. We certainly don't see a spirit leave the body when someone dies. I began to wonder how could all this be if things we can't see aren't real?

Ah, but often they are. Let's give some thought to how sight works. It's one of five senses that convey information from the physical world to our brains. Without sight or hearing we'd be like Helen Keller. We'd have a hard time imagining what the world around us is like. But even with 20/20 vision, our knowledge is only an approximation of what exists. For example, at this moment what you see is reflected light that has passed through the lenses of your eyes and struck the retinae. The retinae have translated the light into impulses and these are sent by the optic nerve to your brain. The brain translates these impulses into a picture of the page of a book that looks like the thousands of other pages of books you've seen.

But there's so much you don't see. You don't see the comparatively huge distances between paper molecules and ink molecules. You probably don't see the tiny cotton fibers, and you surely don't see microbes squirming around that were left by the last person who picked up this book.

Okay, you say. But scientists can see microbes with a microscope, and cotton fibers, and even some of the empty space between molecules. We know these exist.

Well, then, look around the room, and think about other things you can't see. For one, the space is filled with television and radio waves. Think of all the cell phone conversations going on you can't see or hear.

True, you say. But all it takes is a television, radio, or cell phone tuned to the right frequency to know they're there.

Yes. And with the right kind of lens or photographic paper you'd also be able to detect infrared light, which the eyes cannot. And X-rays. And gamma rays. And who knows what else.

A lot of things you can't see exist whether you like it or not. Suppose for a moment that the instruments to detect them had not been invented?

Let's think about a few other invisible things that are unquestionably real. What about a magnetic field? We can't see that or take a picture of it.

We could sprinkle some iron filings on a piece of paper, place a magnet in the middle and shake it gently. Presto, a butterfly shape would form.

How about a gravitational field? That's too big for paper and iron filings, but we know it exists because without it we'd fall off Earth.

What are these fields made of? They aren't material.

And how do they work?

These kinds of fields are curved space. The filings are drawn into the pattern of the space around the magnet. This creates what we call magnetic force. The moon follows the curved space created by the gravitational field around Earth. Earth follows the curved space around the sun and so on. This is what is called gravitational force. These forces are curved space. Perhaps thought forms are curved space, and some curved space thought forms become life on the physical plane. The thought form of a mouse. The thought form of an elephant. The thought form of you and me.

But wait a minute. Space is nothing, right? How can space be formed into a thought? How, from a Scientific Materialist point of view, can space be curved?

It can and is because matter isn't really matter in the hard and solid way we normally think of it, and empty space isn't empty. Everything is connected, and part of one complete whole, just as Stage Four intuition would have us believe. The physics of Einstein tells us matter is energy, and energy is matter ($E = mc^2$). Neither can be created nor destroyed — although each can be transformed from one into the other.

Life is a form of energy. Energy cannot be destroyed. Therefore life cannot be destroyed. Remember that the next time you experience the fear of death.

Contrary to how things may seem, when all is said and done, there really isn't such a thing as solid and separate stuff. Subatomic particles aren't particles in the sense we're accustomed to thinking. They're tiny packets of energy (quanta) that behave both like waves and particles. Quantum physicist David Bohm (December 20, 1917 - October 27, 1992) wrote, "Ultimately, the entire universe (with all its particles, including those constituting human beings, their laboratories, observing instruments, etc.) has to be understood as a single undivided whole, in which analysis into separately and indepen-dently existent parts has no fundamental status."

Anyone wishing to expunge Scientific Materialist dogma from his or her thought processes ought to read Gary Zukav's book, which I mentioned in , *The Dancing Wu Li Masters*. He explains quantum mechanics without using complicated mathematics. Afterwards, the person will no longer doubt the sense of connectedness that has started them on Stage Four of their journey.

Zukav writes, for example:

> *The astounding discovery awaiting newcomers to physics is that the evidence indicates that subatomic "particles" constantly appear to be making decisions! More than that, the decisions they seem to make are based on decisions made elsewhere. Subatomic particles seem to know instantaneously what decisions are made elsewhere, and elsewhere can be as far away as another galaxy! The key word is instantaneously. How can a subatomic particle over here know what decision another particle over there has made at the same time the particle over there makes it? All the evidence belies the fact that quantum particles are actually particles.*

This explains how I'm able to wake up the second before the alarm goes off. My mind, brain, the clock, everything — all of it is seamless. At a deep level, I know what time the clock says, even though I am sound asleep. Once we understand this, and accept it, we are forced to reconsider all sorts of dogmatically held beliefs of Scientific Materialism, from the possibility of telepathy and other psychic phenomena to the very nature of life itself.

One biochemist has indeed done just this. He has developed the field theory into what seems to me a more logical and intuitively satisfying explanation than can be offered by those who hold to the mechanical view. The biochemist's name is Rupert Sheldrake. While physiologists do their best to explain the functioning of plants and animals in mechanistic terms, explanations of some phenomena are sketchy at best. Sheldrake believes the following can be explained by the existence of what he calls morphic fields: Formation of the structure of organisms, instinctive behavior, learning, and memory. To this I would add the uncanny correspondences between temperaments, personalities and life choices often made by identical twins, even those separated at birth. I would also add an aspect of the evolution of plants and animals that has been recognized during the last twenty or so years: that when conditions warrant, changes occur rapidly from the standpoint of geological time.

We've noted that species may remain virtually unchanged for many millennia and then alter dramatically during an epoch when environmental conditions shift. This happens so quickly that scientists often are unable to find evidence of the transition. The eminent authority on evolution, Stephen Jay Gould, wrote, "The extreme rarity of transitional forms in the fossil record persists as the trade secret of paleontology. The evolutionary trees that adorn our textbooks have data only at the tips and nodes of their branches; the rest is inference, however reasonable, not the evidence of fossils."

Sheldrake has broken ranks with his fellow biologists by setting forth the hypothesis that the growth, development and the programmed behavior of organisms are governed by fields which exist much like fields of gravity or electromagnetism and that these fields change and evolve as a species changes and evolves. He calls them "morphic fields," the word "morphic" indicating shape or form. Indeed, these fields contain the *collective memory* of the entire species. He writes:

> *The fields of a given species, such as the giraffe, have evolved; they are inherited by present giraffes from previous giraffes. They contain a kind of collective memory on which each member of the species draws and to which it in turn contributes. The formative activity of the fields is not determined by timeless mathematical laws—although the fields can to some extent be modeled mathematically—but by the actual forms taken up by previous members of the species. The more often a pattern of development is repeated, the more probable it is that it will be followed again. The fields are the means by which the habits of the species are built up, maintained, and inherited.*

As indicated above, one of the main elements of the morphic field of a species is that it contains the entire memory of all the members that have gone before. As touched upon earlier, this can be seen in the development of a human embryo, for example, as it evolves from a fish-like creature through the various stages until it reaches human form. This is how physical characteristics such as the long necks of giraffes are propagated. It is how instincts develop and are passed along. If Sheldrake is right, his theory could form the basis of a scientific explanation for continuation of the existence of an individual after death. If the memories of a species continue, our individual memories must live on in some way after we die as well, whether intact in individual fields, or at minimum as part of the greater field of mankind.

Sheldrake calls his hypothesis formative causation, and it was first proposed in 1981 in his book *A New Science of Life*, and developed further in *The Presence of the Past* (1988). It suggests that self-organizing systems exist at all levels of complexity, including molecules, crystals, cells, tissues, organisms, and societies of organisms such as ants and bees.

Consideration of the existence of morphic fields provides a compelling explanation of how morphogenesis works. The genes supply the right building blocks of protein and the field provides the blueprint. Without this governing (morphogenetic) field scientists are hard pressed to explain something as simple as the shapes of your arms and legs and feet. They believe the information is encoded in the genes but aren't certain where or how. Think about it. Your limbs are made of muscle cells and nerve cells and bone cells and so on. They use the same building materials but have different shapes, just as differently shaped buildings can be constructed with the same type of bricks but with different blueprints.

Rupert Sheldrake is not the only one to have come up with such a theory. A man named Harold S. Burr, Ph.D., (1889 - 1973) did also. Dr. Burr was E. K. Hunt Professor Emeritus, Anatomy at Yale University School of Medicine and a member of the faculty of medicine for more than forty-three years. From 1916 to the late 1950's, he published, either alone or with others, more than ninety-three scientific papers. Dr. Burr maintained that all living things — from men to mice, from trees to seeds — are molded and controlled by electro-dynamic fields, which he was able to measure and map with standard voltmeters. He maintained that these "fields of life," or L-fields as he called them, are the basic blueprints of all life.

These fields may also explain a phenomenon of memory which has neuroscientists puzzled: where it is located in the brain. One way research on this subject has been conducted is to train an animal to do something and then to cut out parts of its brain in an effort to find where the memory was stored. As Sheldrake writes, "But even after large chunks of their brains have been removed — in some experiments over 60 percent — the hapless animals can often remember what they were trained to do before the operation." Several theories have been put forth to explain this including backup systems and holograms, but the obvious one in light of Sheldrake's hypothesis is that the memory may not be in the brain at all. Scientists have been looking in the wrong place. To quote Sheldrake again, "A search inside your TV set for traces of the programs you watched last week would be doomed to failure for the same reason: The set tunes in to TV transmissions but does not store them." In other words, the brain is a physical link to the memory located in our individual morphic field.

The brain is not the only physical link to the memories in a morphic field. Our entire physical body is linked to our field in that it is a projection of that field. That this is so can be seen in the experience of heart transplant recipients, for example, who often report having memories that do not belong to them. One little lady reported having constant cravings for chicken nuggets and beer after receiving her transplant. The problem was, she'd never before had chicken nuggets, and she wasn't a drinker of beer or any other kind of alcoholic beverage. After a recurring dream in which a young man came to her saying he loved her and had given her his heart, she decided to find who her new heart had actually come from. After a good deal of detective work, she learned that it had belonged to a young man, the victim of a motorcycle crash, who'd been found with a box of MacDonald's chicken nuggets and a six pack of beer stuffed inside his motorcycle jacket.[11]

Here is what makes sense to me. A person's individual morphic field — or L-Field if you prefer Dr. Burr's terminology — survives death. Philippe's L-Field was what I sensed that night in Marseille. Your field and mine have existed as part of the whole and have been evolving since the first life on earth. Your field and mine are part of the whole field of all life, and that of humankind, but they each also became separate, differentiated fields once we became aware of ourselves. Your individual field continued evolving as it came to the physical plane time after time in a long succession of bodies. You and I have walked Earth in human form in many different incarnations. For my friend in the apartment in Marseille, the most recent happened to have been as the incarnation I came to know as Philippe Sirot. Eventually, if he hasn't already, he will be born again with a new physical body. All Philippe's memories will come with him to the new body, whether or not he consciously recalls them, and he will most likely be troubled in this next go-round and have issues to resolve, given his suicide and the dangling love affair with Joel that he left behind.

I realize this may be heavy stuff for some readers. Because most of us do not have memories of past lives, it seems logical to assume that this is our first and only visit to planet Earth. But stop and think. Most of us do not remember much, if anything, of what happened to us before the age of four, yet those years surely existed, and what happened then can have an important effect on us in terms of how we relate to the world. Psychologists and psychiatrists will attest to this.

Now, before any staunchly Christian readers toss this book in the trash can in disgust, let me tell them about a man I interviewed on my radio show in the spring of 2008. His name is James A. Reid Sr., and he is a Southern Baptist minister, now retired. He holds a Doctor of Ministry degree from San Francisco Theological Seminary.

---

[11] Thanks for this anecdote go to Gary E. R. Schwartz and Linda G. S. Russek, *The Living Energy Universe*, Hampton Roads, 1999.

For fifteen years he was Chaplain to the Los Vegas strip, where he heard a lot of talk about Edgar Cayce and past lives, which he always dismissed as hogwash. Finally, he got so fed up he decided to write a book denouncing reincarnation as a Biblically untenable doctrine. But Dr. Reid is an honest and mature individual. Once he dug into Church history and the Scriptures he was force to change his view. He ended up writing a book that says the Bible supports the doctrine of reincarnation. It is called, *BORN AGAIN AND AGAIN AND AGAIN: A Bible-Based View of Reincarnation.*

Dr. Reid maintains that for the first five hundred years of the Church, reincarnation was accepted as fact. It wasn't until 553 A.D. that it was condemned by the Council of Constantinople, and then only by a narrow margin. He gives several examples why it appears Jesus and others of his time believed in reincarnation. For example, John the Baptist was supposed by many to be the prophet Elijah reincarnated. Jesus himself said this was so. (See Matthew 11:14.) Once, Jesus asked his followers who people thought he (Jesus) was. They replied that many believed him (Jesus) to be one of the prophets — presumably reincarnated, since the last prophet lived about 400 years earlier. Also, consider the story of Jesus healing the blind man as recounted in John 9:1-12, which begins as follows:

> *As he went along, he saw a man blind from birth. His disciples asked him, 'Rabbi, who sinned, this man or his parents, that he was born blind?'*
> *'Neither this man nor his parents sinned,' said Jesus, 'but this happened so that the work of God might be displayed in his life.'*

Since the man was blind from birth, the only way his sins could have caused his blindness was for him to have sinned in a former life. Jesus did not tell his followers this wasn't possible. To the contrary, he seems to have assumed it was possible, although he gives another reason for the man's blindness.

There are many other references to reincarnation in the Bible but believers overlook them because they have been conditioned to think reincarnation is anti-Christian. Kevin Todeschi, Executive Director of the Association for Research and Enlightenment, said on my radio show in November, 2007, that he as counted eleven such references in Matthew's gospel alone.

Much has come to light about reincarnation in the past twenty or thirty years. So much that today an open-minded individual familiar with the evidence would have difficulty refuting it. For example, Ian Stevenson, M.D. (October 31, 1918 - February 8, 2007), who was Carlson Professor of Psychiatry and Director of the Division of Personality Studies at the Health Sciences Center of the University of Virginia for many years, collected over 2,600 reported cases of past-life memories of which 65 detailed reports have been published. Specific information was matched with the former identity, including family, residence, and manner of death. I have read a couple of his books which were enough to convince me. In some instances a physical attribute on the body such as a birth mark coincides exactly with the wound a person died from in the previous life.

Once you accept the reality of reincarnation, you will begin to see life as a continuum rather than a one night stand, and this will have an effect on how you go about your daily life and relate to the world. Had Philippe realized this, for example, I doubt he would have taken the action that he did because he would have known that he'd have to face a similar situation again, and again, until he got it right. This is how we and everything evolve.

The morphic fields of individual humans blend into the overall morphic field of humankind. Each one affects the whole in terms of where the species stands in evolution. The same is true of species of animals, and this has obvious implications in the explanation of instinctive behavior. The collective field of a species that is hunted — deer, for example — learns over time to be afraid of man. An individual deer does not have to learn this after birth. He is born with it, and we label it "instinctive behavior." It's part of the collective memory of deer which is contained in the morphic field of the species. Adherents to the "survival of the fittest" theory will argue that of the many deer that are born each spring, those that possess a natural inclination to skittishness are more likely to reach the age of reproduction, and this is what has caused the trait to develop into an instinct over time. This makes sense as well, so it's hard to argue. My guess is — since most things have more than one cause — that both theories are correct. I'm willing to bet that someday science will demonstrate that they work in concert in a push-me, pull-me effect.

The fact of a collective morphic field helps explain the behavior of societal insects, fishes and birds. For example, we've all seen swarms of gnats, schools of fish, or flocks of birds behaving as though they were a single organism as they glide through the air or water, turning and diving as though they form one unified whole. Spend some time at an aquarium watching a school of fish. Something is sure to cause a minor explosion in their midst, producing momentary chaos as individuals scatter a short distance from their original positions. But within seconds, they will regroup and become a single moving organism once more.

The behavior of some species is truly amazing, or would be without Sheldrake's and Dr. Burr's theory. Key West silver-sided fish, for example, will organize themselves around a barracuda in a shape that seems dictated by risk. The distance between the school and the barracuda is widest at the predator's mouth and narrowest at the tail, where the threat of being eaten is the least.

In the world of insects, African termites, which are blind, rebuild tunnels and arches from both sides of a breach and meet up perfectly in the middle, and they can do this even when the two sides are separated by a large steel plate that is several feet wider and higher than the termitary, placed so that it divides the mound.

Concerning identical twins, the possibility they may share a morphic field in some way might account for physical similarities and behavioral choices that scientists have been unable to explain.

Beyond the fact of looking alike, which sharing the same field would explain, almost every identical twin can relate anecdotal evidence of a special, perhaps even "psychic," connection with his or her sibling.

A skeptic would argue that this sort of thing can easily be accounted for by the fact of having been raised together. But what about identical twins who were not? In 1979 the University of Minnesota conducted a study in which twins separated for years were investigated and subjected to medical and psychological tests. The results demonstrated astonishing affinities between the subjects even though some had never met. The example of Jim Spring and Jim Lewis, twins who never knew each other and were raised in different Ohio towns, is a case in point. Both married and divorced women called Linda and chose a woman named Betty as a second wife. Each of the two twins named their sons James Allen and each had a favorite dog named Toy. Both had identical blood pressure, sleep and heart-beat patterns. At the age of 18 both had suffered intermittent migraine headaches. Their drinking and smoking habits were identical. Both men also chewed their fingernails.[12]

Be all this as it may, what may be mind-blowing about Sheldrake's hypothesis to those accustomed to thinking of heredity as working solely by the passing of genes through egg and sperm is this: *acquired* characteristics can be passed from one generation to the next. As mentioned above, Dr. Stevenson found that birthmarks and other physiological manifestations often relate to experiences of the remembered past life, particularly when violent death is involved. This might explain the rapidity of changes in organisms when environmental shifts occur. Natural selection would be given a boost enabling a species to adapt more readily, not only because hard-learned survival behavior could be passed on, but because the information would not have to be passed solely from parent to offspring. As new behavioral habits or physical characteristics change the morphic field of the entire species, all its members would become affected.

---

[12] Shepard (1982), page117.

The implications of Sheldrake's hypothesis are incredibly widespread. To give an inkling of those falling outside the parameters of this book, consider this: during the past century athletes achieved ever higher levels of excellence in everything from Olympic track and field to tennis. Improvements in diet, equipment, training techniques and coaching have certainly played a big role, but one now must also consider whether memories located in morphic fields may also be a factor. According to the theory, what has been learned by the pioneers in a sport would become embedded in the morphic field of humanity, and this should make learning as well as body and muscle coordination easier for future participants. This might also account for child prodigies and virtuosos. Could it be, for example, that Tiger Woods is the incarnation of a Twentieth Century golfing great?

Sheldrake's hypothesis of formative causation is controversial, but it is testable by experiment. For example, when a newly synthesized organic chemical is crystallized for the first time (a new drug for instance) there would be no morphic resonance from prior crystals since none of the type existed before. Of the many different ways the substance might crystallize, one actually happens, and a new morphic field comes into existence. The next time the substance is crystallized morphic resonance from the first crystals will make the formation of the same pattern more probable. A cumulative memory will be built up as the process is repeated. Each time the newly established pattern forms, the particular formation will become more habitual and the substance will form more readily. This should be the case each time, no matter in what laboratory or location in the world the crystallization takes place. This tendency is indeed a known fact in the scientific community but other explanations usually are offered in attempts to explain it in a way that will allow researchers to cling to beliefs consistent with Scientific Materialism. The most common one is that fragments of previous crystals are transferred from laboratory to laboratory on the hair or clothes of chemists. Controlled experiments would be simple enough to conduct that could eliminate this possibility.

Given all that cannot be explained by Scientific Materialism, and in light of the theories of quantum mechanics, scientifically demonstrated psychic phenomena, and the late Ian Stevenson's research on reincarnation, what Sheldrake says makes sense. Behind and supporting the physical matter of the universe is an enormous field. Earlier we called it mind, spirit or the Life Force. Thought forms exist within this. Mankind has its own thought form, which Sheldrake calls a field within this larger field, as does each species of plant or animal. Everything — the Earth, crystals, toads — and everyone, all have their own personal field within the larger field of the group of which they are a part. All the fields, from that of the entire universe down to that of a single molecule, are interconnected.

One way it helps me to visualize many fields and one field is to think of the oceans and seas of Earth. Look at a globe. You'll see only one body of water encircling the planet, until you move close. Then the water seems divided into many different bodies.

Behind the outward appearance of a disconnected physical reality, we are indeed connected. This may explain the feeling of eyes on our back, waking up the instant before the alarm goes off, and since time is not a factor in this realm (see the discussion of Thomas Troward's theory in Chapter Two) the possibility of tarot cards predicting a chance meeting with a blond young man. It would also explain the existence of Philippe's ghost. Before I read about Sheldrake's hypothesis I had already sensed something like this. In one of my novels, *The Mt. Pelée Redemption*, the heroine comes to the same realization. She has had an out of body experience and glimpses of the Eternal. The following takes place after she has returned and described the experience to her boyfriend. He has just told her that she must have been dreaming.

> *I decided it didn't matter what Jeff or anyone else thought and turned my attention instead to the display of nature all around. A remnant of the glow of the light from the other side*

must still have been with me because I felt in awe as I took in the scene. We were passing giant bamboo, mountain palms, chestnut and mahogany trees, and were almost engulfed by foliage. It was hot and bugs swarmed and normally I'd have felt uncomfortable because of the temperature and the insects and the humidity or perhaps even frightened by what I would have seen as an alien environment. Instead, I had the sensation of being part of it, of being one with it, the same feeling I'd had when I viewed the sunset from the motorcycle. The Life Force was expressing herself and I was seeing the outside of what was inside, the physical manifestation of the invisible: one thing, completely and utterly connected. Then it came to me with the same unequivocal sense of knowing Jean-Luc had experienced during his revelation. I'd learned the secret of life. Of course, I thought, why hadn't I grasped it before? It is the urge *to* become *I'd sensed in myself for as long as I could remember, which I now realized was the light's desire to express and experience itself. A vision flashed in my mind of a cave, a cavern like we have in the Blue Ridge Mountains of Virginia with millions of stalactites and stalagmites forming intricate and wondrous patterns glistening with tiny droplets of water. The whole was nature and each stalactite or stalagmite a separate soul, or species of plant or animal. Each had its own identity but was also part of the larger formation of rock. Every drop of water was a current life leaving in its path a tiny deposit which helped shape the species, or in the case of humans—the soul. At that moment I understood that the realm of my father's Higher Self was a metaphor his mind had created just as mine had created this cavern, and that his life, my life and your life are like those water droplets. They are expressions of the light and cause something larger to grow, a universe that is becoming. They are sent forth as knights were sent forth to the Crusades.*

The heroine's vision of course is my vision. It is a vision of one giant connected whole that is constantly being expanded by the unique experiences and insights realized by each new life that ventures forth on the physical plane. It was brought about by the "urge to become." In other words, the driving force is the desire of spirit to know and to replicate itself. The nature of this force will be explored in the pages ahead. I will attempt to identify the implications of its existence, and to explain how we can each join with the force to allow it to help us move forward on our journeys past fear and doubt to a life of abundance, fulfillment and personal satisfaction.

Throughout the ages, mystics of all religions have recognized the existence of an unseen dimension. Some have gotten only fleeting glimpses of it, while others have basked in its radiance and experienced the incredible feeling of omniscience for extended periods of time. Yet, for all but a very few, the true nature of the unseen has remained a mystery.

Nevertheless, if Rupert Sheldrake is right, we do know some things about the invisible. First, it seems certain that the underlying message of all mythologies is correct: an invisible plane supports and informs the visible. According to Sheldrake's hypothesis, the universal field and the morphic fields within it give form to the physical world, from the shape of Earth and its gravitational field to the shape of your nose and the structure of a crystal. The field does not remain static but is constantly evolving. The entire morphic history of a species is contained by its field and can be seen unfolding in the growth of an embryo. A species' collective memory and instinctive behavior are components of this field.

Individual memories are contained in the fields of individual organisms. Brains are devices that retrieve memories and allow us to manipulate our bodies — move our fingers and toes — by connecting our minds to them. A least some of a field transcends the individuals of a species. This is most clearly seen in fields that unite colonies of organisms such as certain ants, bees, birds and fish.

Thus, the entire colony operates as one. Indeed, it may be possible that identical twins — as a sort of mini species — share a field at some level, just as at a higher level we as individuals share the field of the species *homo sapiens* and at higher levels still, primates, all life, and the planet. Taken to the highest of all levels, the entire field of the universe can be viewed as one living organism.

*Anyone who has had an experience of mystery knows
that a dimension of the universe exists that is
not available to his senses.*

Joseph Campbell
The Power of Myth

Chapter Five: Nirvanna, The Kingdom and Lucid Living

Everything within the universe is a part of the whole: Earth, each individual species, mankind, and every individual plant or animal including you and me. This vision of oneness mirrors the experience on the Pangbourne Moors described in Chapter One. It is the source of the sensation of unity experienced by mystics throughout the ages. Of this sensation, William Johnston, author of *Silent Music,* wrote:

> But there is a human question which psychology never asks and which leads people to religion; namely, what is at the deepest realm of the psyche? What is the basis or centre or root of all? Put in Jungian terms I might ask: When I go beyond the ego, beyond the personal unconscious, beyond the collective unconscious, beyond the archetypes, what do I find? And in answer to this all the great religions speak of a mystery which they call by various names: the Buddha nature, Brahman and Atman, the divine spark, the ground of being, the centre of the soul, the Kingdom of God, the image of God and so on. They use different terms; but all I believe, are pointing towards a single reality.

You and I now know it is mind, spirit, the Life Force, what Deepak Chopra calls "the field of infinite possibilities," the very fiber of the larger organism of the universe of which we are part. When we recognize this, when we truly feel it in our being, we are compelled to change the way we view all that surrounds us. As Joseph Campbell said, "But then, when the center of the heart is touched, and a sense of compassion awakened with another person or creature, and you realize that you and that others are in some sense creatures of *the one life in being,* a whole new stage of life in the spirit opens out." (The emphasis is mine.)

Let's think for a minute about the unity of all and what it means.

You know about out-of-body experiences. You may even wonder if the phenomenon is some sort of illusion. But if you buy the concept that everything is really just one large organism, then you must conclude that what you are having now is an in-body experience, and that this in-body experience is the illusion.

As was mentioned earlier, the illusion created by the senses is called "maya." You think you are looking at paper and ink that form light and dark areas representing characters and patterns that communicate words and ideas. What you actually are experiencing is an event taking place inside your head. Like a motion picture projected onto a screen at your local cinema, light is picked up by your retinae, transformed into impulses and sent over the optic nerve to your brain, which unscrambles them. This centralized event causes you to think you are encapsulated in your body and that the book you hold is something separate and apart from you, located outside. In truth, the bag of flesh and bones is only a footprint in the sand.

It helps me bring this into focus for myself by comparing this field to something else I know is present but unseen: television transmissions. Television transmissions are of a single kind. Their frequencies fall within a given spectrum. You and I can't see them, but the space around us is full of them. They manifest in many seemingly separated segments that appear on TV sets as television programs. Yet each single frequency is an integral part of the total number, which in combination constitute the band of frequencies used for television.

In the same way, your morphic field and its attendant conscious and unconscious minds are integral parts of the total field and the collective subconscious mind that transcends all humankind. Your portion of the field is manifesting at this moment through a body that until now you may have thought you were contained within. You might think of your body as a television set with only one channel that is tuned to your individual frequency. If it weren't functioning properly you'd be getting all kinds of signals, and the psychiatric community would call you schizophrenic.

You are not the television set, and you do not live inside it. The illusion that you occupy your body is the same one that a bushman from Africa might experience if he saw a television for the first time. He would probably believe the show was located in the set. If he took the set apart, he'd be surprised to find the program wasn't there. It simply does not occupy a given space. It is nonphysical.

Your conscious mind is a mind within a mind within a mind — your conscious mind which includes its unconscious part, your subconscious mind, and the universal or collective subconscious mind. Later, we will turn our attention to Arthur Schopenhauer (February 22, 1788 – September 21, 1860), the nineteenth century German philosopher who observed that specific events and the meeting of individuals, which seemed at the time to have come about by chance, later turn out to have been essential components in a constant story line. Using the a metaphor similar to what Timothy Freke used on my radio show (see Chapter One), Schopenhauer said it is as though one dreamer were dreaming a giant dream in which each of the dream's characters has his own individual dream. But, I believe that it's not so much that individual dreamers *coordinate* with each other. In truth, there's only *one* dreamer and *one mind.* You are connected to this one mind by what in this book I've been called your personal subconscious. Everyone's personal subconscious mind is part of it — just as indiviudal television shows each are part of a single band of frequency called television transmissions. Each dreamer might be thought of as an individual cell that is part of the whole. Each has a conscious mind, and each as a unique subconscious mind. But these merge into a collective mind we all share — saint or sinner, murderer, Sunday school teacher, Ted Bundy, Buddha, Christ, or Vishnu. We each have free will, and can do things that bring pain and suffering to ourselves and to others. But the one mind will almost always have subsequent events work out so that at least some good will come from our ill-advised deeds. As the Apostle Paul said, "In all things God works for the good of those who love Him." (Romans 8:28) Coordination happens effortlessly for the good of all toward the end goal of life in physical form: the evolution of humankind to ever higher levels of self-awareness and to the realization of our true nature as spirit having an in-body experience. The goal is for us to become co-creators — creators in cooperation with the Universal Mind. We hear the same idea expressed in a different way when people speak about God having an overall plan that we cannot possibly understand, and that "He works in mysterious ways."

You will know that you have achieved the shift in consciousness when you feel this at a gut level. This is what the Buddhists seek in their quest for Nirvana, what the Hindus seek in the ultimate union with Brahman, what Moses meant when he talked about his people being servants of God, and what Christ had in mind when he spoke of entering the Kingdom — and thereby becoming one of God's subjects. You will *know* that we are all connected — all one — and that what will bring you a sense of fulfillment is surrendering to and going with the force that some call grace and many think communicates with them by way of an inner voice known as the Holy Spirit.

Not long ago I came across what I consider to be an amusing view concerning the goal of life on earth in a book by the noted biologist, Richard Dawkins — a British ethologist, evolutionary biologist. His book considered the matter of cheetahs and gazelles, and that the former hunt the latter. Fleet-footed cheetah are superbly designed to hunt gazelles. Gazelles, on the other hand, are clearly optimized to evade cheetahs. What, Dawkins asks, is the overall goal of such an apparently self-defeating scheme? Certainly it goes beyond both the cheetah and the gazelle, and for that matter the brief lives of all creatures.

Dawkins concluded that the central purpose of evolution is the survival of DNA, not of the creatures that are the DNA's temporary expression. According to this theory, DNA has been blindly pursuing a plan of survival and reproduction of itself ever since the first molecule of RNA, DNA's elder cousin, got itself replicated in the stew of chemicals during the epoch when life on earth began.

One might expect a Scientific Materialist to come to such a conclusion. For them, RNA and therefore DNA came about by accident. Of course, the odds of this happening are greater than the odds of those monkeys I mentioned earlier accidentally typing *War and Peace.* Nevertheless, if one begins with the assumption held dear by professional skeptics that nothing exists which cannot be measured, then this has to be how the first molecule came about.

Once one accepts, however, that "Spirit is the life, mind is the builder, and the physical is the result," the situation changes. Spirit and mind led to DNA. In other words, *intelligence* is what's behind it all. Even so, it's quite possible that no purpose exists for cheetahs and gazelles outside of the desire of the universe to experience itself. I'm talking about amusement and entertainment. These have value. Why shouldn't they have a place in the great scheme? What purpose — outside of amusement — does a Junior-Senior prom serve? The cheetah and the gazelle may simply be part of the dance. To me this would be a more logical and satisfying explanation than mindless double helixes replicating themselves ad nauseam. Indeed, this idea of the universe expressing itself through its own creation seems to be the prevailing view in eastern religions and in pantheism. The universe just *is.* Its purpose is to amuse itself.

Alan Watts (January 6, 1915 – November 16, 1973) , a Twentieth Century philosopher and interpreter of Zen Buddhism, answered children's questions such as why they are here, where the universe came from, where people go when they die and so on with a parable about God playing hide and seek. Watts would tell them that God enjoys the game, but has no one outside himself to play with since he is all that is. He overcomes this problem of being all, and therefore not having any playmates, by pretending he is not himself. Instead he pretends that he is me and you and all the other people and the animals and rocks and stars and planets and plants, and in doing so has wonderful and wondrous adventures. These adventures are like dreams because when he awakes, they disappear. Watts wrote:

Now when God plays hide and pretends that he is you and I, he does it so well that it takes him a long time to remember where and how he hid himself. But that's the whole fun of it—just what he wanted to do. He doesn't want to find himself too quickly, for that would spoil the game. That is why it is so difficult for you and me to find out that we are God in disguise, pretending not to be himself. But when the game has gone on long enough, all of us will wake up, stop pretending, and remember that we are all one single Self—the God who is all that there is and who lives forever and ever.

It will no doubt be shocking to some to think of themselves as God, but Watts was talking about the core essence that is beyond the ego and deeper within than the personal unconscious, the collective unconscious, the archetypes and so on as was William Johnson in the previous quotation. As Joseph Campbell said, "You see, there are two ways of thinking 'I am God.' If you think, 'I here, in my physical presence and in my temporal character, am God,' then you are mad and have short-circuited the experience. You are God, not in your ego, but in your deepest being, where you are at one with the non dual transcendent."

By the way, I must admit I feel uneasy using the term God when speaking of the field because it is a confusing word, often loaded with emotional baggage, that means different things to different people. In our western culture it generally conveys the Stage Two idea of the big cop in the sky. For Stage Four Christians, Jews and certainly Muslims of the Sufi variety, God is present — immanent — in all things. God is the field. Without Him nothing else could exist. Yet He would continue to exist even if nothing else did. Alan Watts clearly was using the word in the transcendental — mind, spirit, Life Force, field of infinite possibilities — sense, as was Joseph Campbell. From here on I'll use the word in the same way. I'll also use a new term of my own, already touched on — the Big Dreamer.

If each of us is God, according to Watts we will eventually wake up and find out what our purpose — if there is one other than playing hide and seek. Nevertheless, in an effort to get our minds around what we're about in the meantime, let's continue to explore the possibilities.

We have learned that the field constantly is changing and evolving. This seems to argue against the concepts of determinism and predestination which have come in and out of vogue among theologians over the years. Nevertheless, a question we might ask is whether the field is moving toward a predetermined goal or state of being. Is the field on a path to a particular destination? Are we really to be co-creators? Is this the goal? If so, does spirit know the way it will get us to that point and simply is unfolding? Is there a road map so that everything and every event is known in advance?

Apparently not. There may be a final end toward which the field is headed, but it does not appear that the way to this has been known from the beginning because the most direct path is not being followed. For example, thousands of species of animals and plants have become extinct with the result that thousands of dead ends have been reached. What purpose, for example, did the dinosaurs serve?

Okay. They contributed to the oil and coal reserves. Without them we may have burned up all the forests by now.

Well, then, how about the Irish elk? His thirteen-foot-wide antlers certainly must have looked grand standing atop his majestic head, but the only purpose they served was the extinction of the animal who wore them when his environment shifted.

Charles Darwin (12 February 1809 – 19 April 1882) observed that evolution does not move ahead in a way that seems to have been predetermined. He expounded on this in his writings on orchids. He maintained that self-fertilization is a poor strategy for long-term survival since offspring carry only the genes — and, I would add, perhaps only the morphic field — of a single parent. As a result, plants with flowers that have both male and female parts usually evolve mechanisms to ensure cross-pollination. Darwin used orchids to illustrate the astonishing variety of ways that have evolved to attract insects, to insure that pollen adheres to a visitor and that once attached the pollen will come in contact with the female parts of the next orchid visited.

Orchids use the common components of ordinary flowers to fabricate the intricate devices that are required — components which are usually fitted for very different functions. Orchids are jury-rigged, so to speak, from a limited set of available parts, proof they are evolved from ordinary flowers. Thus, neither the course of their evolution nor even their existence as a species seems to have been planned from the beginning of time.

Another example is the panda's thumb.

If you've ever been to the National Zoo in Washington, you've probably watched the giant pandas eating bamboo leaves. They take stalk after stalk and slide them between thumb and forefinger, stripping them, then popping this mouth-watering high-fiber food in their mouths. You may have wondered how these big guys got thumbs since primates are the ones with opposing digits. Pandas belong to the family Procyonidae (raccoons, kinkajous, et cetera) of the order Carnivora, one of the hallmarks of which is that all five digits on the front paw point forward and have claws for ripping flesh.

On close inspection you'll find that the panda's thumb is not a thumb at all but a "complex structure formed by marked enlarge-ment of a (wrist) bone and an extensive rearrangement of musculature." Not having the thumb needed to make bamboo eating easy, the panda took what he had to work with and evolved one of a makeshift variety, according to biologist Stephen Jay Gould (September 10, 1941 – May 20, 2002), who also wrote, "The panda's thumb provides an elegant zoological counterpart to Darwin's orchids. An engineer's best solution is debarred by history. The panda's true thumb is committed to another role, too specialized for a different function to become an opposable, manipulating digit. So the panda must use parts on hand and settle for an enlarged wrist bone and a somewhat clumsy, but quite workable, solution." Gould added, "Odd arrangements and funny solutions are the proof of evolution — paths that a sensible God would never tread but that a natural process, constrained by history, follows perforce."[13]

From this we might conclude that either the field does not know where it is headed, or perhaps that the specific route it is following to get there doesn't matter. All that matters for the moment are solutions that work and thereby keep the journey alive.

What is clear in all this is that mind, spirit and the Life Force foster growth and in so doing search for solutions. It also seems certain that the theories of determination and predestination are off base, as the fossil record demonstrates. Solutions can't be found until problems are encountered. Once it was clear, for example, that the Panda would benefit from a thumb, the intention was somehow impressed upon the subconscious mind of the Panda — his group soul — and ultimately in the mind of the Big Dreamer — since there really is only one mind. A thought form was created and out of a bump on the wrist came a thumb. The same is true of the giraffe's neck. ("Hey, if I had a longer neck, I could reach the really good stuff way up there.") A recent example is that of the Tasmanian devil, reported on in a July 15, 2008, Associated Press article. Faced with an epidemic of cancer that cuts their lives short, Tasmanian devils have begun breeding at much younger ages than one would expect. The case was reported on by researchers at the University of Tasmania in Australia.

"We could be seeing evolution occurring before our eyes. Watch this space!" zoologist Menna Jones of the university was quoted as having said.

Tasmanian devils live on the island of Tasmania, south of Australia. They weigh 20 to 30 pounds and were named devils by early European settlers because the furry black marsupials produce a fierce screech and can be bad-tempered.

Since 1996 a contagious form of cancer called devil facial tumor disease has been infecting these animals and is invariably fatal,

[13] Stephen Jay Gould, page 20-24.

causing death between the ages of two and three.

In the past devils would live five to six years, breeding at ages two, three and four, but with the new disease, even females who breed at two may not live long enough to rear their first litter.

Jones, who has been studying the animals' life cycles since before the disease outbreak, noted that there has been a 16-fold increase in breeding at age one. She reported her findings in the July 14, 2008 edition of *Proceedings of the National Academy of Sciences.*

The disease could cause the devils to become extinct in 25 years or so, she said, but this change to younger breeding may slow population decline and reduce the chance of them disappearing.

Darwin's theory of natural selection is no doubt part of what is going on here, but this case and that of the Panda's thumb suggest something more at work. The speed at which organisms adapt, as in this case, argues for something more. This something more is spirit — the Life Force — and mind — subconscious/subjective — spurred on by the intent of a conscious or objective mind. It would make more sense to me if these forces together with natural selection are what produce the end result.

Let's take a brief look at the history of evolution. Before planet earth came into being an incandescent nebula was dispersed over a vast expanse of space. This condensed into a central sun surrounded by a family of planets. Eons of slow geological formation followed. Eventually, Earth became inhabited by the lowest forms of life in the sea. From this came an unhurried forward movement that brought things stage by stage to the condition in which we know them now. This progression clearly demonstrates the nature of the evolutionary principle. Evolution does its work by creating such great numbers of each kind of organism — many of which have tiny variations — that only those best suited to the environment survive. We may say, then, that cosmic intelligence works by a law of averages that allows a wide margin of accident and failure. In ordinary nineteenth century scientific speak this is the "survival of the fittest." The reproduction of fish, for example, is on such a scale that they would choke the sea if every single individual survived, but the margin of destruction is correspondingly enormous. Thus the law of averages simply keeps up the normal proportion.

But with humans and other higher forms of animal such as the panda with his "thumb," reproduction is by no means so enormously in excess of survival. True, accident and disease cut off some number of human beings before they are old enough to reproduce, but this is on a very different scale from the premature destruction of hundreds of thousands and the ultimate survival of one. It seems indisputable that as intelligence advances, the individual ceases to be subject to a mere law of averages and is more and more able to control the likelihood of his own survival. This is true on a day to day basis as an intelligent creature uses his wits to survive, and it appears true that as the intelligent creature sees what adaptations would result in easier survival, the intent of the creature's objective mind becomes impressed on the subjective mind and this in turn goes to work to produce the desired physical result in future offspring. This would account for the rapid adaptation of certain species during times of catastrophic climate change. It would account for the panda's thumb and the Tasmanian devil's rapid change in breeding capability.

Remember this whenever you feel a situation is hopeless. Like the thirsty crow in Aesop's fable who filled the pitcher with pebbles to bring the water level up to the place he could reach it with his beak, the first step is to use your brain. Identify a possible solution. Form the intent. Push forward. Support in the form of "breaks" — i.e. grace — will start coming your way. Believe me, you can count on this. I've experienced it time after time.

But let me caution you to stay flexible. The best solution may not be the one you've identified. Or the best way to arrive at the solution may not be the specific route you thought you ought to take. The wise thing to do is to go with the flow. Don't struggle against it. You know approximately where you want to end up, and it's important to do something. Action on your part is essential, so push in the direction that seems right. But if unseen hands seem to be guiding you in a slightly different direction, then by all means see where they lead. Keep in mind that you're privy to only one piece of the puzzle.

Let's return now to our discussion of the end game. Where can we find clues as to what spirit is up to?

How about those who have pondered this question deeply throughout the ages? In the final chapter of his book, *The Religions of Man,* Huston Smith who is among the preeminent religious studies scholars in the United States, came to a conclusion which may prove instructive. He writes, "Does not each [religion] contain some version of the Golden Rule? Do they not all regard man's self-centeredness to be the source of his troubles and seek to help him in its conquest? Does not each acknowledge a universal Divine Ground from which man has sprung and in relation to which his true good is to be sought? If all truth essential to salvation can be found in one religion, it can also be found in each of the other great ones."

Joseph Campbell echoed this: "All religions have been true for their time. If you can recognize the enduring aspect of their truth and separate it from the temporal applications, you've got it."

By "temporal applications," by the way, he meant those parts of a religion which stem from the culture and customs of its times.

What do the various religions say about where things are headed and why? Is there one, or are there components of one or more, that fit what we know about the field?

Let's take a look first at Hinduism, one of the oldest and largest religions (about 500 million followers). It is thought to date from about 4000 years ago. Unlike Christianity, Islam and Buddhism, it had no single founder. Hinduism came into being over time in the Indus River valley and other parts of western India and is completely decentralized with no hierarchy of clergy and no supreme authority. As Hinduism developed, it continually absorbed and reinterpreted the beliefs and practices of the different people with whom it came in contact. As a result, it differs in many ways from one geographical area to another. Generalizing is perhaps ill advised and full of possible pitfalls, but at the risk of incurring the wrath of some of its practitioners, I will plunge ahead and do so anyway.

Hindus believe that behind the ever-changing physical world is one universal, unchanging, everlasting spirit known as Brahman. The soul, or Atman, of every being in the universe, including the gods, is part of this spirit and inseparable from it.

Sounds pretty close to what we've been discussing, doesn't it?

Hundreds of gods exist but they are all of the same divinity, just as humans are, because everyone and everything is part of the oneness of Brahman. Only the veil of maya — the illusory world of the senses — prevents man from understanding and grasping this.

The concept of many gods is quite different from our western idea of the big cop in the sky — God with a big G. In some ways, Hindu gods might be compared to the Judeo-Christian idea of angels. They are not prime movers but arise out of Brahman as channels for its energy. Brahman is the ground of being from which everything comes. As a metaphor, this does not seem so very far from what we have been calling mind, spirit, Life Force, or the field.

So where do Hindus think things are headed? What is the purpose of it all?

According to Hindu belief, the course of the universe through time is cyclical. Every event has happened before and will happen again. This applies not only to the life of the individual in his rebirths, but also to the history of society, the lives of the gods, and the evolution of the entire cosmos. Each person has lived many times and the fortunes of the soul in each rebirth are determined by its behavior in former lives. This is the law of karma — cause and effect. It states that no sin ever goes unpunished and no virtue remains unrewarded. If a man does not receive his punishment or his reward in this life, he will do so in a future one.

On the surface it seems unfair that we would be punished or rewarded for something we did in another persona in another lifetime that we don't remember. But given enough lifetimes and therefore enough experiences things would indeed even out over time.

Another way to look at this is to envision the entire spirit of mankind as one life and each individual — past, present and future — as an incarnation of the one. Jesus may have had this thought in mind when he said, "Whatever you do to the least of these my brothers, you do to me." In the end, all our actions cancel out. Even so, the Hindu interpretation of reward and punishment may simply be an ingenious way to keep order, or as Joseph Campbell said, a "temporal application."

Hindu society is fragmented into several thousand castes, which comprise a hierarchy based on occupation and hereditary standing in the community. These castes range in size from a few dozen to a few thousand people. Although in modern times this is changing, traditionally a Hindu born into one caste was not able to change from one to another during his lifetime. He had to marry within his caste and would most likely possibly carry on his caste's traditional occupation. All the castes in a region are ranked according to social status, with Brahmins, or priests, at the top of the hierarchy. As a consequence of the doctrine of karma, the majority of Hindus have traditionally felt that one's position in the hierarchy is a direct result of one's behavior in previous lives. If a man performs the duties of his caste diligently, he may improve his caste position in a future birth. For most Hindus this was the goal of life at least until recently. But to us Westerners, particularly in America where class mobility is the norm, toeing the line with the goal of improving our social and economic position next time around hardly seems worth the effort. Like the highest caste of Hindu, we need something more to strive for. This leads to the question, what do the Hindus in the top category seek?

The top stratum is concerned with Moksha, or release from rebirth. There are three ways to break out of the cycle of reincarnation: 1.) A life of deeds appropriate to one's station in life. All actions must be performed selflessly, without regard to personal gratification. This leads to detachment from the self and union with Brahman. 2.) Uncompromising devotion and faith to a personal god.

This brings the believer closer to Brahman and can generate the insight of the unity of all things necessary to see beyond maya. When this happens, the soul is released. 3.) Direct insight into the ultimate truth of the universe — the unity of all things. This requires renunciation of all worldly attachments and a rigorous course of ascetic and mystical practice, such as yoga.

It appears, therefore, that the ultimate goal and destination for Hindus, where they believe all are headed and will someday arrive if they persevere, is what Alan Watts said. They will wake up and realize they each are God — or in the terminology of Hinduism, that they are Brahman. The illusion that they are not at one with Brahman, the sense that they are separate and distinct individuals who exist apart, is the illusion — maya — that must be overcome. Only one awareness or consciousness exists — Brahman — but it has been subdivided into many parts. Your slice is your individual mind. This is separate because it evolved over eons out of the Universal Mind. Eventually, when our individual minds merge with the whole, our consciousness will expand to include the whole.

Buddhism, which came out of Hinduism, teaches followers that they don't have to work their way up caste by caste from one reincarnation to the next for liberation from the wheel of life and death. Buddhists believe an individual does not even have to die.

Buddha — which means, "The Enlightened One" — was a historical figure who lived about 500 BC. His given name was Siddhartha Gautama. The story goes that at his birth it was predicted he'd become either a great emperor or a great teacher. Four signs would show him which course to follow.

Siddhartha's father preferred the emperor role for him and took great pains to prevent him from seeing signs that would influence him to be a teacher. As a result the boy was raised in luxury. But at the age of 29, he finally saw the signs his father had hoped would never come his way: old age—a decrepit old man, sickness — a diseased man, death — a corpse, and true serenity — a wandering religious mendicant. Siddhartha realized the first three signs stood for the presence of suffering in the world, which he perceived as doubly terrible because he believed, as did other Hindus, that man was continually reborn. Suffering was for all eternity. As a result, he left his family and set out searching for enlightenment. He took up with five ascetics but after six years got fed up and decided to sit under a tree until enlightenment came. He sat there for 49 days during which time he withstood the temptations of Mara, the Buddhist devil. On the morning of the forty-ninth day, he achieved enlightenment and union with Nirvana, which is the ultimate detachment from the world. With Nirvana comes an end to suffering. This is the ultimate goal of Buddhists.

But is Nirvana the end and the sole purpose of the evolution of a man or woman? Buddhism does not attempt to answer this. The fact is, Buddha refused to discuss metaphysics and never told his followers whether he believed life after death existed for those who had achieved Nirvana, or whether the world was eternal, or where it might all be headed. Apparently, he did not want his followers distracted from the hard road toward enlightenment. This is illustrated in Buddha's parable of the arrow:

> *It is as if a man had been wounded by an arrow thickly smeared with poison, and his friends and kinsmen were to get a surgeon to heal him, and he were to say, I will not have this arrow pulled out until I know by what man I was wounded, whether he is of the warrior caste, or a brahmin, or of the agricultural, or the lowest caste. Or if he were to say, I will not have this arrow pulled out until I know of what name of family the man is—or whether he is tall, or short, or of middle height; or whether he is black, or dark, or yellowish; or whether he comes from such and such a village, or town, or city; or until I know whether the bow with which I was wounded was a chapa or a kodanda, or until I know whether the bow-string was of swallow-wort, or bamboo fiber, or sinew, or hemp, or of milk-sap tree, or until I know whether the shaft was from a wild or cultivated plant; or whether it was feathered from a vulture's wing, or a heron's or a hawk's, or a peacock's; or whether it was wrapped round with the sinew of an ox, or of a buffalo, or of a ruru-deer, or of a monkey; or a razor-arrow, or an iron arrow, or*

a calf-tooth arrow. Before knowing all this, that man would die. Similarly, it is not on the view that the world is eternal, that it is finite, that the body and soul are distinct or that the Buddha exists after death that a religious life depends. Whether these views or their opposites are held, there is still rebirth, there is old age, there is death, and grief, lamentation, suffering, sorrow, and despair. . . .

I have not spoken to these views because they do not conduce to absence of passion, tranquility, and Nirvana. And what have I explained? Suffering have I explained, the cause of suffering, the destruction of suffering, and the path that leads to the destruction of suffering have I explained. For this is useful.

Therefore, my disciples, consider as unexplained what I have not explained, and consider as explained what I have explained.

Nirvana is a kind of peace, a state of mind or consciousness, rather than a place. It comes from knowing on a gut level what you and I now know on an intellectual level: that we and everything are one. It means getting in touch with the subconscious mind or soul and allowing oneself to be guided by this. Once a person does, the pain of existence vanishes and instead is replaced with joy. In the words of Joseph Campbell, "(Nirvana) is right here, in the midst of the turmoil of life. It is the state you find when you are no longer driven to live by compelling desires, fears, and social commitments, when you have found your center of freedom and can act by choice out of that. Voluntary action out of this center is the action of the bodhisattvas — joyful participation in the sorrows of the world. You are not grabbed, because you have released yourself from the grabbers of fear, lust, and duties. These are the rulers of the world."

A bodhisattva, by the way, is an individual who has achieved Nirvana, or at least has come to the brink of it but turned away to participate voluntarily in the sorrows of life. He has come back into the game, so to speak, in order to help others find their way out of it.

So how does one reach Nirvana? According to the Buddha one must know and live by his "Four Noble Truths":

1) *The Noble Truth of Suffering:* suffering is inherent in all life in the experiences of birth, old age, sickness and death; in union with

the unpleasant; in separation from the pleasant; in failing to obtain what one wishes; in clinging to existence.

2) *The Noble Truth of the Cause of Suffering:* suffering is brought about and people are born again and again because of craving or desire. This includes the craving or desire for any and every thing such as sexual lovemaking, food, and drink, and other matters of the flesh. As long as we crave the trappings of the world, we cannot escape from the world and will be reborn.

3) *The Noble Truth of the Cessation of Suffering,* which is the cessation of craving by the forsaking and relinquishing of craving so that one may be set free.

4) *The Noble Truth of the Path that Leads to the Cessation of Suffering (The Eightfold Path):* right view, right thought, right speech, right action, right livelihood, right effort, right mindfulness, right concentration. By following the path, craving is extinguished and deliverance from suffering (and into the state of Nirvana) is achieved.

It seems to me that this emphasis on suffering and a desire to escape from it may to a large degree be a product of the place and time the Buddha lived, another "temporal application." And no wonder. If you want to see the type of suffering that he and his followers wanted to avoid, you do not have to travel back in time to the world of 500 BC. A trip to the India of today or to practically any Third World country will do the trick. Gruesome is hardly an adequate word to describe the suffering.

For us in the West, a more accurate description of our condition can be found in the first three words of Scott Peck's book, *The Road Less Traveled,* "Life is difficult." Once we accept this, things usually don't seem nearly as bad as they did when we thought life was supposed to be a bowl of cherries. Life may be difficult, but difficulty is not nearly as unpleasant as suffering. Difficulty we can live with. Without difficulties, how would we know when times are good? As Khahil Gibran wrote in *The Prophet:*

Your joy is your sorrow unmasked.
And the selfsame well from which
your laughter rises was oftentimes filled
with your tears.

And how else can it be?

The deeper that sorrow carves into
your being, the more joy you can contain.
Is not the cup that holds your wine
the very cup that was burned in the potter's oven?

And is not the lute that soothes your
spirit, the very wood that was hollowed with
knives?

When you are joyous, look deep
into your heart and you shall find it is only
that which has given you sorrow that is
giving you joy.

When you are sorrowful look again
in your heart, and you shall see that in truth
you are weeping for that which has been your
delight.

Some of you say, "Joy is greater
than sorrow," and others say, "Nay, sorrow
is the greater."

But I say unto you, they are inseparable.
Together they come, and when one
sits alone with you at your board, remember
that the other is asleep upon your bed.[14]

Joy and sorrow are both integral to the game. But though all of us would like to minimize our difficulties, I have a feeling life would be dull if we did away with them entirely. It would be nice, however, to jettison the sense of frustration we often live with in this modern world. That gut-level realization of oneness with the field can enable

---

[14] Gibran (1923), pages 29-30.

us to do just that. Moments of joy would become more intense and be savored. Sorrows would be looked upon philosophically. Indeed, a sense of union with the universe would empower us. Once we come into harmony with all that is by forming an alliance, or merger, between our conscious, ego mind and our subconscious mind or soul, we put ourselves in position to live the fulfilling life we were born to live. And what a feeling of wonder this can be.

Alan Watts said of the realization:

> *In immediate contrast to the old feeling, there is indeed a certain passivity to the sensation, as if you were a leaf blown along by the wind, until you realize that you are both the leaf and the wind. The world outside your skin is just as much you as the world inside: they move together inseparably, and at first you feel a little out of control because the world outside is so much vaster than the world inside. Yet you soon discover that you are able to go ahead with ordinary activities—to work and make decisions as ever, though somehow this is less of a drag. Your body is no longer a corpse which the ego has to animate and lug around. There is a feeling of the ground holding you up, and of hills lifting you when you climb them. Air breathes itself in and out of your lungs, and instead of looking and listening, light and sound come to you on their own. Eyes see and ears hear as wind blows and water flows. All space becomes your mind. Time carries you along like a river, but never flows out of the present: the more it goes the more it stays, and you no longer have to fight or kill it.*[15]

Sometimes in the interval between wakening and sleep, I experience what Watts described. For me, it is as though creation is a giant expanse of soft, gray-white foam — actually millions of tiny bubbles, translucent and glowing. I understand that this is "the underlying tissue of life."

---

[15] Watts (1966), page 125.

My awareness is centered in one of the bubbles, which seems both tiny because it is at one with the larger mass, and large since it fills my individual consciousness. At once, I understand that I'm at one with the whole—all that separates me is an infinitely thin membrane—and at the same time, I am me, the individual who woke up in a crib fifty some odd years ago and wondered who he was this time. Since my mind is cordoned off, I have my own perspective. But I realize that all I would have to do is relax my attention to become absorbed into the whole and its larger awareness. I can experience this briefly. But if I were to allow myself to do so at length, I feel as though I'd become fully absorbed into such a blissful state that, in effect, my separate consciousness would be obliterated. At such moments, I realize that fear and doubt are the biggest obstacles to a life of full self-actualization and that by joining forces with the larger part of myself — the whole — anything is possible.

With this in mind, let's peruse some of the teachings of a carpenter who lived some 2000 years ago in the Middle East.

Whatever you may think of the religion which has grown up as a result of his life, the man named Jesus appears to have been one who lived as a true bodhisattva. He chose to participate voluntarily in the sorrows of life in order to teach others and lead them out of suffering. By age of 30, at the beginning of his ministry, there can be little doubt that he had achieved what the Buddha called Nirvana—the sensation I described above. In all probability, he was able to move in and out of this state at will. Once we have an appreciation for this, the majority of his sayings come into focus. The excerpts here are from the NIV translation of the Bible. For example, Jesus must have believed that all of us are one:

> *Whoever welcomes this little child in my name welcomes me;*
> *and whoever welcomes me welcomes the one who sent me.*

Luke 9:48

Most of what he taught falls into one of three areas. 1.) That faith brings peace. 2.) That the power of belief is awesome. 3.) That love and service toward fellow man are the paths into the Kingdom.

He sees that all life is orchestrated — by the Universal Mind or Big Dreamer, which he called his Father — for the good of the whole, and that people and creatures that pursue their intended purpose will receive what they need to live. This is true for lower organisms and for each of us as humans:

> *Therefore I tell you, do not worry about your life, what you will eat or drink; or about your body, what you will wear. Is not life more important than food, and the body more important than clothes? Look at the birds of the air; they do not sow or reap or store away in barns, and yet your heavenly Father feeds them. Are you not much more valuable than they?*

Matthew 6:25-26

On the power of belief he said:

> *Everything is possible for him who believes.*

Mark 9:23

> *I tell you the truth, if anyone says to this mountain, 'Go, throw yourself into the sea,' and does not doubt in his heart but believes that what he says will happen, it will be done for him. Therefore I tell you, whatever you ask for in prayer, believe that you have received it, and it will be yours.*

Mark 11:23-24

Notice the tense changes here and think back to our discussion of belief in Chapter Two. Jesus tells us to believe we have *already* received what we ask for, and if we do, we *will* receive it — in the future. Obviously, he clearly understood how the mind creates.

About love and service:

> *"The most important (commandment)," answered Jesus, "is this: 'Hear, O Israel, the Lord our God, the Lord is one. Love the Lord your God with all your heart and with all your soul and with all your mind and with all your strength. The second is this: Love your neighbor as yourself. There is no commandment greater than these."*

Mark 12:29-31

> *. . . whoever wants to be great among you must be your servant, and whoever wants to be first must be slave of all.*

Mark 10:43-44

One of the things that stymies non-Christians is the Christian doctrine that Jesus was God incarnate. We have seen, however, we all are one in spirit. Each is a spark from the fire we call God. In other words, we are each a piece of God, hiding from him to be sure — but at one with God, nonetheless. This is difficult to grasp only when our concept of God is that of the Big Cop, and Jesus as the Big Cop in the flesh.

According to Karen Armstrong, author of *A History of God*, the doctrine that Jesus actually had been God come to earth in human form was not adopted until over three hundred years after his death. Even the Apostle Paul, who supplied more New Testament writings than anyone else and did more than any other individual to get the Christian Church off the ground, never called Jesus "God." He called him "the Son of God," but this is a Jewish figure of speech of the time. For example, consider the following quotation of Jesus (Matthew 5:43-45):

*You have heard that it was said, 'Love your neighbor and hate your enemy.' But I tell you: Love your enemies and pray for those who persecute you, that you may be **sons of your Father in heaven**.*[16] *He causes his sun to rise on the evil and the good, and sends rain on the righteous and the unrighteous.*

I've added the emphasis. Not only does Jesus believe we all can be "children of God," but this quotation seems to demonstrate his understanding of the law of karma, which says that we get back what what we give out, and that no one and no thing exists apart from the whole. We all take part in the dance and are part of all that is, whether or not we behave as we should toward our fellow man. By striking back at those who annoy or harm us, we perpetuate discord and unhappiness for ourselves as well as others. One key to entering the Kingdom of God — tapping into and allowing ourselves to be guided by the Universal Mind — is to rise above the day-to-day fray and to see things and act from a unified point of view. We wouldn't get angry with our foot or elbow if it weren't behaving the way we thought it should.

To do this requires us to change how we think. Making this shift, allowing it to happen, can be compared to answering the call to adventure written about earlier. This takes courage because we must be willing to give up where we are in our understanding of life, as well as ideas that may have been held dear, so that we can climb to a new plateau. Nowhere is this more evident than in Chapter Three of the Gospel of John. Let's turn our attention to it.

It's generally accepted by Bible scholars that the Gospel of John was written by John the Apostle, the disciple to whom Jesus was closest and the person referred to throughout this Gospel as "the one Jesus loved." I suspect that few people today, or in his own time, comprehended the true meaning of what Jesus was saying most of the time, but if anyone did it was John. His Gospel is an attempt to

---

[16] A better translation might be *"children* of your Father in heaven."

demonstrate that Jesus was the Messiah whom the Jews had been expecting. In Chapter One of his Gospel, he promulgates that Jesus is the "Word," and that had been with God since the outset when God created the universe (Genesis 1:1) and spoke light into being by saying, "Let there be light." (Genesis 1:3) John seems to be arguing that metaphorically, at least, Jesus was God's vocal cords or "mouthpiece," to borrow a term from the old gangster movies, who had come to Earth in human form to tell people what God wanted them to know. Considering how closely Jesus was in touch with the subconscious, I believe John's portrayal is accurate.

John also states in Chapter One of his Gospel that John the Baptist was the prophet whom the Jewish Scriptures — the Old Testament — said would come before the Messiah in order to pave the way. This was important because many at the time were followers of John the Baptist and believed that he, not Jesus, was the true Messiah.

In Chapter Two of John, Jesus turns water into wine at the wedding feast and then throws the money changers out of the Temple, as well as those selling animals for sacrifices. The wedding symbolizes the marriage of the Messiah — the bridegroom — and Israel — the bride, which had been prophesied by the prophet, Isaiah, hundreds of years earlier. It seems logical that the two incidents (wine and Temple) were placed back to back in order to demonstrate the two sides of Jesus: 1.) The side that embraces and radiates love and joy, and feels deep concern for each individual in that he saves the host from the embarrassment of running out of wine, and the guests disappointment of a premature ending to the wedding celebration. 2.) Jesus' unbridled passion for God, and his determination to make God available to everyone. You see, the Sadducees had turned the Outer Temple into a market. The Outer Temple originally had been intended to be a place that *everyone*, including women and gentiles, could come to pray to and offer praise to the one true God. This got the Sadducees really ticked off at Jesus, and probably caused secret glee on the part of the Pharisees who were also among the priestly class and often disagreed with the Sadducees on one thing or another.[17]

Chapter Three of the John Gospel opens with one of these priests coming in secret to speak with Jesus in order to find out about him—probably to satisfy his own curiosity. Here is the text from the NIV version of the Bible.

> *There was a man of the Pharisees named Nicodemus, a member of the Jewish ruling council. He came to Jesus at night and said, "Rabbi, we know you are a teacher who has come from God. For no one could perform the miraculous signs you are doing if God were not with him."*
>
> *In reply Jesus declared, "I tell you the truth. No one can see the Kingdom of God unless he is born again."*
>
> *"How can a man be born when he is old?" Nicodemus asked. "Surely he cannot enter a second time into his mother's womb to be born."*
>
> *Jesus answered, "I tell you the truth, no one can enter the Kingdom of God unless he is born of water and the Spirit. Flesh gives birth to flesh, but the Spirit gives birth to spirit. You should not be surprised at my saying, 'You must be born again.' The wind blows wherever it pleases. You hear its sound, but you cannot tell where it comes from or where it is going. So it is with everyone born of the Spirit."*
>
> *"How can this be?" Nicodemus asked.*
>
> *"You are Israel's teacher," said Jesus, "and do you not understand these things? I tell you the truth, we speak of what we know, and we testify to what we have seen, but still you people do not accept our testimony. I have spoken to you of earthly things and you do not believe; how then will you believe if I speak of heavenly things?"*

---

[17] Later Jesus also alienated the Pharisees, who were ardent keepers of the Law, by arguing in essence that they had lost sight of the spirit and purpose of the Law and had allowed themselves to become caught up blindly in rituals.

As you have guessed, this is where the expression, "born again," which also can be translated, "born from above," comes from. It is perhaps one of the most misunderstood phrases in our society today, both inside and outside the Christian Church. Jesus is speaking of the shift in consciousness that occurs when a person realizes his or her connection to the Divine. Like the rich man in Chapter One, a person cannot be "born again," or "enter the Kingdom" without making a conscious decision to answer the call. God knocks, we make a decision to accept the invitation, and a relationship is formed that must be maintained and nurtured through regular prayer, mediation or, as Christians often say, a daily "walk with Jesus." Remaining steadfast to the path the Divine would have us follow is an important part of this walk. To ignore the direction we receive is to deny the relationship, which will eventually become severed.

Above, Jesus speaks of being born of "water and the Spirit." Water represents purification, as in Baptism, and the Jewish custom of ritual washing and bathing. The Spirit, as in the Holy Spirit, is the presence of God on earth. To be born of water and the Spirit results in a "turning away" from the egocentric nature we've developed during our stay on planet Earth since we exited the womb, and instead, voluntarily becoming a loyal and joyful subject of the "Lord" as part of His Kingdom.

The "wind" he speaks of is the air in our lungs, life, or better yet, the Life Force. No one knows where it comes from or where it goes. But those who are "born again" have tapped into it and allow it and the subconscious mind to guide them.

Picking up where we left off above, Jesus goes on to say:

"No one has ever gone into heaven except the one who came from heaven — the Son of Man.[18] Just as Moses lifted up the snake in the desert, so the Son of Man must be lifted up, that

---

[18] "The Son of Man," is how Jesus refers to himself throughout the Gospels.

everyone who believes in him may have Eternal Life. For God so loved the world that he gave his one and only Son, that whoever believes in him shall not perish but have Eternal Life. For God did not send his Son into the world to condemn the world, but to save the world through him. Whoever believes in him is not condemned, but whoever does not believe stands condemned already because he has not believed in the name of God's one and only Son. This is the verdict: Light has come into the world, but men loved darkness instead of light because their deeds were evil. Everyone who does evil hates the light, and will not come into the light for fear that his deeds will be exposed. But whoever lives by the truth comes into the light, so that it may be seen plainly that what he has done has been done through God."

Apparently, among his adversaries and followers only Jesus has experienced this close relationship with God, this awareness of being one with all, (i.e., only he has "gone into heaven"), so only he is in a position to speak of it authoritatively. Few today who know about such things would question that Jesus had extraordinary insight and was well into Stage Five spiritually, in that he was able to switch his perception back and forth between the universal mind and the material world. But this may not be the entire meaning of his words. Another possibility may be that somewhere along the line, Jesus had a near death experience, "went to heaven," and was sent back with a mission. Denise Linn, author of a number of books including her most recent, *Past Lives, Present Miracles*, recounted just such an experience on my show in spring 2008. At the age of seventeen, Denise was riding her bicycle along a country road in Ohio when what turned out to be a serial killer came along and shot her several times with a pistol. He left her for dead, and she did die in the hospital, but was resuscitated. Denise described the experience of dying and passing into a beautiful realm of light where she was greeted by heavenly beings. She said she felt she had returned home and wanted to stay. But she was told to return because it was not her time. As you might expect, this changed her life.

Others have experienced almost exactly the same thing. Betty Eadie indicates in her book, *Embraced by the Light,* that this is what happened to her. A similar experience which took place in World War II is described in detail in a book entitled, *Ordered to Return.* In December, 1943, 20-year-old Army private George Ritchie died of pneumonia. Nine minutes later, he came back to life profoundly changed. What happened to him while his dead body lay under a sheet changed his life profoundly. During that time he was given a tour of "heaven," and ultimately, he was "ordered to return." He became a psychiatrist as a result and spent most of his life helping those experiencing spiritual problems. Even so, Dr. Ritchie did not go public with the story of his journey into the afterlife dimension and back until late in his own life because he was afraid no one would believe him. His fear was that his credibility, and with it his ability to help others, would be lost. I've had three or four more people on my radio show who have told similar stories.

A third possibility is that unlike the vast majority of us, Jesus recalled the time before his birth and even his previous lives. Some other quotations attributed to him indicate that this may have been the case. He may have been what some refer to as an "ascended master" who was sent to earth with a mission. We will discuss this possibility when we take a look at what goes on in the interlife — the time between one life and the next.

Returning to our analysis, Jesus next forecasts his death on the cross (he will be "lifted up"), which will have the result of calling attention to his message so that "everyone who believes in him shall not perish but have Eternal Life." What follows is the most famous verse in the Bible (John 3:16). Please read it one more time: "For God so loved the world that he gave his one and only Son, that whoever believes in him shall not perish but have Eternal Life." In my "red letter" Bible this is attributed to Jesus as a direct quote. Even so, this does not seem to me to be the way a person talking about himself would speak. I suspect these words come from the writer of this Gospel — John.

No matter whose words they are, by and large the Church has taken this verse to mean, and has taught throughout the centuries, that anyone who believes: A.) That Jesus actually lived, B.) was the Son of God/God incarnate, C.) was crucified as a sacrifice for our sins, and D.) arose from the dead — is saved and will go to heaven.

I see nothing wrong or destructive in believing these things. I've come to believe they are true myself in a symbolic way. But the idea that Jesus was literally a blood sacrifice given to purify humankind is in my opinion a "temporal application" of the First Century civilization in which he lived. Back then, the Jews made sacrifices of "pure" animals — spring lambs, doves and the like. So did pagans. Sacrificing a "pure" animal to bring oneself closer to or to win favor with God or "the gods" was pretty much standard operating procedure. Jesus was thought to be pure and without sin. That he was a sacrifice that washed away the sins of all humans who accepted his crucifixion as such made perfect sense back then.

Defining "believes in him" as "A" through "B" also misses the mark in my opinion. To me, believes in him means, *"Believes what he teaches."* Nor do I think that belief in "A" through "D" alone will gain anyone entry into the Kingdom. What will get a person through the gate is that all important *shift in consciousness.* It is being "born from above," or, in other words, answering the call when God knocks, and forming that relationship. It is the gut level knowing that all is one and we are an integral part of it.

To me "believes in him" means "believes what he says." If asked, of course, practically any professed Christian would say he or she wholeheartedly believes everything Jesus ever said or taught — but actions often tell a different story. Let me hasten to add that many Christians do believe, and do act accordingly. And many form that crucial relationship with the divine.

But by putting the emphasis on the belief that certain events occurred and that circumstances surrounding Jesus were true exactly as reported, rather than on the ideas and concepts of Jesus's teachings, I believe that the Church has misled many into thinking they are "saved." In fact, if this is as far as they go they are not saved. After they cross over after death, these misguided folk will find that they have a lot of work on themselves yet to do. As has been touched on already, the real goal is the evolution of our consciousness to the point when we realize who we are — an inseparable part of the universe experiencing the whole — so that we become conscious and purposeful co-creators.

Later in the passage is the phrase, "has not *believed in the name* of God's one and only son." To believe in a person's name was a Hebrew expression of the time that meant to believe thoroughly in a person, i.e., their very essence, their beliefs, and what they stood for. A person's name encompassed the person's entire being.

Now if this is so, why would someone be condemned who does not believe in what Jesus was saying and what he stood for?

Jesus taught that the only way to enter the Kingdom is to form that relationship. (Be "born again.") If a person doesn't believe that, he or she isn't going to form a relationship, and without the relationship, he or she isn't going to enter the Kingdom. He or she is not going to experience lucid living. It's that simple. The person has condemned him or herself.

As previously mentioned, Jesus was, in Buddhist terminology, a bodhisattva, someone who has achieved Nirvana, but has returned to help others find the way. He was God incarnate and he was the only begotten son in that he embodied what is known as Christ Consciousness, the very highest level of consciousness encompassing awareness of reality as it truly is. Consider the verse:

"Light has come into the world, but men loved darkness."

What does this mean?

Simple. Most people don't like to admit when they're wrong, and they certainly aren't going to let on that they are bad or evil — even to themselves. That's why we have all those skeptics out there grasping at straws to shoot down every case of the paranormal that gets documented. They are in denial.

People need to get honest with themselves if they are to enter the Kingdom of Heaven — in other words, live lucidly. The shift allows them, perhaps for the first time, to see themselves as they really are. Without the ability to distinguish right from wrong — without the ability to tell light from darkness — a person may remain stuck in darkness. Apparently, this becomes literally true in the tunnel between this astral plane and the next, after death. Those who return from this experience report lost souls who cannot see the light they must go toward if they are to pass through the tunnel. These souls appear lost in the darkness, permanently separated from God.

Later, in Chapter Three (verses 35-36) of John, John the Baptist is asked his opinion of Jesus. Among other things, he says:

> *The Father loves the Son and has placed everything in his hands. Whoever believes in the Son has Eternal Life, but whoever rejects the Son will not see life, for God's wrath remains on him.*

John the Baptist recognized that Jesus had a special relationship with the transcendent, that Jesus was in contact with a higher intelligence, and that this intelligence came through him, i.e., "has placed everything in his hands." In essence John said, "Believe what Jesus says. Follow his teachings and Eternal Life will be yours. 'Reject' what he says, and you reject the relationship that you, too, could have with God." It's a choice. Believe what Jesus says, or *reject* it. Acceptance opens the way to perfect mental health. Rejection means keeping hidden away what then will appear in the form of panic attacks, depression, and many physical illnesses — from heart attacks to cancer. Indeed, God's wrath remains on those who stay in denial and keep issues buried.

At the risk of being redundant, let me say that by "entering the Kingdom of Heaven," and allowing oneself to be "born again," or "born from above," Jesus was talking about opening one's mind to the universal mind within. There is really only one mind so it is always present. It's what the Quakers, quoting from 1 Kings, call "the still small voice." But many people — Hitler, Bundy, and O.J., in fact perhaps most people — choose simply to ignore it. This is understandable. When we start listening, we open ourselves to the truth about ourselves. And the truth can hurt.

Yet, by opening ourselves to the truth, we also open ourselves to fulfillment and true happiness. It may take time, it may take effort, and it may be painful to see ourselves as we really are, but by bringing ourselves to light, we put ourselves in position to jettison old baggage. We can shed the mistakes and attendant accumulated karma and begin anew. What would otherwise require lifetimes of going in circles, lifetimes of learning the hard way and repaying old debts, can be accomplished in much less time and with a sense of joy and discovery that those who keep the door closed will never know.

The Kingdom is available to the living — of this there can be no doubt. Jesus makes it clear that it's not necessary to die or to wait for the second coming. This fact has been missed by many — though certainly not all — throughout the ages. The Gospel according to John is not the only place such references can be found. Once you become aware, you'll see them throughout the other Gospels as well.

Consider the following:

And (Jesus) said to them, "I tell you the truth, some who are standing here will not taste death before they see the Kingdom of God come with power."

Mark 9:1

The Kingdom of God does not come with your careful observation, nor will people say, 'Here it is,' or 'There it is,' because the Kingdom of God is within you.

Luke 17:20-21

The passage above can also be translated, "the Kingdom of God is *among* you," since the Greek word used means both "within" and "among." Indeed, the Kingdom of God is "within and among" all of us but most of us are blind to it. Perhaps this is because one requisite for entering the Kingdom is to set aside the tendency we all have to view the world from an egocentric position and instead to adopt an attitude of humility:

> *I tell you the truth, anyone who will not receive the Kingdom of God like a little child will never enter it.*

Mark 10:15

And with this comes the realization that you are one with and led by the transcendent. Here is Luke 22:70:

> *They all asked, "Are you the Son of God?" He replied, "You are right in saying I am."*

Jesus was the Son of God and the rest of us can be also. He was God incarnate because he was the Christ Consciousness embodied in flesh. The way to heaven is to achieve this. Consider that this may be what Jesus was saying in these verses (John 14:6-7):

> *Jesus answered, "I am the way and the truth and the life. No one comes to the Father except through me. If you really knew me, you would know my Father as well. From now on, you do know him and have seen him."*

With the shift in consciousness comes the realization that we are each part of something much bigger. Then it is possible to allow oneself to be guided by our subconscious mind or soul, which is in touch with the universal mind, the Big Dreamer. The ego — our sense of identity — remains but gives up its central role and willingly turns over the reins. To enter the Kingdom is to become a loyal subject. It is to say, "Thy will be done," and mean it. Paradoxically, this turning over sets a person free. The way to rapid spiritual growth has been opened in part because of a new ability to see the world clearly. This connection to the truth enables us to sort what is important from what is window dressing. It enables an individual determine his or her intended destiny.

Let's say you make the shift. Because of your new, objective viewpoint, you'll be able to evaluate your talents honestly and to determine your likes and dislikes. Before, these were determined to some degree by what others thought of you and what you ought to be doing. You'll come to know what you do best, what you are on earth to do. You'll see how this serves the whole. By serving others in a way no one else can, fulfillment and joy will manifest with very little effort. Perhaps for the first time, you'll be going with the flow and following advice given to you a long time ago:

"Row, row, row your boat gently down the stream.
Merrily, merrily, merrily, merrily. Life is but a dream."

Before it incarnates, each soul enters into a sacred contract with the Universe to accomplish certain things. It enters into this commitment in the fullness of its being. Whatever the task that your soul has agreed to, all of the experiences of your life serve to awaken within you the memory of that contract, and to prepare you to fulfill it.

—Gary Zukav
The Seat of the Soul

Chapter Six: Why You Are Here on Earth

Did we incarnate and enter the physical realm with a specific mission or missions to accomplish as stated by Gary Zukav on the opposite page? Many believe so. If so, some aspect of ourselves would have to have existed before we were born. Let's examine this.

To the Scientific Materialist each individual human is an assembly of parts, the same as my thirty year old Volkswagen convertible. We are built of a brain, heart, blood vessels and muscles. It has fuel injectors, pistons, a crankshaft and valves. It was put together in a factory. We were assembled in the womb. Fortunately, I've taken care of it so it has outlasted many of its contemporaries and enjoyed a relatively good existence for a car.

Humans, too, seem to be subject to the same whims of fate. One may be lucky and be born to a wealthy, well-educated family in the West or unlucky and enter the world in Somalia, Afghanistan, or some other Third World nation where living conditions are miserable and opportunities for a good life are largely nonexistent.

Or is it luck? We know from our review of the facts so far that a human being is not an assembly of parts. Rather, behind, supporting, and giving life to the physical body is a thought construction — an assembly of memories that exist in the medium of mind or spirit. To put it in Rupert Sheldrake's terminology, our physical bodies are projections of individual morphic fields in combination with the fields of other members of our species. Our bodies are not made of separate pieces. Each is a unified whole. The human body's abilities were shaped by the evolution and experiences of our species in an unbroken chain dating to the first life on earth. We are each separate only to the extent that we identify ourselves as such. On a deep level we are all totally at one with the Life Force and Universal Mind from which we sprang. Indeed, as we each grow spiritually and move through the stages described earlier, we will each come to sense our

133

connection to all of creation. If we answer the call to adventure when it comes, we will experience growth that will lead to a new way of seeing the world. This shift may be accompanied by a sudden insight, an epiphany, as experienced by the woman as a child on the Pangbourne Moors written about in Chapter One.

As an individual who has had this insight grows in wisdom, experiences life, and moves into and through middle age, the idea of fate as whimsical and arbitrary will increasingly seem contrary to personal experience. The Nineteenth Century German philosopher Arthur Schopenhauer observed in one of his essays, for example, that when an individual reaches an advanced age and looks back over his or her lifetime, the lifetime will seem to have followed a consistent plan as though composed by a master storyteller or novelist. Specific events and meeting of individuals that seemed at the time to have come about by chance turn out to have been essential components in a constant storyline.

If this is so, and my personal experience says it is, we are compelled to ask who wrote the story?

In Twentieth Century jargon, Schopenhauer would have said that it was an individual's subconscious mind. He would note that our dreams are composed by part of us of which we are unaware. He'd argue that our whole life is created by a subconscious aspect of ourselves that he labeled the *will within*. This *will within* merges with those of others so that the whole of human existence comes together like a symphony.

The truth is, only one organism with one single mind exists, and this mind is having the dream we call reality. We have trouble understanding this because we are each an aspect of the organism — you, me, and everyone. Our individual perspectives are from where we sit in relation to the whole. We each possess a unique point of view. This point of view constitutes our own personal reality, the circumstances of which our subconscious minds create. Yet our individual subconscious minds are part and parcel of the whole, the universal subconscious, which is the Big Dreamer himself.

This idea is not new. More than 400 years ago John Donne wrote, "No man is an island." Our lives are intertwined. As a piece of the continent of mankind, we have roles to play that affect other parts of the mainland. An individual we meet apparently by chance becomes a key player in the story of our life, just as in turn we play key roles in the lives of others whether or not we realize it.

What is the part of us, our personal puppeteer with its unique point of view, that compels us to play our different roles at different times in the giant dream of humanity? And why aren't we aware of it? Was this part created at the moment the egg, the sperm and the morphogenetic fields of our mother and father united with our own unique morphic field? Did it develop as our egos developed, a sort of parallel construction? We've said that an unconscious part of our conscious mind exists that stores the memories and programming of this life. The other part of ourselves that is beyond our conscious awareness is our subconscious mind. This is our personal morphic field built up through our own evolution that began when life began. This part is our puppeteer. It is privy to the big dream. It knows the end game. Its goal is growth and evolution because it is at one with the Big Dreamer.

Perhaps you, too, have made or were about to make a decision based on some ego demand or urge, the part of us that becomes afraid, that lusts, that rationalizes, and worries what others will think. Something inside said you would live to regret the decision if you followed through. At that moment you were in touch, however briefly, with your subconscious mind.

One mind exists, and it is divided into three gradations: The mind of the Big Dreamer, which encompasses the entire medium that we call mind. Our individual subconscious minds. And finally, our conscious minds, also known as the ego mind. The conscious mind also has an unconscious part which contains the memories and the programming of this lifetime. The conscious part of our ego mind is our objective mind that by definition has self awareness. It is the part that tricks us into thinking we are separate. But we are not separate. From our perspective, life may appear to be chaotic and random, but everything is coordinated at the subconscious level. We each have our roles. Things click along when we are playing them. When we get off the track of the dream, however, things go awry. Life gets messy.

Perhaps you know someone, as I do, who married a person he knew deep down he was going to divorce. Unfortunately, the feeling didn't poke through into conscious awareness until the day the invitations were mailed. Even so, there was still plenty of time to call off the wedding. But he didn't. Two years later, after he and his bride had split, he came to the realization he'd — his ego had — talked himself into going through with the marriage because he didn't have the courage to tell the girl or his friends and his parents and her parents that the marriage would be a mistake. Embarrassment is typical of an ego concern. Had he listened to his subconscious mind, he would not have lived through the nightmare that ensued. But his ego mind blocked communication through the mechanism of denial because the truth was not what it wanted to hear.

Elisabeth Kübler-Ross, the Swiss-born physician and author of the perennial best-seller *On Death and Dying*, has been in attendance and helped ease the deaths of scores of patients. She's studied the near death experiences of many more. She has spoken of her own mystical, out of body experience and is generally acknowledged as one of the world's leading authorities in this area. She has come to the conclusion that this inner voice is very real. In a 1977 lecture given in San Diego and published the same summer in the *Co-Evolution Quarterly*, she said, "If you listen to your inner voice, your inner wisdom — which is far greater than anybody else's as far as you are concerned — you will not go wrong and you will know what to do with your life." It is too bad my friend had not been exposed to these words, or if he had, that he did not heed them.

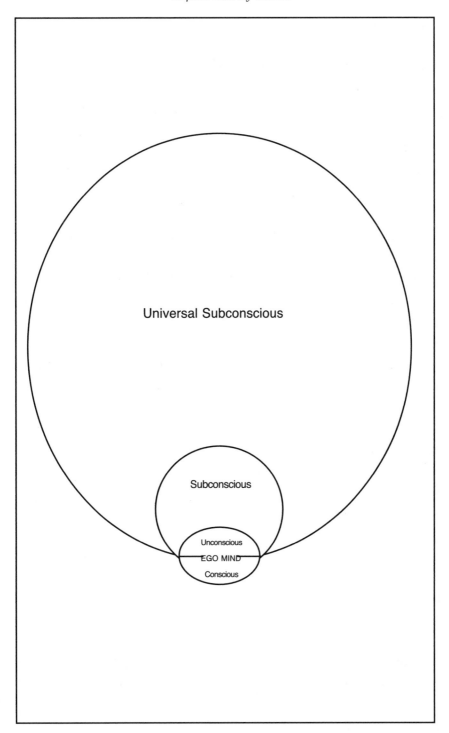

How can we get in touch? By answering the call to be "born from above." By recognizing that we are a part of the whole and that we have a conduit to the mind of the whole within us. As this becomes real for us, we move into the Kingdom of God — the condition of knowing and sensing our connectedness on a gut level. Over time our ego or lower self will come together in harmony with our subconscious mind. This cannot help but happen, and when it does we will experience the major payoff of our struggle upward on the spiritual path: a life where the pieces fit, where we understand why we are here, our purpose and how we are to achieve it. Fear will fade and finally vanish. As time passes, we become patient, collected, and serene. We are able to live in the eternal now and, perhaps for the first time, truly to experience and enjoy life in the physical world.

We all have egos, the part of us that has developed in this lifetime from an unfocused awareness in our early days in the crib to the part of us that contains the memories of this life. It is the part that worries, that fights for life, for achievement, for glory and for recognition. In contrast, the subconscious mind is not concerned with the trappings of the physical world. It seems to have been around for a long, long time, since the epoch of mankind's evolution from a species driven by instinct into a species characterized by self-awareness and free will. It may have been around longer. It does not experience fear or worry because it knows it will continue to exist throughout eternity. It possesses no desire whatsoever for self-aggrandizement.

This fits nicely into the theory of morphogenetic fields advanced by Rupert Sheldrake. Life itself has a morphogenetic field that first became differentiated from the overall field when DNA formed into one-celled creatures. This field evolved and changed over the eons as life took ever more complicated forms. Along the way, different parts of fields followed different paths of evolution. What has become my field and what has evolved into your field followed the path of primates. Each of us has a corner of it — figuratively, since the field is everywhere at once like TV transmissions. Ours dates from when we became differentiated from other primates via self-awareness. Your field, which is also known as your soul, just keeps on evolving as it continues reincarnating time after time.

In researching reincarnation, I've found that libraries are well stocked on the subject. Since becoming interested in this, I have met and come to know well two different people who make their livings by helping others remember past lives and then release buried memories that are holding them back. In some cases, thousands of years have passed since a debilitating incident took place. I've visited the School of Metaphysics in Missouri and watched trained readers of the Akashic records report on past lives of workshop attendees. Additionally, I've read four books written by different past life therapists and edited a fifth. Rather than relate what is contained in those, however, I will give you a quick summary of a case reported in the 1988 book, *Many Lives, Many Masters*. I've chosen this because the author, Brian L. Weiss, M.D., cannot be accused by anyone of being a Looney Tune. He is a Phi Beta Kappa, magna cum laude graduate of Columbia University who received his medical degree from Yale, interned at New York's Bellevue Medical Center, and went on to become chief resident of the department of psychiatry at the Yale University School of Medicine. At the time of the case covered in his book, he was head of the department of psychiatry at Mount Sinai Medical Center in Miami Beach.

Weiss is a medical doctor and a scientist who has published widely in professional journals. Ethnically Jewish, he was a skeptic who had no interest in reincarnation. He was fully aware that most of his colleagues in the field do not believe in such things and waited six years before giving in to the feeling that he had an obligation to share what he had learned. He had much more to lose than to gain by telling the story of the woman called Catherine (not her real name) who came to him in 1980 seeking help for her anxiety, panic attacks and phobias. Read his book. I'll hit only a few highlights.

For eighteen months, Weiss used conventional therapy, which means that he and Catherine talked about and analyzed her life and her relationships. When nothing worked, he tried hypnosis in an effort to find out what she might be repressing that would account for her neuroses. Forgotten events in her childhood, in fact, were revealed that seemed to be at the root of several of her problems. As is customary in this type of therapy, she was instructed to remember them after she had been brought out of the hypnotic state. Dr. Weiss discussed what had been uncovered in an effort to dispel her anxieties. But as days went by, her symptoms remained as severe as they had ever been.

He tried hypnotism again. This time he regressed her all the way back to the age of two, but she recalled nothing that shed new light on her problems. He gave her firm instructions, "Go back to the time from which your symptoms arise." Nothing had prepared him for what happened next. She slipped into a past life that took place almost 4,000 years ago. Weiss was astounded as she described in detail herself, her surroundings and others in that particular life, including specific episodes, and in later sessions entire lifetimes, which seemed to be the root causes of problems. In all, she said she had lived 86 times. This, by the way, indicates she was a very young soul in that most who have gone through this type of regression therapy have lived hundreds of times.

Weiss continued using hypnosis in an effort to rid Catherine of her neuroses. In weekly sessions that spanned several months, she recalled and recounted in detail the highlights of twelve previous lifetimes, including the moment of death in each. People who played a role in one lifetime often reappeared as someone else in another, including Dr. Weiss himself, who had been her teacher some 3500 years ago.

Catherine had not had a happy existence over the last forty centuries. The overwhelming number of memories from her past lives were unhappy and proved to be the roots of her present day symptoms. Bringing them into her consciousness and talking about them enabled her to recover. Considering the number and intensity of her neuroses, psychotherapy would normally have lasted years before she was cured. In fact, her symptoms disappeared within months. She became happier and more at peace than she had ever been.

Weiss is an experienced psychotherapist who has dealt with thousands of patients. He is convinced that Catherine was not faking. She was unsophisticated and of average intelligence, a young woman who made her living as a laboratory technician. He thinks it quite impossible that she could have pulled off such an elaborate hoax and kept it up every week for months. Think about it. She was a physically attractive twenty-eight year old woman of average intelligence. She had a high school diploma and some vocational training. Could she have faked her neuroses? Could she have faked gradual improvement from one visit to the next, all the way to a state of being completely free of them? It hardly seems likely. Also, and this is where the plot thickens, she conveyed information about Weiss's father and an infant son, both of whom had died. Weiss is convinced she could not have known anything about them through normal channels.

This message from the other side leads to what some may find the most amazing aspect of her story: the spaces between past lives. Once, after having been murdered, she floated out of her body and was reborn very quickly. At the end of her next life, she described an experience remarkably similar to that related by thousands who have been clinically dead and come back to life. She rose out of her body, felt at peace, and was aware of an energy-giving light. It was at this time in this session that spirit entities spoke through her to Dr. Weiss for the first time. In a loud, husky voice and without hesitation Catherine said, "Our task is to learn, to become God-like through knowledge. We know so little. You are here to be my teacher. I have so much to learn. By knowledge we approach God, and then we can rest. Then we come back and help others."

Although Catherine was able to recall her past lives after she was brought out of a hypnotic state, she was never able to recall, nor was she particularly interested in remembering, the conversations Dr.

Weiss had through her with several different spirit entities. These "masters," as he came to call them, spoke through her primarily for his benefit and only indirectly for hers. I will not go into detail about these exchanges; you may wish to read his book. Essentially, they told him that we incarnate into the physical world to learn what cannot be learned on the nonphysical plane. In that realm, whatever is felt or imagined instantly appears real or greatly magnified. The slightest ill will toward someone becomes rage. The smallest feeling of affection turns to all encompassing love. If you imagine a demon, a thought form of it will suddenly materialize before you. If you picture in your mind a lovely sunset viewed from a secluded beach, you will find that you are there. It is because of this that we need the thickness of matter. Matter slows things down so we can work them out. Earth is a school. The most important things we come here to learn are charity, hope, faith and love, as well as to trust and not to have fear.

Funny. This sounds an awful lot like Jesus or the Apostle Paul, doesn't it?

Let's leave Dr. Weiss for the moment and dig into the workings of reincarnation. What you are about to read at first seemed as fantastic to me as it may to you. Nevertheless, like Dr. Weiss, I feel compelled to share.

When the Life Force or spirit is withdrawn from anything, be it an animal, plant, person or object, the Life Force continues to exist, but the object it supported no longer is animated by it. That thing ceases to be alive — informed by the Life Force — and turns to dust. This is true of what we normally consider living things such as plants and animals, and it is true of what we may have thought until now were inanimate objects such as rocks, moons, mountains. Although the process of decay and return to dust takes longer for the latter, it will nonetheless happen in time when the Life Force is no longer present.

As Claire DuMond came to know in my novel, *IN MY FATHER'S HOUSE*, the secret of life is *the urge to become*. In other words, life is imbued with raw organizing ability that pushes it to evolve into ever higher forms. Finally, when the sensation of being separate comes about, a soul — or an individual subconscious mind — is born.

Your subconscious mind may have evolved on Earth, or it may have evolved elsewhere. As for myself, I've had a flash of memory that might be compared to an epiphany, which I believe is an indication of my own personal history of evolution. This moment of recall lasted perhaps for 30 seconds during which I "relived" all my prehuman lives in rapid succession, from life as a fish-like creature in some primeval sea, through reptilian forms, to a furry lemur-like creature that lived in a tree. This seems to fit. When a soul has learned all it can in one form, it seeks a new experience that will allow it to continue its upward push. Ultimately, it will grow and develop until it reaches a perfected state.

We live in a multi-dimensional reality, though under normal circumstances our physical senses allow us to experience only height, width, depth and the passage of time. Souls are evolving in other dimensions, and they are evolving on other planets in other solar systems of this universe. While recognizing that your soul could be much older than life on earth, one view of how souls evolved along with life on this planet will be presented in the paragraphs that follow. This is by no means intended as the last word on the subject and is meant only to give you one plausible explanation of the evolutionary path a soul may have followed.

A theory accepted by some followers of eastern religions is that souls which began their journeys here have been around in some form since the beginning of life on Earth. They did not become differentiated, however, until the epoch recounted in the myth of Adam and Eve. Scientists would probably estimate this to have occurred about 100,000 years ago. This was when we reached a point in the evolution of our minds that we were self aware. We saw ourselves as different, separate and distinct from the rest of nature. Unlike birds and animals of the forest or the savanna, we no longer relied on nature and instincts to direct our behavior. Our minds could override what instinct said to do.

This is what the story of Adam and Eve is about, the splitting off or separation from the field that resulted in self awareness and free will. God told Adam and Eve not to eat the fruit of the tree of knowledge of good and evil. The snake, which represents Adam and Eve's all too human nature, or ego mind, said to go ahead and eat. Rather than consult God before taking action, Adam and Eve acted as humans usually do today, and proceeded to do as they pleased. By exercising free will in this manner, they severed their connection to God, and humankind has been suffering the consequences since. We have, in effect, cast ourselves out of the Garden, with the result that we are no longer able to tap effortlessly into the abundance and joy that nature is always ready to bestow on us.

The way back, of course, and the major point of this book, is to reestablish a relationship with our personal subconscious mind and thus our connection to the transcendent. But this is a digression. The point here is that the origin and evolution of souls in this particular scenario would have followed the course of evolution from one-celled animals in the sea, to creatures who first walked on land, to tiny mammals, to pre-apes, to *homo sapiens*. It was as *homo sapiens* that we became differentiated. The Adam and Eve step was absolutely necessary. But we've been on this step now for about a hundred thousand years. Since the course of evolution is a spiral rather than a straight line, our next plateau is to return to the state the first man and woman enjoyed, but on a higher level. The time has come for many on earth to reconnect with the whole, while remaining aware of their separateness and maintaining free will. Metaphorically, they will return to the Garden and this time remember to keep God in the loop. When this happens, the bad times will be behind us. Our every desire will be fulfilled.

Some will argue that reincarnation isn't likely because there are so many more people alive today than in the past. The population of earth has exploded in recent centuries. If humans aren't humans unless they have a soul, and if a human soul must be built up through many incarnations, then where, they wonder, did all these souls come from?

It seems to me that there are several possible explanations. One is that souls which evolved on earth are incarnating more frequently now than in the past. In other words, they are spending less time in the state between lives. One therapist who has helped many recover from psychological problems due to past life traumas indicates that with respect to his clientele, the duration between lives ranges from a high of 800 years to a low of ten months.

Or, it could be that many on earth today are experiencing their very first human incarnation — that new souls are being created from universal mind.

Another possibility is that souls are pouring into this world from all over the place, that evolution of these souls up to this point may have occurred elsewhere for many alive today. Morphogenetic fields are composed of information as opposed to energy. According to quantum physics, unlike energy that must travel and diminishes in intensity with distance, information is everywhere in the field at once. It is non-local. This, by the way, coincides with Thomas Troward's theory concerning thought and life or spirit covered in Chapter Two. Since a thought form is everywhere at once — non-local — souls can come from anywhere in the universe; no travel time is required.

Parenthetically, we can expect life forms that have evolved on other planets to be similar to those on earth, provided physical conditions of the planet are similar. I say this because this is true of life forms that evolved in Australia after that continent became separated from the rest of the world's land mass. We see equivalents of dogs (dingoes) and cats and other animals in the land down under that are not exactly dogs or cats. They are marsupials, not mammals. So on a family tree, they would be placed closer to the opossum than to the animals they resemble. Water prevented the spread of genes of cats and dogs but not their morphogentic fields. These are everywhere at once — unhindered by water. These fields have influenced the shapes and forms of Australian creatures — though their genes may be quite different. When you think about it, those strange creatures might just as easily have evolved on another planet since physical contact with the rest of the world had been cut for millions of years.

Let us now consider the process of evolution of a human soul. When a new human soul starts out, the number of foolish or evil actions, thoughts and words the soul is responsible for far exceeds those of the good variety. This is understandable. It is also where the law of karma comes into play, as a basic learning tool provided by the universe. According to the law of karma, every thought, word or deed must produce a definite result, good or bad, and the result must be felt by the person responsible. Experiencing the law of karma is one of the ways we learn. It is one reason many lives in physical form are necessary. We usually do not live long enough for all our acts and deeds to play out in a single life.

The Bible tells us, "As you sow, so shall you reap," or as an old friend of mine in the ad business was often heard to say, "What goes around comes around." I believe that Jesus was talking about karma, for instance, when he said:

> *Do not judge, and you will not be judged. Do not condemn, and you will not be condemned. Forgive, and you will be forgiven. Give, and it will be given to you. A good measure, pressed down, shaken together and running over, will be poured into your lap. For with the measure you use, it will be measured to you.*

Luke 6:37-38

A selfish act on your part that causes misery to someone else earns a unit of bad karma. This must be repaid by your suffering from a similar action at the hands of another person, either in this lifetime or in one to come. A kind act on your part earns a unit of good karma. The result of this action can be either the erasing of a unit of bad karma or experiencing the same amount of kindness from someone else. You might say that karma is the metaphysical law that's equivalent to Newton's law of physics — for every action there is an equal and opposite reaction.

When I first learned about this and the truth of it took hold, I began to think back over my life and to remember things I'd done to others that had caused them pain. A number of instances of thoughtlessness, and two or three of outright cruelty, came to mind. I truly felt remorse and was thrown into a kind of depression. It was as though a black cloud hung over me and my future. I could almost feel the pain I'd caused and went about wondering how I'd ever repay these debts. At that time, I didn't know the therapeutic and practical value of confessing my sins directly to God, or to Christ, and asking forgiveness. Rather, I was convinced that I was doomed to suffer the same level of misery that I'd inflicted.

One day, I was running along the Canal of Burgundy during a summer sojourn to France. I came to a stop and said, "Please, God, Please. Even out the score. Give me a level playing field. Make whatever needs to take place happen so that these debts are paid."

A Jewish friend later told me that Jewish prayers to wipe the slate clean include the phrase, "But not through pain or suffering." Now he tells me. I learned firsthand that you get exactly what you ask God for when what you ask will result in spiritual growth. In this case, what I asked for started coming three days later when I was back in the States. I took my daughter's brand new ten speed bike for a test spin down the hill in front of our house. My foot slipped, caught on the pavement, and the metal pedal completely severed my Achilles tendon. The result was a ghastly wound. I spent almost two weeks in the hospital, had two operations, suffered a great deal of physical pain, and was in a cast from the tip of my toe to the top of my thigh for eight weeks. It took nine months before the wound was completely closed, then another nine before I was able to walk without a limp.

But that was not all. While I was still in the cast, my wife announced that the spark had gone out of our marriage. She was sick of living in the United States. She was leaving me, filing for divorce, and taking my daughter with her to live in France.

As a parent, I can imagine that the death of a child may possibly be the worst possible experience one can endure. If this is so, then having your only child, age twelve, taken to live 3,500 miles and six time zones away is number two. It was not a good year, but at least the slate was wiped clean. As you might expect, I developed spiritually. Adversity is a great teacher. The experience also taught me that it is possible to get in touch with the Big Dreamer and to have a request granted. I do not advise you, however, to follow the same course because I now believe the process of arriving on a level playing field with respect to karma does not have to be so painful. This is partly due to the fact that the purpose of karma, the law of cause and effect, is not retribution in and of itself. The Big Dreamer finds no joy in extracting "an eye for and eye and a tooth for a tooth." Rather, as with most things connected with the subconscious mind and universal law, the purpose of karma is to foster spiritual growth. Sometimes an "eye for an eye" is the only way to make a point. This is especially true during the early part of our spiritual journey. Then, the only way we will fully understand the consequences of our actions, our thoughts, and our intentions will be to experience those consequences firsthand. When O. J. Simpson comes back in another life as a woman and is brutally murdered by a bigger, stronger person with a knife, chances are he will finally "get it" deep down in his soul.

The end goal of the law of karma, you see, is the shift in consciousness that I've been harping about. It is the "aha!" experience, the gut-level realization of what one has done when one realizes that he and others are the same person — not literally at this moment, perhaps, but certainly at another moment, or in a different incarnation. This is likely what Jesus was driving at when he took a child in his arms and said, "Whoever welcomes one of these little children in my name welcomes me; and whoever welcomes me does not welcome me but the one who sent me." (Mark 9:37) And, when speaking of the hungry, thirsty, and the downtrodden, he said, "I tell you the truth, whatever you did for one of the least of these brothers of mine, you did for me." (Matthew 25:40)

In these quotations, Jesus is saying we are all from God and of God, and we all have played or will play every role and part in the dance of creation. This being the case, to help or harm another is to help or harm yourself at some point in your past or future. It is also to help or harm God.

How is is possible to help or harm God? There is only one screen of awareness on which the moving picture of reality plays. In aggregate, the total screen is God's awareness. Each person's awareness, on the other hand, is a tiny sliver of the larger screen.

Does one who has committed murder in this or a previous life have to experience the same violation? I believe that meditation, study, reflection can lead to higher level of consciousness that, combined with true repentance, can avert having to live through "eye for an eye" retribution. The universal subjective mind doesn't judge and it doesn't hold a grudge. Being subjective, it doesn't even sit around and analyze. If retribution is no longer needed for growth, it will not happen. This is one of the key messages of Jesus. He came to show the way, his way, to Christ-consciousness and everlasting life. The attainment of the Christ Consciousness triggers the "law of grace," and this dissolves the need for a karmic boomerang. Spiritual consciousness "fulfills the law," to use Jesus' phrase, in the sense that it annuls the erroneous thinking that was the source of the wrongful action. "I come not to destroy the law," is what Jesus might have said "but to teach you how to fulfill it through an elevated spiritual consciousness."

Full attainment of this consciousness is not easy. "Remember," Edgar Cayce said in one of his readings, "there is no shortcut to a consciousness of the God-force. It is a part of your own consciousness but it cannot be realized by a simple desire to do so.

149

Too often there is a tendency to want it and expect it without applying spiritual truth through the medium of mental processes. This is the only way to reach the gate. There are no shortcuts in metaphysics, no matter what is said by those who see visions, interpret numbers, or read the stars. They may find urges, but these do not rule the will. Life is learned within the self. You don't profess it; you learn it."

How, specifically, does one learn it? Regular meditation and prayer. Fasting. Study of the Scriptures and books such as this. Rendering service to one's fellow men. All these will be helpful. Depending on where a persons stands in the evolutionary process, regular practice of these acts may be all that is required. But I personally have been at it twenty years in a concentrated way and can say with honest conviction that I still have a good way to go. Every now and then when things seem to be going wrong, I suffer bouts of fear and doubt. If I were fully there, I wouldn't. Even so, I am putting my talents to use, and I do feel fulfilled in this regard. I have a solid, comfortable, affectionate marriage. I share and revel daily in the joy of healthy, happy, well-adjusted children. My greatest shortcoming seems to be the almost subconscious fear that if I don't push myself financial disaster could be right around the corner. Perhaps this stems from growing up poor. Nevertheless, I'm making progress. I have faults, but I know it. Some would say I'm patient, but I know I'm too quick to anger. I'm making an effort to correct this. If I stay at it, perhaps full mastery of life may not be all that far off. This life? The next? The one after?

I believe I may have entered this life at a level of evolution higher than I now have achieved. But for the first half of my days in this incarnation, I was sliding backward, losing ground. Having come to my senses, I've been able to make up much of the lost ground quickly because in effect, all I've had to do is "remember" (re—member) what I already knew and recapture the level of consciousness.

Apparently, I'm not the only one who has been guilty of backsliding. Edgar Cayce did so as well in a life he spent in Colonial

America. It's the reason he could only put his psychic powers to use when he was in a self induced trace.

This story was told to me by an expert on the Cayce readings, a psychotherapist named Peter Woodbury, who was on my radio show in November 2007. Apparently, Cayce had achieved the consciousness shift we've been talking about and had developed his psychic abilities in an incarnation in ancient Egypt in which he had been a high priest. Later, in a life he spent in Colonial America, he put his psychic abilities to use in an inappropriate way. As you can imagine, as a true psychic he was very good at cards, and that's how he made his living — bilking others out of their hard-earned cash. He apparently was also a womanizer. Because of this, in his next life as Edgar Cayce (1877-1945) he had to go into a self-induced trace in order to access his psychic powers. In fact, he was known as "The Sleeping Prophet." That way he couldn't use his powers for personal gain. But this didn't stop him from trying. He wanted to build a hospital, which seemed a worthy cause, and so he located what he described as a "mother load" of oil on some land out west. Nevertheless, one thing after another, such as equipment failures and the like, kept the oil right where it was — far down under the ground. Cayce spent his whole lifetime with money troubles. You may know that he never charged for his psychic services, although he did accept donations.

Backsliding is a potential danger an old soul must face when he or she incarnates. But as is always the case, the consequences of the ill-advised exercise of free will be used by the Big Dreamer as an opportunity for spiritual growth. In his 1877 to 1945 incarnation Cayce helped many to evolve through his work as a psychic. This work goes on today in the form of books written as a result of his explanations of the true nature of reality given in his psychic readings, as well as through the work of the organization he founded, The Association for Research and Enlightenment. In my case, the experience of having to crawl back helped prepare me to write this book. If I had come into flesh with prior knowledge intact,

I'd have faced two problems in sharing it. First, it would have been *a priori*, or part of me and my makeup, and therefore difficult to verbalize. Second, It would not have been gained in the white-hot crucible of a society of doubters and skeptics. But because it was acquired gradually, over the years, I am able present it knowing what sort of objections might have to be overcome. After all, I had to overcome them myself before I accepted as truth the knowledge I present here.

Having regained what I have to share in this lifetime, I can do so in the context of this lifetime and the time in history that we share. My sincere desire and intent is to help you, too, to re—member what you once knew, and to help you soar to a new level of understanding. But let me quickly add that growth cannot be mechanically induced. Unless and until the heart is sufficiently tenderized, practicing charity, for example, will be in the Apostle Paul's apt phrase, "as tinkling brass." The rich man who gives it away with the idea of buying his way into heaven has bought nothing. It's what is in the man's heart that counts. What he truly gives, he keeps, because of the joy he feels. But don't misunderstand. This doesn't mean he should not give, even though he does not feel joy. Perhaps his deed may be the act his soul needs to start it on the proper path. But this won't let him to skip a grade. Souls in kindergarten, spiritually speaking, cannot jump ahead to college.

Let's think for a moment about the new soul with very little understanding. In the early incarnations, this entity will go about creating much havoc. Fortunately for him or her, no one is expected to suffer more in one lifetime than he can stand. Units of bad karma that aren't worked off by good deeds or a poke in the mouth are carried forward to be worked out in future lives.

Think about a person you know or have come in contact with who has what you now recognize to be a young soul. The individual appears to have very little conscience. He or she simply cannot hear the still small voice and thinks nothing of spraying his housing project with bullets just for the fun of watching broken glass tinkle to the ground. During the early incarnations, a person like this will pile up more karmic debt than he works off. In effect, this karma represents lessons he or she must learn. As time goes by and he continues to incarnate, the connections grow between his subconscious mind and his ego. He or she learns the lessons and finally "gets it." Now that the lines of communication are open, conditions continually improve. At last, the right wavelength is found and the mother ship comes in loud and clear. This is why a person with an old soul appears to have a highly developed sense of right and wrong. Many people today have reached this state. You probably are one. If so, a short jump is all that's required to make to that shift in consciousness.

This book probably won't do much for those with young souls, nor will they be likely to have read this far, anyway. Past-life therapists tell me that often such individuals incarnate with no life plan. Their lives are chaotic at best and purposeless at worst. Having stuck with me this far, I suspect you have a relatively old soul and may be on the cusp of a breakthrough. This being the case, it's highly likely you came to earth with special talents to use for the benefit of humankind and have an important purpose or goal to accomplish. If you have achieved Christ Consciousness in a previous life, your visit to earth this time is to help others do the same. If you have a ways to go, it is to face and overcome certain problems or to work out karma from a previous incarnation. The way to drop the karmic baggage that's holding you back is to recognize why you have it, see the error in your thinking, and to move to a higher place. You might say it's by turning the other cheek because you know that's the right thing to do that you finally offload it.

Speaking of flow, I've heard a number of people who profess to be New Consciousness thinkers repeatedly make statements to the effect that "everything is working just as it should" at any given moment. Perhaps this is to remind themselves not to be concerned with outcome, but rather to concentrate their energy on doing what they are here on Earth to do. I agree with this approach. I've never been successful making money, for example, by *trying* to make money. And believe me, there are times when I've tried very hard. To the contrary, I've made a lot of money by concentrating my effort on what I do well and "just doing it," to borrow the Nike slogan. Each time I've let the chips fall wherever, things have indeed worked out to my benefit, provided I was doing what I now see I'm here to do.

Even so, I do not agree that *everything* is always working out for the best at any given moment. Though I rarely say anything, these kinds of statements sometimes rankle me because they are contrary to the law of free will. On the material plane, each human being is free to choose, and therefore, is free to make mistakes. Dumb mistakes. Mistakes in calculations. Mistakes in judgment. We are free to be just plain cruel or stupid. Thomas Troward pointed out that the universe operates by laws. Violate the laws, whether or not you even know the laws exist, and you will suffer the consequences. If you don't believe this, watch what what happens when an unsuspecting child sticks his finger in an electric socket. Metaphysical laws are as consistent as those of physics. For example, it is a law that what you believe will happen will happen. So believe you are going to go bankrupt, and you will go bankrupt.

Wait a minute, you may say. I've thought terrible things might happen and they didn't.

The key here is that you "thought they might happen." You no doubt *hoped* they wouldn't. Hope is a kind of belief. It is a belief in possibilities. You believed this might happen or that might happen. You were sending the subjective mind mixed messages, and fortunately for you, hope was stronger and won the day. You'd have been better off to *believe* you would succeed and not take chances.

Some people think there's a fairy godmother looking after them, or maybe a guardian angel, and that's okay. Perhaps it's true. But whether or not there is, if you believe she will take care of you, you'll be taken care of. I tend to think it's the law of belief at work although I do not refute the possibility of "divine intervention." I've experienced what seemed to be nothing less. Perhaps belief can bring about what appears to be divine intervention due to our limited understanding of how the world really works. Jesus is said to have turned water into wine, to have walked on water, and to have fed 5,000 people with a few fish and some loaves of bread. And had a lot left over. I've heard firsthand reports from people I trust — one the founding partner of a large law firm — of miracles similar to this being performed today. And of course there is Katie the Gold Leaf Lady, who is living proof the mind can create something out of what appears to be nothing. If Katie's mind can create brass, why wouldn't Jesus be able to do the things he is reported to have done?

Keep in mind, however, that no set plan for the universe is in place, as the Panda's thumb indicates. Things aren't automatically going to work out right. Edgar Cayce indicated that things can go awry even though they have been planned with the clarity that surely must exist on the spiritual plane. He assured us, for example, that the process of birth and rebirth does not always work as intended, and that sometimes errors are made. Cayce said that we choose our parents and our circumstances from what is available at any given moment. The circumstances may be far from perfect, yet we may elect to go ahead anyway and, figuratively speaking, keep our fingers crossed. The fallout might be that a soul may discover, after having made a choice and been born, that the parents are not living up to expectations they seemed to have offered before birth. Realizing that its own inner purpose for the incarnation may be frustrated by the altered circumstance, the soul may decide to withdraw. Cayce said that this may be the cause of at least some infant mortalities.

For detailed descriptions of what happens between incarnations, and the process of selecting parents and circumstances, read the books, *Journey of Souls,* by Michael Newton, Ph.D., Llewellyn, 1994, and *Life Between Life* by Joel L. Whitton, M.D., Ph.D., and Joe Fisher, published by Warner Books, 1986. The authors of each are past-life therapists. Both provide interesting information, although I found the one by Dr. Newton to be slightly more enlightening. Essentially, groups of souls numbering a dozen or so who are at the same level of development work in what might be called clutches. Each group has guides or teachers to help them. The guides are a level or two farther along the evolutionary path than those in the group and do not incarnate as often. These guides are at work virtually all the time, behind the scenes during an incarnation and at the head of the class in between — not unlike your high school math teacher. Members of the clutch often incarnate at the same time, in the same place, often in the same family, with the goal of helping one another accomplish specific tasks, work out karma, or learn specific lessons.

Soon after bodily death, a soul's guides or teachers, or what also might be described as elders — up to three, according to Dr. Whitton in *Life Between Life* — will expose the newly returned entity to a detailed review of his or her just-completed life. These elders do not judge the entity. The entity judges him or herself — actually feeling the pain or the distress, as well as the joy, that he or she may have caused others. The elders or guides make comments and suggestions. They are usually non-judgmental in their approach and often provide comfort to the entity, who may find the review gut-wrenching. This is very likely to be the case if a number of mistakes were made, or if opportunities were wasted that might have led to the accomplishment of goals that had been set forth for the life.

This seems a good spot for a couple of anecdotes that relate to this. When he learned I was writing this book, a friend told me something that happened to change his life when he was a teenager. He had an unhappy home and was deeply depressed. His mother was wacky, and she and his father constantly argued. He had almost no friends. It was so bad, and things appeared so hopeless, that he was seriously contemplating suicide. One night, after he'd gone to sleep with suicide on his mind, he had the sensation of being shaken awake. He opened his eyes and saw two strangely clothed men. They grabbed him and whisked him upward, directly through the ceiling and the roof — or so it seemed. He now realizes he had passed through the tunnel we've heard so much about into a kind of limbo where the three of them had a chat.

"Don't do it," one of them said.

"Do what?" he asked.

"Don't commit suicide."

He looked at the man sheepishly and frowned.

"It won't do you any good," the other said. "If you do, you'll just be sent back again, and again, until you get it right."

My friend understood precisely what they meant. If he ended his life prematurely, he'd have to be born into the same circumstances over and over — like the character in the movie *Groundhog Day*, who had to live the same day again and again until he finally got it right.

Another friend, a therapist with a Ph.D., uses past life recall to help his patients get over their phobias and neuroses. He has explored his own past lives, and says he's been able to remember back about 15,000 years to the time before he came to this planet. At that time, he was engaged in an intergalactic war — sort of like Star Wars, I guess. He and his crew were captured just as they were about to blow up a planet inhabited by the enemy. He and the crew subsequently were sent to earth for incarceration and rehabilitation, and he's been here ever since, forced to reincarnate over and over again. He'd like very much to break out of the cycle but, so far, hasn't been allowed. He believes he is part of a small percentage of the population of our world who are prisoners in a penal colony. For them, Earth might be compared to Devil's Island in the South Atlantic off the coast of French Guiana, which was a French penal colony from 1895 to 1938. Instead of criminals from France, however, prisoners like him from other worlds are put here to "get them off the streets," so to speak. He's calculated the total number of prisoners on earth at about five million.

Returning to our description of the interlife, quite a bit of time may be spent between incarnations, during which an entity will study his most recent past life as well as other lives he or she has lived. As souls become more highly evolved, they tend to spend more time between incarnations than do less evolved souls. They are more cautious about picking the circumstances of upcoming lives. Also, compatible parents don't come along as frequently for the more evolved souls. In the meantime, the soul may use the time to hone particular talents or skills.

Once back in flesh on Earth, a soul may accomplish what was planned for a particular incarnation more rapidly than anticipated. This was the case for one of Dr. Whitton's subjects. With nothing left to accomplish in the lifetime, some sort of premature death would normally have occurred so that the soul could return for rest and recycling. Instead, the living soul was given a new assignment and was allowed to stay on Earth and continue evolving. This way, the remainder of the incarnation was made fruitful and productive, and what would have been viewed as an untimely death by us mortals was averted.

It is important to know that taking on a new assignjment is possible. This means we don't have to die just because we've accomplished the objectives set forth before birth. In effect, we can begin a new incarnation without having to go through the bother, drama and trauma of death, rebirth, childhood, adolescence, and so forth. If science indeed finds keys that unlock the mechanism of aging, this could become the norm, provided people understand that the purpose of life is spiritual evolution — their own and others'. I say this because it seems only logical that people who decide to retire and play golf all day, every day, will have a serious illness, accident or something else happen in order to get them back on track and productive once again.

Back to the interlife. When the time comes for rebirth, the panel of judges will review or help identify objectives and lessons for the next incarnation, perhaps giving the entity a choice of a couple of different families in which to incarnate. The soul must agree to the selection, although it appears that this agreement is often given reluctantly. The upcoming incarnation is then planned much as a writer might outline the plot of a novel. The elements must be in place and the supporting characters ready and waiting. The entire process can be tricky. Race, nation, region and familial circumstances are factors. Someone who was a bigot in a past lifetime may come back clothed in the race they were prejudiced against in order to experience the other side of the equation and to learn from the karma they created.

Amnesia of the time between lives is important. If we know what's coming, the purpose will be defeated. Fortitude and courage, for example, will not be acquired if the harrowing experience and outcome are known in advance. For lessons to be internalized, they must occur spontaneously, without foreknowledge. So as a new ego begins forming, amnesia sets in — starting when a baby begins to bring its surroundings into focus.

Most of us who have been around babies and small children instinctively know that they have just arrived from some heavenly place. I saw this clearly in my own children. As long as their needs are met, including food and a a lot of good, healthy interaction with people who love them, they appear absolutely delighted to be here. Their faces almost seems to glow. The quality I have in mind has been recognized by poets down through the centuries. It was best captured, in my opinion, by William Wordsworth in the fifth stanza of his poem "Ode." This work is perhaps best known by the subtitle, which is, "Intimations of Immortality from Recollections from Early Childhood."

Our birth is but a sleep and a forgetting:
The Soul that rises with us, our life's Star,
Hath had elsewhere its setting,
And cometh from afar:
Not in entire forgetfulness,
And not in utter nakedness,
But trailing clouds of glory do we come
From God, who is our home:
Heaven lies about us in our infancy!
Shades of the prison-house begin to close
Upon the growing boy,

But he beholds the light, and whence it flows,
He sees it in his joy;
The Youth, who daily farther from the east
Must travel, still is Nature's Priest,
And by the vision splendid
Is on his way attended;
At length the Man perceives it die away,
And fade into the light of common day.

Whether this little person "trailing clouds of glory" makes progress in this incarnation or whether he fulfills his destiny or slides backward, will depend in large measure on the efforts and abilities of his parents. Consider for a moment how important it is that we create a loving environment in which a child can flourish and develop and pursue "natural" talents. Indeed, we can make it easy or difficult and, in the process, create a good deal of negative or positive karma for ourselves. In a very real way, our parents are our guides at least until we're grown. It is an awesome responsibility.

All that our invisible guides can do is provide us with guidance when it is sought and help create favorable conditions for us to "pursue our bliss," as Joseph Campbell said many times. Of course, the subconscious mind will remain a subpart of the universal subconscious doing its best to keep the communication lines open. But each of us is born with free will. We always have the option of going against what our intuition or "better judgment" tells us.

A major point of this chapter is that you are here for a reason. Your birth was not an accident. You have a choice. You can try to find that reason and live it, or you can do as you please, and perhaps get so far off track you'll never get back. You are a soul with a body, not a body with a soul. Maybe you have made some mistakes. If so, it may not be too late to correct them, especially now that you know you are the driver and not the vehicle.

It's hard to doubt that we are all here to evolve. Some do so rather quickly. For others, it takes longer. Some may never make it.

But why? What is the purpose behind it all?

In his book, *The Seat of the Soul,* Gary Zukav argues that the purpose is the rounding out and eventual perfection of the soul. He wrote, "When the soul returns to its home, what has been accumulated in that lifetime is assessed with the loving assistance of its teachers and guides. The new lessons that have emerged to be learned, the new karmic obligations that must be paid, are seen. The experiences of the incarnation just completed are reviewed in the fullness of understanding. Its mysteries are mysteries no more. Their causes, their reasons, and their contributions to the evolution of the soul, and to the evolution of the souls with whom the soul shared its life, are revealed. What has been balanced, what has been learned, brings the soul ever closer to its healing, to its integration and wholeness."

Let us ask the question. We now know that we are here to realize our true nature as spirit and to become co-creators, but is that the end of the line?

Somehow I doubt it. If we think about this long and hard it will occur to us that perhaps the transcendent, the Universal Mind, the "one life," has set about the task of reproducing itself. Think about it. As Richard Dawkins observed in his study of cheetahs and gazelles, propagation is an underlying theme of nature. Every organism from the smallest amoeba to the biggest whale has this as a primary objective. Why shouldn't the universe, the largest organism of them all? Perhaps at some point in our development, long after this life is finished, we will not only be the universal mind or field, we will be a new reality.

Perhaps a less grand view is that we will be fully evolved beings whose function is to help in the construction of new realities, new universes. This idea was held by the occultist, W. E. Butler (1898-1978). He said, "We're going to be universe builders in company with God. We are going to be tools, instruments in the hands of the Eternal as His will prevails in the universes which He has formed and in which He lives, moves and has His being and which He is bringing back to perfection from their fallen state. And you and I have the privilege of being coworkers with Him and with the whole of creation which is part of His work."

In the next chapter we will look at ways of identifying our missions and getting in touch with our subconscious minds.

Chapter Seven: Creating Your Reality

Our thoughts, beliefs and actions create our reality. Dreams are evidence this happens instantaneously in the world of spirit. On earth, in the physical realm, the density of matter provides an environment where we can learn through trial and error how to create, because the density of matter slows things down. Our subconscious mind or soul records what we learn. Nothing is lost in the many cycles of reincarnation. A soul retains the self-assurance that comes as a result of success and the inner strength and compassion that are born of sorrow. Even the effects of the destructive experiences one suffers are brought forward into each new life. This was certainly the case with Catherine, Dr. Weiss's patient, who was cured of her phobias and neuroses after recalling them under hypnosis and examining them with his help.

Under normal circumstances our power of recall cannot conjure up specific events, but their fruits are no less than the sum total of our personality. They combine to form the basis of who we are. This should not be so difficult to accept. Few of us remember specific events in our lives that took place before the age of four or five. Yet few would argue that our early lives do not influence who and what we are as adults. So it is with past lives.

Once this is recognized, however, I believe it is possible to overcome current or past life difficulties without having to dredge up these difficulties for examination. As for myself, I've learned detailed information about three past lives — one about 200 years ago and the other about 300 years ago and another about 2700 years ago — from psychic readers at the School of Metaphysics. A reader at the School also has consulted the Akashic records about my dharma[19] and explained to me how it was acquired through

---

[19] Dharma is the special ability a person has to share and to use to serve others. Mine is "omni perception," which is the ability to see all sides of any situation and to picture the whole even when only a small part is available or visible.

concentrated effort over many lifetimes. The majority of one lifetime, for example, was spent mostly in a ship's crow's nest developing psychic as well as visual perception abilities. I'm fairly certain as a result of what I've learned about myself that I've lived hundreds of times. No doubt I've experienced just about anything and everything that can be imagined. Name it, I've probably done it or had it done to me. Surely, I've paid dearly for mistakes along the way. If I hadn't asked for the slate to be wiped clean on that trip to France, I'd still have some to pay. What I now realize, however, is that these mistakes could have been "forgiven" without having to go through the terrible time that I went through.

In understanding how this can be, the first thing to understand is that these errors exist only in the past and nowhere else. The Universal Mind does not dwell on the past. It doesn't hold a grudge. Your personal subconscious will not put you through unnecessary trial. The past might be compared to the wake of a boat. When you look back, you see where the boat has been. But the wake does not have to have anything to do with where the boat will go in the future.

The next thing to realize is that you are the pilot of the boat and can make it go where you wish. The wake does not have to influence your direction. Your effectiveness at directing your life, however, is subject to one caveat. You will find yourself in old familiar waters, repeating old adventures and mistakes, if you don't change the setting of your compass. This is why adopting a new way of seeing the world is so important. Your outlook on life is the mental equivalent of your compass setting. If you don't reset it, your personal subconscious may decide you need the shove that repaying karma can create.

Let's say your compass is set correctly and your heart is right. You have forgiven everyone for what they may have done to you and have sincerely asked for forgiveness for your transgressions. You have truly turned away from your old ways and embraced Jesus's directive to "Love the Lord your God with all your heart and all your soul and with all your mind . . . and your neighbor as yourself,"

(Matthew 22:37), and to "Love your enemies and pray for those who persecute you that you may be sons of your Father in heaven," (Matthew 5:44). Once you have done all this and are starting to feel good about it, your past errors will remain right where they belong — in the past. They have been released and can be forgotten. Your mental compass has been reset. Your heart is right. Now your new guidance system, your subconscious mind, has been set free to direct you to a new world of abundance and fulfillment.

In the subtitle of a book I wrote a few years back, I called the information like this "secret" because it is not readily found or available in North America today. You will not see it taught in any public school. Except perhaps for the School of Metaphysics and others like it, it is not a part of a university curriculum. Yet, this knowledge is perhaps the most important you can possess. This knowledge can enable you to avoid a life of sorrow, today, and it can help you avoid many future lives of sorrow. It can stretch your productive and abundant years of life. It can bring about the life you dream about.

Let's say that right now you're riding on a bus or sitting on a beach. Look up and glance around. Each individual you see is traversing an evolutionary course that spans many lives and according to his or her actions and experiences, is either retreating from his true nature as spirit or advancing toward it. From life to life, each is followed by the good or the bad he has created. You don't have to do the same. You can take a shortcut. You can dump that excess baggage. You can do so through study, mediation, prayer, and by joining a group of seekers like yourself. Give them your support and allow them to give you theirs. Learn this from one who has paid an expensive karmic debt the hard way. Learn that you have a shortcut available.

Sometimes the payback of a karmic debt will arrive without advance warning. If it cannot be avoided, it is best to consider it an opportunity to learn and grow. Here is what Saint James, the younger brother of Jesus, had to say about this: "Consider it pure joy, my brothers, whenever you face trials of many kinds, because you know that the testing of your faith develops perseverance. Perseverance must finish its work so that you may be mature and complete, not lacking anything." (James 1:2-4.)

Elisabeth Kübler-Ross echoed this in 1977 when she said, "All the hardships that you face in life, all the trials and tribulations, all the nightmares and all the losses, most people view as a curse, as a punishment by God, as something negative. If you would only realize that nothing that comes to you is negative. I mean nothing. All the trials and tribulations, the greatest losses, things that make you say, 'If I had known about this I would never have been able to make it through,' are gifts to you. It's like somebody has to temper the iron. It is an opportunity that you are given to grow. This is the sole purpose of existence on this planet earth. You will not grow if you sit in a beautiful flower garden and somebody brings you gorgeous food on a silver platter. But you will grow if you are sick, if you are in pain, if you experience losses, and if you do not put your head in the sand but take the pain and learn to accept it not as a curse, or a punishment, but as a gift to you with a very, very specific purpose."

Almost every Christian is aware of the Apostle Paul's words, "A man reaps what he sows." (Galatians 6:7) That we create our own reality is a truth we must digest before we move to a higher level. This is as true here on Earth as it is in the nonphysical side of reality. Back at the turn of the Twentieth Century, in a little book called *As a Man Thinketh*, James Allen wrote, "The outer world of circumstance shapes itself to the inner world of thought, and both pleasant and unpleasant external conditions are factors which make for the ultimate good of the individual. As the reaper of his own harvest, man learns both by suffering and bliss." And on the following page he said, "Even at birth the soul comes to its own, and through every step of its earthly pilgrimage it attracts those combinations which reveal itself, which are the reflections of its own purity and impurity, its strength and weakness." Allen's observation should prompt each of us to examine our circumstances for clues as to what we need to do to accomplish what was set out for us before we were born.

We can begin by examining the circumstances of our birth and the parents and family to whom we were born for clues. As detectives with the goal of determining our missions, once we figure out why our soul chose our circumstances, we will be a step closer to the specific reason, or reasons, we are here.

One of my missions was to write. My father and my mother were in the advertising business, a business of words and ideas. I've had an interest in writing for as long as I can remember. My parents allowed me to develop in my own way, and to "follow my bliss." In other words, the conditions were in place.

Ultimately, perhaps, a major reason I'm here is to write this particular book. Yet this would not have happened if I hadn't come to realize I'm not alone in the endeavor. The truth is I'm a conduit. I've been led to the information presented here. My subconscious mind, the part of me that is in touch with the big dream of life and the Big Dreamer, has guided me. For as Jesus said, "Ask and it will be given to you; seek and you will find; knock and the door will be opened to you. For everyone who asks receives; he who seeks finds; and to him who knocks the door will be opened." (Matthew 7:7-8.) To this, James later added, "If any of you lacks wisdom, he should ask God, who gives generously to all without finding fault, and it will be given to him." (James 1:5.) So, listen up. When you're pursuing spiritual growth and seeking to get yourself on the track of your destiny, all you need do is ask for guidance. Then, expect an answer. Be attentive. One way or another the answer will come. The trick to recognizing it lies in cultivating the quality of discernment. As James also said, "But when he asks, he must believe and not doubt, because he who doubts is like a wave of the sea, blown and tossed by the wind."

Soon we will discuss techniques you can use to get in touch with your subconscious mind. At that time I will ask, what is your bliss? What have you been interested in for as long as you can remember? How does this fit with the circumstances into which you were born?

Are you now doing what you like? Does what you do help others in some way?

But, before we get into this, there's likely to be baggage you're carrying around that needs discarding. This baggage is what leads to the doubts James was talking about. This baggage falls into the category of destructive attachments you may have, feelings of guilt about your own past actions, and underlying fears that have been programmed into you. You will be blocked and will not achieve your potential in this lifetime as long as you hold on to this. So now, the time has come to clean the attic.

The first thing to do is forgive. Forgive yourself and forgive others. Karma is created by your thoughts, conscious and subconscious. This includes thoughts toward yourself. Both love and hate make bonds. Bonds of hate lead to the worst kind of destructive behavior.

If you are in an abusive relationship, get out of it. Get out of it and forgive the abuser. As long as you hold onto bitterness, it will come back to you. Forgive. Pray for the one who has abused you. Pray that God's peace, serenity, and love, will come to that person.

Perhaps your parents pushed you in a direction you didn't want to go. Even though it may have happened long ago, it may still be having a negative effect on you. What possible good can it do to hold on to the feelings? You're perpetuating a bond that eventually will have to be worked out if not in this lifetime, then another. Dissolve it today. Forgive.

Let me tell you a story that help will show the way.

Once I worked with a man who was the most unlovable person I have ever met. It was almost impossible for me to like him. He was mean, spiteful, and petty. I'd known him a long time before I found myself working with him, and his reputation backed up my appraisal of him. By a series of what seemed coincidences, he became my partner in an advertising agency. Not only that, he owned the largest share, over fifty percent, and ultimately was able to call the shots. We disagreed at almost every turn. Not surprisingly, he unwittingly turned out to be one of my greatest teachers.

About six months after we came together in business, I traveled to New York to visit with the editors of *Advertising Age* and *ADWEEK* and the ad columnist for the *New York Times,* among others, in an effort to drum up publicity for our little agency. I had breakfast meetings, lunch meetings, after-work-drink meetings, and was dragged from one place to another by our publicist. All Of this meeting and greeting gave me a splitting headache, partly because she talked so much and so fast, and partly because I had to be "on" the whole time. Some people would surely enjoy this sort of thing, but I'm the sort who prefers to sit by the fire, sip a scotch and soda, and read a good book. But I was doing what needed to be done for the benefit of the agency, which included myself, my partner, and all our employees.

The morning I returned to my office in Richmond, I opened the *New York Times* to the business section and realized that lightning had struck. My picture was at the head of the advertising column. It must have been a very slow day for news in the ad game. Three-quarters of the text was devoted to our little upstart agency in Richmond, Virginia. What a coup to be featured in the Gray Lady herself, where the presidents and ad managers of companies all over the United States would see us. Practically any ad agency owner would have given up his first born for this kind of publicity. Reprints would be run off by the thousands and sent to every client prospect from Nova Scotia to Tijuana. I was ecstatic. I was certain my partner would be doing back flips.

But no. He was angry. His name wasn't mentioned in the article. How dare my name and photo appear in an article in the *New York Times* and *his* name not be mentioned? He was the creative director, wasn't he? His name was on the door same as mine only ahead of it, wasn't it? He owned *more stock,* didn't he?

Wait a minute. I didn't write the story, I told him. Of course I'd talked about him in the interview. I'd sung his praises. The columnist and I had talked an hour. He had selected what he wanted to write about. A lot of what I'd said had found its way onto the cutting room floor.

This didn't matter. That he was not included was somehow my fault. Not only was he now even more impossible to live with than usual for the next week or two, I learned later that he actually had pulled our publicist into his office, shut the door, and rather than give her the pat on the back she deserved, had threatened to fire her if another story on the agency ever appeared without his name in it.

Needless to say, having this guy as a partner was no fun. It got so bad I began to dread coming to work. Perhaps he and I had karma from a former life to work out, I don't know. I wasn't aware of such things then. But in retrospect, I believe we would still have some to work out if I hadn't followed the course I recommend for you if ever you face a similar situation. I'd recently learned that one of the things Jesus had told people to do was to pray for their enemies. I knew this wouldn't be easy, but I thought at least I ought to try. So, I prayed for this guy. I meditated about him and his situation. I could see the chaos inside. He was like a nerve ending dangling and exposed, ready to touch something, anything, and streak off like a heat seeking missile. I asked God to bring him comfort and peace. I prayed that his splintered soul would be healed and made whole. I asked God to come into his life, to slip into his heart and show him the way to peace and tranquility. Every time he upset me, I would pray this prayer at the first opportunity.

Something happened that I hadn't expected. I found that these prayers helped *me.* I found that I no longer could feel animosity toward him. I couldn't harbor anger once I'd prayed for him. The anger melted. The burden lifted. I felt light, buoyant.

This would have been reason enough to have done all that praying, but to my astonishment, it was not the only good that came about. Within two months, he called me into his office and announced that he was retiring. To say that I was surprised would be a gross understatement. He was only 54 and had never so much as hinted at the possibility.

Doctor's orders, he said. He'd had a heart attack a few years before, and a stress test had revealed that blockages recently had reformed. They were still at the point where they could be taken care of without high-risk surgery, but his doctor had advised him to get out of the business before it killed him. He had to slow down, take it easy, and get away from the stress.

I bought his share of the business. I paid more than I should, but that didn't matter. Suddenly, my working life was a pleasure again. My brother joined me in the business and we were able to build up the agency and sell it. Enough was generated to allow me to try my time at writing full time, which was something I'd always wanted to do. But the real kicker, the most amazing thing is, my former partner was able to do something he'd always wanted to, which was paint. Fine art was a passion he'd neglected in favor of the ad game and the almighty dollar, so he was able at last to devote time to his real purpose and "follow his bliss."

A feature article appeared in the paper about him not long ago. Apparently, he has become a success in this new career. I imagine the blockages are a thing of the past. He certainly looked healthy. No doubt his stress level is down to zero, which means he was led to the peace and tranquility that I had prayed that he would find.

The lesson this man taught me is to forgive. You can do this, too, by praying for whomever you feel has wronged you. Pray that they will find whatever they need to make them whole. And when you do, what seems like a miracle may happen. Rather, if you hold onto ill feelings, the animosity you harbor toward them will return to you as surely as a lead ball dropped from a tower will hit the ground.

The need to forgive includes forgiving yourself. Ask for God's peace to come to you. Pray for those you've harmed. Ask forgiveness in prayer. Allow yourself to feel sorrow for your deeds. Then give that sorrow to God. Promise never again to do such a thing. Mean it. Do what you say. Make amends if possible.

I know from experience that self-forgiveness can be the most difficult kind to give. If you have done something you truly regret, images of your actions may haunt you. Nevertheless, you must get past this. You must move on if you are to develop and grow spiritually. Otherwise, you will be blocked because you are haunted by doubts.

Remember as we have already discussed, the wake need not guide the boat. You've got a new compass now. Give the memories to Jesus. Ask him to take them, and he will. For as he said, he is all people. Seek his forgiveness, and he will give it. Know that his forgiveness is their forgiveness.

What else can you do to get rid of negative baggage? I suggest that you find a group whose members are at the same place as you on their journey. Become part of this circle of seekers. You need the support and the prayers of people who accept you for who and what you are.

In deciding where to look, take into account where you were born and into what family and cultural surroundings. Your subconscious mind selected these things. For this reason alone, it does not seem to me that the right choice for someone born and raised in the Midwest of America, for example, would be to join an order of Buddhist monks. Not that Buddhists don't have answers. I believe that the three major religions I know something about — Buddhism, Hinduism, and Christianity — each sprung from knowledge and understanding of the same central truths. But from having studied the Gospels and the teachings of Jesus, I believe one need not go far beyond the New Testament to find answers and understanding that can lead to a life of fulfillment and abundance.

The problem with religions, and this includes Christianity, is that they are based on someone else's interpretation of The Truth as related by the founder of the religion. Jesus taught his disciples and the Apostles. The Apostles, such as John, wrote down his teachings. John did his best, I'm certain, to capture every word correctly, but even so, what he wrote is secondhand. Then a group of Church leaders took what John wrote and created doctrine — in other words, what is acceptable and proper for their members to believe. Finally, a pastor interprets this to his flock.

Anything that's gone through iterations and interpretations is likely to reflect the mores and values of the age and the society in which it was created. In other words, it may be full of temporal rather than timeless stuff.

If you're lucky, you will find a church with a pastor who has his own relationship with God. I have found such a church, and I can tell you, when you do, you will be getting firsthand information. What I have found may be rare. Nevertheless, it is worth an effort it to find the right one. In the United States are churches that range from those headed by Stage One Jim Baker and Jimmy Swaggart types, or pedophile Catholic priests who use Christianity as a cover for their wickedness, to those led by a pastor well into the Stage Four or Five, and attended by people who are for the most part well into Stage Four. I know of no way to know which is which until you visit one and discover firsthand. So don't just visit one, visit a bunch. See which, if any, send off vibrations that resonate with yours. If your intuition is at all developed, one sermon may be enough for you to know if you have hit upon the right place.

I also urge you to discover God for yourself. This will happen as a result of *the shift,* and through prayer, meditation, and study of the Scriptures and other spiritual works. Don't rely on my interpretation or on anyone else's. What is revealed directly from God will become a part of you. It cannot help but result in significant growth.

Do not be swayed by what others may think. Keep in mind that the media are almost always one-sided in their depiction of Christians and other believers because they are run for the most part by Stage Three Scientific Materialists, who delight in showing the Stage Ones with their hands in the pockets of simpletons and Stage Twos who think everyone else has to believe exactly what they believe or they're going straight to Hell. Look for a Stage Four church. As you visit and talk to members, be open and receptive. Listen as others explain what Christianity means to them, and try not to get hung up on terminology. Words aren't what's important. What's important is the truth behind the words and what's in the hearts of people. You don't have to agree on every point. They don't have to agree with you. What's important is for people to be accepting of one another, even when they disagree. To be a true Christian means to love your neighbors and to have compassion for your enemies. See if they practice this.

By following Jesus, you begin to leave behind in the wake of your boat the wrongs that you may have done. Just think. You can dump all that karma, the entire negative bank balance, from lifetimes of errant behavior.

Here's something else to think about. Being a member of a spiritual brotherhood of some kind also may prove beneficial when the time comes for you to make the transition from the physical to the nonphysical. I'm reminded of my mother who told me about the time, back in 1918 when she was twelve years old, that she was put on a train in Arizona. She was to travel alone all the way to boarding school in Canada. The trip would take eight days, and a number of train changes would be required. Her father, a Mason, removed his pin, and put it on her, telling her to wear it always where others could see. If she had a problem, someone would help. It worked. She traveled all the way across the United States from the far Southwest to Quebec. Many times along the way she was helped by total strangers. She had tapped into a brotherhood and become part of a group that takes care of its own.

When the time comes for you to make your journey into the next dimension, perhaps it won't hurt to have your own version of a Masonic pin.

In summary, by whatever means you can, forgive yourself and forgive others. Allow a group of fellow travelers on the path to help you. When these steps have been taken, you will have made tremendous progress. As you proceed, meditate on other truths. For example, consider how our attachments to people and the trappings of the physical world hold us back, and bring us back again and again. Buddhists place a lot of emphasis on this and there is something to it. It is one reason Jesus said that it is as difficult for a rich man to enter the Kingdom of God as it is for a camel to pass through the eye of a needle. He did not mean that anything is inherently wrong with being rich. The error is to become *addicted* to wealth. The young man who came to him seeking Eternal Life had failed to keep the first commandment, which is to put no other gods before the one and only God. Wealth had become the young man's god. As in his case, the love of and pursuit of wealth can sidetrack us and thereby block us from reaching our potential. When faced with answering the call or protecting our wealth and status, most will choose the latter. Fear of what we might lose keeps us mired in the status quo and prevents us from allowing our egos and our subconscious minds to merge. Until we rid ourselves of this fear and attachment, we will not live life to its full potential.

Okay. Let's assume you have forgiven yourself and others. Let's even say you have cut the bonds of karma and have overcome your attachments. What else may be holding you back?

Try tuning in to your moment-to-moment stream of consciousness and observing what makes you worried, anxious, resentful, uptight, afraid, angry, and so on.

Saint James said we should be glad when we face trials. Trials can be opportunities to build strength, self control and perseverance. In addition, the emotions these trials generate can be signals which identify fears and attachments that have you blocked. Try to step outside yourself and identify unsettled emotions, tugs and urges which have become part of your programming.

Unsettled emotions are a form of interference that stands between you and being in touch with your subconscious mind. As long as they plague you, it will be almost impossible for you to distinguish between communication from your subconscious mind and a buried fear conjured up by your ego mind.

To deprogram yourself, slow down and consider what triggered a negative emotion. Did your temper flare? Why? Why was it so important for things to go a certain way? If you retrace what you felt back to its cause, in most cases, you will come to a particular variety of fear, and it's been said that only two fears are instinctive: the fear of high places and loud noises. Others were acquired, and whatever was acquired can be disposed of.

Fears usually can be grouped under one of six headings: the fear of poverty (or failure), of criticism, of ill health, of the loss of love, of old age, and of death.

I've listed the fear of poverty (failure) first because in many ways it can be the most debilitating. It is self-fulfilling, in that traits develop that bring it about. For example, are you a procrastinator? An underlying fear of failure is probably the root cause and can be counted upon to produce that result.

Are you overly cautious? Do you see the negative side of every circumstance or stall for the "right time" before taking action? Do you worry (that things will not work out), have doubts (generally expressed by excuses or apologies about why one probably won't be able to perform), suffer from indecision (which leads to someone else, or circumstances, making the decision for you)?

Are you indifferent? This generally manifests as laziness or a lack of initiative, enthusiasm or self control.

Step back and listen for internal voices that say "can't" or "don't" or "won't" or "too risky" or "why bother?"

How do you get rid of them? Shoo them away.

Whether you are the president of a company, or a bum on Skid Row, the only thing over which you have absolute control is your thoughts.

You may say, I can't control what thoughts pop into my head. True. You may not control what thoughts arise, but you can decide whether to discard one or to keep it. You can decide that it is counterproductive and throw it away, or you can turn it over and over in your mind, nurture it and let it grow. Whatever thoughts you keep will expand and eventually manifest themselves.

Beginning now, each time you catch yourself with a negative

thought, a thought that says "you can't," "it's not possible," "maybe someone else but not me," get rid of it.

But you say, "I'm poor, I'm not a good student, I'm not a good salesperson, I'm in the lower third of productivity."

You are what you are because of your thoughts. Your subconscious mind wants the best for you, but your ego is holding you back because of the way it was programmed.

If what I've been writing about on this page is a serious problem for you, go out and buy some self-help tapes that will plant positive thoughts in your mind in place of the negative ones. Play them to and from work and before you go to sleep at night. Use self-hypnosis tapes. Play them over and over for at least a month. Get all that junk out of your head, and replace it with thoughts that are positive.

What about the other fears? They're to be discarded in the same manner. If you suffer from fear of criticism, for example, it probably came about as a result of a parent or sibling who constantly tore you down to build himself up. You'll know this is a problem if you are overly worried about what others might think, if you lack poise, are self-consciousness or extravagant. (Why extravagant? Because of the voice which says you need to keep up with the Joneses.) You must rid yourself of inner voices that tell you to think even twice about what others will say. Simply eliminate them.

Let's think for a minute about the fear of criticism. There have been places and times in history when what others thought was worth worrying about. My great, great, great, great, great, great, great grandmother, Susannah North Martin, for example, was accused of being a witch and hanged in Salem, Massachusetts, in 1692. She was an old lady. Probably, she looked like a witch. But her downfall was the stir she caused after her husband died. She was able to run the farm successfully without a man around. Think of the talk. Such a thing wasn't possible, or so they believed, without the use of witchcraft.

The opinions of Susannah's neighbors mattered a great deal.

They led to an unpleasant and untimely death.

What about today?

In Iraq or Iran one might have to watch out what your neighbors think or what the "virtue police" hear about you, but this simply is no longer a valid concern in developed countries. What others think or don't think of you or anyone else is their problem. Yet worrying about what they think can cause a great deal of misery, create karma that will have to be worked out, and cause interference between your conscious and your subconscious minds that blocks the channel of communication.

Remember my friend who ignored his subconscious mind and got married anyway? Can you imagine the pain he brought himself and his bride? He was worried what people would say or think. He let those inner voices overrule what his intuition was telling him and got married to avoid criticism. He lived with the woman a year and then went through an unpleasant and expensive divorce.

This is what he allowed the fear of criticism to do.

What about the fear of ill health?

To rid yourself of this, it should be enough to know that what you worry about and think about happens. Ever noticed that it's the people who talk about illness, worry about illness, are preoccupied with this or that possible illness, think they feel a pain here or there or were exposed to some germ, who are precisely the people who stay sick most of the time? The power of suggestion is at work.

Suppose you're a tennis buff. You're in a big match, and it's close, and you arrive at a crucial point. Your opponent is serving. Yell out, "You're playing great today, Morris. Don't blow it. This is a big point coming up. Whatever your do, don't double fault." You've started him worrying. Watch him double fault. It's dirty. It will create negative karma. But it works. Their subconscious minds are creating the reality they dwell upon.

How about the fear of the loss of love? This one manifests itself in the form of jealousy and is self-fulfilling like the others. The person you try so hard to hang onto feels smothered, with the result that you end up pushing that person away. Try being yourself. Give them love, but give them room. It they leave you, they would have done so anyway. You can now move on to a truly meaningful relationship.

Next is the fear of old age. This is closely connected to the fear of ill health and the fear of poverty because these are the conditions a person really is concerned about deep down. The power of suggestion is hard at work here, too. If you think you're too old to do this or that, you will indeed be too old.

Consider this. My nine month old son is the same flesh and blood as my wife and me. I saw him when he was born, still connected by an umbilical cord. I clipped it myself. My wife was thirty-six at the time; I was fifty-four. Yet the cells in my body, and in my wife's body, and in my son's body all were the most recent in an unbroken chain of cell division that goes back to the first life on earth. All the cells—my wife's, my son's, and mine — are at the end of a chain that is precisely the same age: billions of years. "Spirit is the life, mind is the builder. The physical is the result." Those telomeres get shorter and shorter because you think that you should look and feel older as the years go by. The physical body is the overcoat of the mental body. It gets old and decrepit because you expect it to.

When you've learned all you can from this life, the time will come for you to check out. And check out is what you will do. No one says you have to be old. As for myself, I plan to keep taking vitamin E and believing that this will postpone aging indefinitely.

Now we've come to that final bugaboo, the fear of death. As you now have seen, there's nothing to fear except having been fearful in this life. Consider the millions who have had near-death experiences and are no longer afraid to die. They're convinced they'll be greeted by by their guides as well as by loved ones who have gone before. They look forward to being bathed once again in the all-encompassing light which many have described as total, unconditional love. Most do not expect to experience pain. It has been reported by many that the spirit exits the body the instant it looks as though death is inevitable.

Only a handful who have had hellish experiences worry about what they may encounter in the nonphysical world. These folks need to know what you know. Each of us creates his own reality. We experience what we expect to experience, what we think we deserve. In the physical world, this takes time. In the nonphysical world of spirit, which is the medium of the mind, we instantly create our reality, just as we do in dreams. If we expect Hell, the Hell we believe we deserve is the Hell we will get. If we expect Heaven, our vision of Heaven is what we will have.

Anyone who has ever had a lucid dream will understand what I mean. As discussed in Chapter One, such a dream is one in which a person realizes he's dreaming. I've had many and I look forward to them because it's more fun than Disney World. As soon as you're aware you're dreaming, you can begin to compose the dream, determine the players, the surroundings, the action. Want to fly over the Grand Canyon? All you have to do is "think" this. Fly over is what you will do, no airplane required. Like anything it takes practice, but I've gotten so I can swoop and turn and loop the loop.

Want to attend a cocktail party populated by Hollywood stars? You'll be there with Robert DeNiro or Julia Roberts. These characters will, of course, be your own thought projections.

You are a dreamer in the big dream of life, and you can make your waking dream lucid as well. Until now, you may have thought you were at the mercy of conditions outside yourself, that you've either been lucky or unlucky, that chance has brought you where you are. This isn't true. You've brought yourself to this spot, either consciously or unconsciously. If this is not where you want to be, you've arrived because your ego self was programmed incorrectly. You're out of touch with your subconscious mind. Perhaps you hear snippets from it every now and then but ignore what it's trying to say because of other voices which beat it back with "can't," "don't," "shouldn't," "too risky." These are the words of your ego. Your subconscious mind wants much more for you. Your subconscious mind knows more is possible. Let it lead you to fulfillment and abundance.

Once you wake up, once that shift occurs, the deprogramming process can begin. After it's complete, you'll be in position to bring your ego self and your subconscious mind together to work in harmony. You'll reach a higher state of consciousness, the Kingdom of God, Nirvana, or whatever terminology you prefer to describe this state. You will know on a gut level the connectedness of all things. As sure as intentions led to a longer neck for the giraffe and the Panda's thumb, your intentions will bring what you desire. Through your intentions, you'll be able to create your surroundings and direct the outcome of each and every adventure. You'll be a lucid dreamer in the dream of life.

In the next chapter, we'll explore how.

*If we can locate, at the very center of silence, our individual
"still small voice," we will have found our greatest ally in life.
Because, if we listen to that voice with an open heart, it will
guide us through the most challenging crossroads of our lives: in
work, in love, in distinguishing right from wrong.
We need only trust the voice that speaks to us out of the silence.*

Robert Lawrence Smith
A Quaker Book of Wisdom
(William Morrow, 1998)

Chapter Eight: Getting in Touch with Higher Guidance

The ego often is considered the enemy of the soul or subconscious mind, but the truth is the ego is essential. It creates and maintains our boundaries, our sense of where we end and others begin. Without it, we indeed would perceive ourselves as all that is — God — just as a newborn in his crib may consider himself to be the center of the universe. An individual must have a clear understanding that he or she is a separate being before a sense of oneness with the field is viable or healthy. Otherwise, we may believe we are justified in doing exactly as we please, treating the world and others as extensions of ourselves who exist to serve us alone. Narcissism is the term psychologists use to identify the mental condition brought about by the arrested development of the ego. Antisocial behavior often results.

A properly developed ego, on the other hand, allows us to open ourselves to spiritual development. It takes courage to venture into the unknown, which is precisely what we must do. A healthy ego, properly nurtured since birth, helps us view the world as safe. But an ego that has stopped growing at the mental age of, say, two or three will cause its owner a great deal of discomfort. It will immediately raise and wave red flags and jump up and down at the slightest contemplation of venturing outside familiar surroundings. The ego must grow as we grow so that we become secure in our sense of self. Then, it can become the container that can house the soul without threatening mental, emotional, or physical collapse. Without a well-constructed container, a well-developed ego, our journey to the upper levels of spiritual development is impossible.

Why have so many thoughtful men and women come to the conclusion that we must push the ego aside in order to get in touch with the divine, the Universal Mind? They have misunderstood what the ego is and its relationship, or more accurately its lack of a relationship with the personal subconscious mind. Those who possess underdeveloped egos are threatened by contact with what lies within themselves because of buried fears. An ego believes its first job is self-preservation. The weak ego is afraid that exposure to new, unfamiliar truth would simply be too painful for its owner to bear. Thus, problems buried in the personal unconscious mind surface in indirect ways such as dreams, phobias, or neuroses.

The primitive, arrested ego is also self-centered. It wants to take credit for the achievements of others and of the hands of grace— even to the extent of denying the possibility of the existence of anything beyond itself. The ego can turn on an individual and bring action to a stop by pushing just the right buttons.

As previously discussed, the simplest way to deal with the underdeveloped ego's campaign of terror is with detachment. Don't think of the ego as part of you that must be lost for advancement to be made but rather as a part that needs to be strengthened. Think of a fearful ego as a child who needs reassurance or as a student who needs education. This is usually a matter of increasing awareness of where fear has determined your actions. If you are not where you want to be, it is probably because the unconscious rule of fear has taken over and chauffeured you there. Slow down. Put on the brakes. Meditate about your condition. Think about destructive behaviors you repeat. Bring them to light. Try to figure out how you got where you are. What were you afraid of? What did your small self convince your big self you couldn't do? In so doing, educate your ego and yourself. You must become strong enough to bring yourself in touch with your subconscious mind and not feel threatened. Otherwise, your ego will make a concerted effort to stop the action by jamming all communication.

Your subconscious mind connects you with the universal subconscious. It is the individual dreamer who is in contact with other dreamers and the Big Dreamer — the One Life of which each person is a facet. It is that part of us that has existed from the beginning of our journey, the time that we became a separate entity, our own little corner of the morphic field. Your subconscious mind is what provides a sense of meaning and value and what comes through us to create a sense of intimacy with another human being or another creature. Our subconscious mind is reaching out to us when we feel the need to know the meaning of life or of our own lives. It is reaching out when we feel a hunger to experience our connection to all that is. It reaches out when we contemplate our mortality.

It led you to this book.

The existence of our subconscious mind is most apparent when we are in a period of transition. This may be as we undergo a change during one of the seven-year cycles of our maturation,[20] it may be when a child is born, when the death of a friend or loved one occurs, or in the period preceding our own physical death. Many cultures and virtually all spiritual brotherhoods have rituals and myths to aid in and soften these transitions. The lack of rituals and myths, the relative lack of regard for the spiritual dimension in our secular society, can make these passages difficult and lonely.

The techniques which follow are not meant to take the place of these rituals and myths. They are meant to provide practical, day-to-day methods for growing closer to your subconscious mind with the ultimate goal of uniting it with your ego to form a true, undivided Self. When this occurs, you will have reached the end of the rainbow. You will experience a sense of wholeness as though you've arrived home at the end of a long journey. Your life will be transformed by a principle in harmony with the objectives of the Universe. You will be aided and guided by unseen hands. You will be in a position to choose because you will sense outcomes before taking action. You will bring the course of your life into harmony with your destiny.

All this sounds very grand and godlike, but the truth is, this is our natural state, the state of all creatures in the wild. Without the slightest thought, birds, bees, ants and monarch butterflies allow

---

[20] See the book, *Passages*, by Gail Sheely, Dutton, 1976.

themselves to be guided by nature. The subconscious mind, or soul, of swallows brings them back to Capistrano on the same day every year; it directs herds of wildebeest across the African plains. It guides the migration of whales.

Man was the same before the mythical Garden of Eden. He was fully in touch with nature, guided by instincts and higher forces. To put it another way, he was at one with God, the Big Dreamer. But by becoming self-conscious, by becoming aware of himself as separate and apart, he pulled the plug that connected him. What he believed himself to be became his reality. He was separate. He now had free will and was capable of making mistakes, and because he was by nature lazy and self-centered, he could not help but do so.

Many today have arrived near the end of a journey. We are at the end of the period in our evolution when it was necessary to concentrate on the development of the ego. Now our goal must be to maintain our separate identity while uniting with our subconscious mind. When this is done, our journey will be complete.

Most of us have been conditioned since birth to discount what is often described as intuition. As a result, we've developed a habit of not listening to the voice of our subconscious mind. If we are to reconnect, the first step is to acknowledge that intuition is real, that our subconscious mind exists, and that it is possible to be in touch. This "being in touch" is characterized by a sense of knowing, but not in the ordinary way which requires a subject (you) and an object (what is known). For example, you know that California is on the west coast of North America. That's subject and object knowing. It exists outside of you. With "being in touch," no separation exists between knower and known. An example might be your "knowledge" of how to ride a bicycle or how to ski. Unless you are an instructor, and through trial, error, and study have learned the right words to say, it will be very difficult for you to explain what you know to another. You just *know*. Riding a bike or skiing is *part of your being*, like intuition.

When we know something intuitively, we tap into that larger, universal being that is in us. We *are* the all, which includes California and North America, so we *know* where they stand with respect to each other.

To get my mind around this, it helps me to visualize the All as a huge assembly of compartments, each of which represent an individual subconscious mind, and the totality of which represents the universal subconscious I've been calling the Big Dreamer. This mass is a hologram, each unit containing all the information of the larger mass. And so we have the universe, and we have the "universe in a grain of sand." Each person is a small compartment. Each person is the whole. By switching perspectives back and forth between the small and the large, one knows the will of the Big Dreamer and is able to manifest works and abundance in concert with His will. When one has achieved this, one has achieved Mastery of Life.

One does not need to have reached this point, however, to play on the Big Dreamer's team and reap the benefits. At lower levels of play, relevant messages come as insights and intuitions.

Earlier in this book I wrote about the time I glanced at a door-prize ticket and knew instantly I'd won, even before the numbers were read. The sensation I had was: *winner*. No subject, no object. This sensation has been labeled Psychic Intuition, and I experienced it in the area of my solar plexus. It felt as though the string of a viola located inside me had been struck.

Not everyone receives intuitive insights or messages from their subconscious mind in the same way. Some hear voices. After learning I was writing this book, for example, a friend of mine, the founding partner of a large law firm, confided in me about several instances of this phenomenon that he has experienced. One took place between spring and fall semesters of law school when he was at a coming out party at a country club. The debutantes were making their bows, being presented to society, but he was not paying a great deal of attention. He was standing with a group of friends talking and laughing, much more interested in joking around than in the girls dressed in white doing curtsies. Out of the blue a voice said, "Here comes the mother of your children." The tone was like, "Wake up, stupid, and look over there." He wasn't sure whether the voice had come from inside or outside his head and said, "What?" The voice returned with, "The mother of your children is coming." He turned to look. Taking a bow was a young woman he'd met before, but did not know well at all. He had no plan or desire to get married. He thought this girl was attractive but had no interest in her at that time. Two years later they walked down the aisle. As the voice had told him, she became the mother of his children.

The reception of extrasensory signals in the form of words, a sound or some form of language is called Psychic Hearing or Clairaudience. This can be subtle, similar to what one "hears" when one talks to himself. It also can be loud and clear the way my friend experienced it.

I remember a time when people were sure that hearing disembodied voices meant a person was crazy. That's why people who hear them usually don't say so — unless they are. But another friend, who is definitely not crazy, also receives messages from his subconscious mind in the form of spoken words. This man was the successful owner of an advertising agency before he retired. He tells me that he consults his subconscious mind on just about everything, takes a moment to listen, then gets an answer.

Let me relate a story that this friend once told me. He had purchased a new sports car and had just driven it home from the dealership. The car had come straight from the dealer's garage, where it had been prepped. He took a few moments to admire it. It looked absolutely terrific — shiny and new.

He and his wife were about to embark on a trip of about 250 miles and were planning to take the new car, so he pulled it into the driveway and up to the front door, turned off the engine, and loaded their suitcases. One bag had to be tied onto the luggage rack. Then, he and his wife climbed into the car. He took a moment to consult his subconscious mind, as was his custom.

He tilted his head. "Everything a-okay?" he asked silently.

The voice said, "Check the oil."

"Excuse me?" he said.

"Check the oil."

He got out and checked the oil. It barely came to the bottom of the dipstick — was more than two quarts low. The engine would have been badly damaged if he'd driven the planned 250 miles.

Another way messages are received is called Psychic Vision, or clairvoyance. This is a form of ESP which expresses itself as a picture, symbol or visual impression. Traditionally, it is associated with receiving visual insights either through meditation or in dreams. You probably are aware of psychics who help police by visualizing the scene of the crime or the location of the body. You may have had experiences with clairvoyance and not realized it. Have you ever had, for example, a mental image of an old friend and then received a phone call or letter from that person?

If you wish to develop your ability at clairvoyance, read a book by Stephan A. Schwartz, *OPENING TO THE INFINITE: The Art and Science of Nonlocal Awareness* (Nemoseen Media, 2007). Mr. Schwartz was on my radio show in summer 2008. One of the amazing stories he told is about the predictions made by a college seminar class about the capture of Saddam Hussein in 2003. On November 2, 2003, after being taught the basic skills of remote viewing, 47 of those who'd attended the seminar agreed to "Describe the location of Saddam Hussein at the time of this capture or discovery by U.S. or coalition forces." The students' data was collected and analyzed including points of consensus concerning the physical location as well as things that were not likely to be predictable such as Hussein's appearance on the day of his capture. The data were photocopied and distributed to a number of people and then turned over to a third party, Herk Stokeley, Director of Atlantic University. Stokeley placed the data in an envelope, which he sealed in front of a notary, who affixed her seal across the envelope's flap. It was then placed in a vault.

Hussein was captured about six weeks later on December 13, 2003. Remote viewing said he would be beneath an ordinary looking house on the outskirts of a small village near the city of Tikrit, and that the house would be part of a small compound that is bordered on one side by a dirt road and, on the other by a nearby river. Two large palm trees would mark the ends of the house. All this turned out to be true.

Remote viewing predicted Hussein would be found crouching in a subterranean room or cave that is reached by a tunnel. This was true.

Remote viewing said Hussein would look like a homeless person with dirty rough clothing, long ratty hair and a substantial and equally ratty salt and pepper beard. This was true.

Remote viewing said he would have only two or three supporters with him at the time of his discovery. He had two.

Remote viewing said he would have a gun with him. He had a pistol.

Remote viewing said he would have a quantity of money. He had $750,000 in cash.

Remote viewing said he would be defiant but would not put up any resistance, that he would be tired and dispirited. This was true.

This case seems like more solid evidence that the erroneous scientific tenet that thought and mind is contained within the brain needs to be done away with once and for all. For example, Schwartz quoted U.S. Army Major General Edmund R. Thompson, who was deputy Director for the Management and Operations for Defense Intelligence from 1982-84 as having once said, "I never liked to get into debates with the skeptics, because if you didn't believe that remote viewing was real, you hadn't done your homework."

Clairaudience, Clairvoyance, what else is there? Well, how about Psychic Intuition, the instantaneous sense of knowing that I experienced when I won the TV? It is perhaps the most common form of reception. Degrees of this exist, ranging from a fleeting snippet which occurs spontaneously to a permanent gut-level realization, a sense of knowing that continuously flows. The ultimate state is one in which the receiver "knows" himself to be creation, all-that-is, one and inseparable.

Psychic intuition is the main way I stay in touch with my subconscious mind. It has taken me years of working at it, but I've developed an almost continuous connection that gives me moment-by-moment guidance. The times I run into problems are the times I let down and allow my ego mind to take the helm. It's easy to know when this has happened because a jab of fear, or flash of anger, accompanies the ego's takeover. This sends up a red flag, and I stop and count to ten. A few moments of meditation often is enough to put the ego back in its place, but at times I know that it's best for me to break off whatever I'm up to, and wait until the next day to make decisions.

Does this mean a person should no longer use his rational mind? Of course not. The rational mind has its place. But we need to recognize its limitations. The rational mind can be compared to a computer. It can sort the data (anything you have read or experienced), cross-tab, analyze and spit out an answer. Unfortunately, no matter how competent your mental computer is, the answer may not be correct because the analysis is limited to data that consciously entered your mind. But this limitation doesn't make it valueless. I use my rational mind to function on the mundane level. If I see a red light, I stop. If I see green, I go. You won't see me touch a hot stove, spit into the wind, or lick a frozen metal flag pole. A quick scan of my data base is enough to decide matters such as these.

But the subconscious mind, on the other hand, should be consulted on big issues because it isn't limited in any way. It is plugged into the infinite knowledge of the universe. It has direct access to the dream and the Big Dreamer. It encompasses the whole and possesses all knowledge, down to the amount of oil in the crankcase of a particular car's engine.

How does one cultivate this relationship? Like any good relationship, it must begin with trust. Your ego must feel confident enough to allow your subconscious mind to come through.

The ego is looking for control. In my own case, I've convinced myself (my ego) that I do not and cannot have control, anyway. No matter how much I'd like to, or how hard I try, absolutely nothing is under my direct control except my thoughts. To believe otherwise is self-delusion.

Do you believe, for example, that you are in control of your children, that you can control their behavior through threats of punishment? Wait until you are out of sight, then see how much control you have. The fact is, you must teach your children to control themselves. Trying to control others is a colossal waste of time and energy. In fact, I once read that anything a person feels he must control, in reality controls him. The twang of the viola vibrated inside me. Take this to heart, and you're on your way.

Start slowly and ease into your new relationship with your subconscious mind. Talk quietly, or mentally, with it. Tell it you are ready, that you want it to enter your life. You want to form a partnership. You might begin by setting aside a few minutes each day. Call this your quiet time. Dedicate up to a half hour once or twice a day from now on. It can be the most productive and important period you spend each day.

Sit back and relax or lie down. Allow yourself to enter a state of consciousness that's different from what you're used to during normal waking hours. You might buy a tape or two on meditation to help you relax, but for the first week or so don't meditate. Daydream. This may be enough by itself to create the conditions for insights to come through. Think of a quiet place, perhaps somewhere out in nature, where the temperature is perfect. Perhaps there's a blue sky and a gentle breeze. Allow yourself to go into a kind of trance, to drop to a deeper level of consciousness. Let your mind go wherever it takes you.

You may find that you begin identifying your true purpose and mission in life. Daydreams are often fantasies about who we really are or what we can be. They may be closer to the truth than what you thought was the truth until now.

Ask yourself what you would do if you could expand to your full potential. What is your bliss? (I'm not talking about your ego desire to sit on the beach and play gin rummy, I'm talking about how you would like to be involved in life, not watch it mosey by.)

Some people have a regular quiet time without even realizing it. It might be when they exercise or jog. For me it is a walk I usually take in the morning before I write.

No matter when or how you elect to spend time getting in touch, ask yourself, how do your fantasies connect with the circumstances into which you were born? What games did you play as a child? How did you entertain yourself? Have you any interests that go back as long as you can remember?

After your quiet time, take a few minutes to jot down thoughts and ideas that came to you. Ask yourself, are you now doing what you like? Does what you do help others in some way? With your background and training, what could you do? If you could have whatever you want, be whatever you want, what would that be? How would this help others?

Take notes each day for several days. What themes recur? Keep writing things down. A pattern will emerge. Stay with it. Develop recurring themes into a vision. Whatever this entails at first may seem impossible, but your internal naysayer may simply be your ego talking. Don't let your ego get in the way just because it is terrified. Stroke it. Tell your ego you're not going to quit your day job. Not this week, anyway. You may modify your vision as you proceed, but don't start out by watering it down because of the seemingly "practical" voice of your ego. Your subconscious mind already has the end result in mind. It knows. Let it help you bring this into focus.

The subconscious mind also knows how your vision can be achieved. Let yourself be shown the way. Ask for guidance in your daily quiet time. Sometimes the information you need will come immediately. Often it will not. Ask. Be patient. An answer is on the way. It may arrive in several days, or even a week later.

In general, women are able to get in touch with their subconscious mind or intuition, more readily than men. (This is the source of the "old wives' tale" of woman's intuition.) The reason is, in our culture, women usually are in closer touch with their emotions, and intuition is a kind of emotion or "feeling." Feeling what emotions are communicating is one way to "listen." It also may be that women are more receptive by nature, but I suppose the real problem with men is that many have been programmed from birth to deny or suppress emotions. The strong silent type has long been the role model to which a man must aspire. But men should not become discouraged. Everyone, male or female, has a masculine and a feminine side. Men may have to work harder, but everyone can feel emotions. It may take longer for men to "receive" an answer, but they can do it. If I can, anyone can.

Often, I'll ask a question of my subconscious at night before I go to sleep. If possible, I phrase the question so that a yes or no answer is sufficient. I conclude by saying, "When I wake up tomorrow, let me realize the best course. Give me a sense of knowing."

This almost always works.

You may be wondering, how can I tell if my subconscious is telling me something or if it's some other part of me? Many different feelings and conflicts are going on within me at any given time.

In the last chapter, we discussed how to identify the flak thrown up by your ego. This flak revolves around worry and is usually fear based. It almost always has a harried, frantic sense to it. Disregard this garbage. It has nothing to do with your subconscious mind. Your subconscious mind is never worried. It does not know the meaning of fear. It is serene by nature. It is not the part of you that judges or says you must follow the rules. It doesn't use the word "should." "Should" and "ought" simply aren't part of its vocabulary. Communication from the subconscious mind has a lightness to it, a sense of, "This is right. It fits." It floats on a current of air like the blithe spirit in Shelley's poem.

Your subconscious mind never says you need something outside of yourself to make you happy — certainly not alcohol or drugs, or some other person, not a new car, not a mink coat. It is not the one that says, "If only I could get a promotion, or win the lottery, or score a touchdown, then I'd have what I need." It doesn't say these things because this part of you knows that everything you need is already inside. This is what your subconscious will help you discover.

If a voice or feeling has a sense of urgency to it, it probably has to do with some earthbound fear or addiction. When you are bombarded with this kind of interference, release it. Let it float away. Go under this flak. Messages from your subconscious mind have to do with what is right in the long run. If you ask for the answer to a short-term problem, you'll get an answer that will serve the long haul. You may not understand at the time why you are led in a given way, but you will when you look back. You'll see it had to do with inner things, with what is of true value, not with what will remain forever on the physical plane.

Being guided moment to moment by my subconscious mind has become a way of life for me, but I do not expect that everyone reading this book will instantly be willing to plunge into this kind of an all-out relationship. So ease into it a day at a time. Try making minor decisions to test how it feels. For example, suppose you go to a party and a feeling says this is not where you want to be. Your ego may counter with, "You can't leave. What would people think?"

Leave. Go home or where your inner voice directs you. When you arrive, calm yourself. Check how you feel. If you were following higher guidance, you'll feel light. More alive. You'll have energy. Remember this because in the future, even after you've made a big, life-changing decision, you'll experience this same sense of buoyancy after following direction from your subconscious mind. If you are off course, you'll feel drained, blocked, maybe even depressed. When you experience these feelings, it's time to reconsider.

As you work at listening to and practice following these messages, they will get stronger. After a time it will become easier to sort out ego-based voices from communication that stems from a higher source. Start with matters that aren't all that important and let your confidence build. If you persevere, you will come to a point where you are willing to let your life be guided in this way.

As you know from discussion earlier in this book, laboratory tests have demonstrated that scientists who don't believe in intuition are unable to replicate experiments involving intuition and ESP that have been successfully conducted by scientists who do believe. So the first and most important step is to believe that intuition is real. Next, you need to realize that we human beings spend a lot of time in denial. We often don't recognize the truth when we see it because we don't want to. It may be too painful, or we might have to change a bunch of other beliefs if we recognized the truth, and that would require effort. So before you dismiss new information, no matter how it comes to you, stop and ask yourself if you are doing so out of convenience or have solid evidence to back up the denial.

Understand that the truth cannot hurt you. As long as you identify with that timeless part of you that is deep within and realize that you've been around since the beginning of time and will be around until the end that will never come, the truth may ruin your day or your week — but it can only set you free in the long run.

Also, whenever you feel the need — but at least a couple of times a day — remember to take steps to align, or some would say, entrain your mind. Our minds consist of many layers. Deep within they are each connected to the universal subconscious where all knowledge can be found. Through quiet meditation, it is possible to center yourself and thereby align the various layers of your mind so that information can easily flow from one to the next until it reaches conscious awareness.

Finally, when insights come, look for consistency. Does the insight match the facts, or does it fly in the face of them? Look closely. And be honest with yourself. I won't try to tell you this whole business of allowing yourself to be guided by intuition isn't a little scary at first. But once you start down this path, you won't want to turn back. You'll experience anew sense of freedom.

Steps to Developing Intuition

1. Believe intuition is real. Laboratory tests have demonstrated that scientists who don't believe in intuition cannot replicate experiments that have been successfully conducted by scientists who do.

2. Realize that humans spend a lot of time in denial. We don't recognize the truth because it may be too painful, or might force us to change our beliefs. So before you dismiss new information, ask yourself if you have evidence to back up your denial.

3. Understand that the truth cannot hurt you. It may ruin your day, but in the long run it will set you free.

4. Ask for guidance and be open minded. "Ask, and it will be given."

5. Entrain your mind through meditation. Your mind consists of layers. You must align them so that information can flow from the deepest up to conscious awareness.

6. We all hear inner voices that can be compared to old tapes. These are parents or former teachers. "You should do this, you shouldn't do that." Go past them to the voice of intuition. This has serenity, a peacefulness that never tries to manipulate. Learn to recognize the difference.

7. Finally, when insights come, look for consistency. Do they meet the facts or fly in the face of them? Look closely. And be honest with yourself.

I guarantee it will be an adventure. A hero's adventure. And you'll arrive on a higher plane of understanding.

Perhaps right now, today, you feel a sense of frustration with your life. You know something's wrong, that you'd be happier doing something else, but you don't know what. Begin consulting with your subconscious mind. Remember what James, Jesus's brother, said: "Ask." Ask to be shown the way. Keep asking if you don't get an answer right away. In matters of spiritual growth, this always works. You can be confident you will get an answer, and if you run with it, that things will change. There can be no other result. Your ego self will be terrified. Tell it to hang on and trust. Your subconscious mind is a gung ho type who knows no fear. It's more than willing to lead you into the unknown.

And be prepared. You almost certainly will reach a point, as I did, when you will doubt that you have made the right move. You may even doubt that such a thing as a subconscious mind, and a higher power, exists. This will happen because it is part of the script. Read Joseph Campbell's *Hero with a Thousand Faces*. The hero's crisis, the period of uncertainty and doubt, has been an important element of the hero's adventure from the beginning of time. So just keep on plugging, and eventually the hands of grace will come to your aid. You'll be guided along miraculously as the Life Force, the opposite of entropy, folds in behind to support you. As you move ahead, ask for awareness. Ask for a sense of knowing what to do next.

You might ask this at night before bed, as I often do, or during your daily quiet time. You may receive an image, a feeling, or an answer in words right on the spot. You may draw a blank. If so, go about your business, but expect an answer. Trust that an answer is on the way. This may come in a dream or from outside yourself. You are part of one big dream, remember? Your mind and the Universal Mind are one — everywhere at once and non-local. The answer can come from anywhere. So be attentive.

Answers that come from outside me usually arrive in written form. A phrase or paragraph in a book I'm reading will seem to stand out. The medium could be almost anything: a fortune cookie, a comic strip, the Bible, Dear Abby. Whatever it is will strike a chord. It will be accompanied by that sense of "knowing" and possess meaning with respect to my current situation.

How does this work for me on a daily basis? Let's say a question or problem occurs in the morning while I'm working. When lunchtime comes and I'm out and about, I'll take a side trip to the library or a bookstore. I'll go to whatever shelf seems appropriate and take down whichever book grabs my attention. I'll open the book at random. Usually, the answer will be on the first page I turn to. If not, I'll close the book and open it again. If the answer still isn't there, I'll try another book. Seldom do I pick up more than three books. Many of the quotations used here were found this way.

A friend tells me his answers usually come from other people. It could be something the preacher says in a sermon on Sunday. Or my friend might be at work in conversation about something totally unrelated, and a sentence or phrase a person says will jump out at him. He has his answer. The meaning for him may have nothing to do with what the person talking was attempting to communicate.

Ask your subconscious mind to direct you to a better life. Let it show you step by step. Don't try to force it. Don't *make* yourself make decisions. Just let things take place. If you allow yourself to be guided, things will happen. Remain flexible. Trust. Things probably will not occur the way you expect, nor will you end up exactly where you originally thought you would. If you travel down a path only to find a dead end, look around for the open door. It will be there. You were led down that path because that's where the door is.

Your subconscious mind knows what it's doing. It won't let you starve. At times things may look bleak, though, so be prepared. You may wonder what's taking so long. You don't want to know how impatient I can be. The subconscious almost seems to delight in cutting things close — scheduling events to occur in the nick of time.

Something may happen that at first seems a disaster. For example, you might lose your job. If so, this is part of the plan. The crisis has come, so keep plugging. Don't turn back. You could turn into a bush or a pillar of salt. A better opportunity will come along.

Let me give you an example from when I was doing my best to build up the ad agency I mentioned earlier. The National Rural Electric Cooperative Association account went into review. It seemed ready-made, since my staff and I had considerable experience in the electric utility field. It was a million dollar account, not huge but not small, and it was located in Washington, D.C., only a two-hour drive from our offices. The people at NRECA were friendly, and they seemed to like us. The fit looked good on paper. Nevertheless, something told me the account was not right for us. At the time I was still listening to my ego fears, to the "shoulds" and "shouldn'ts" and "don't be sillys." The latter rang loud and clear, so we pressed ahead. We needed the business. What could possibly be wrong? This was a national account with an excellent credit rating. The people were fun to work with. They liked us. We liked them. So what if something "just didn't feel right?"

That sense continued nagging me, but my ego assured me we'd win the business. This part of me was so hopeful, I allowed my company to invest inordinate manpower and to make out of pocket expenditures on a trial project that would take years to recoup. I told myself we needed to make the investment and was assuaged because during the process we became quite friendly with the advertising staff. Before long, they were sending all the right signals. I was practically counting the money we would soon be making to earn back our investment when the ad manager paid me a personal visit. Over a very expensive lunch, she told me our agency would not be awarded the account. A higher up in the organization, whom we hadn't met, had overruled her wishes and the wishes of her staff. The business would go to an agency in Baltimore.

Part of me was devastated. Part of me said, "I told you so." But my intuition being dead right isn't the kicker. Two months later the Virginia Power account went into review. This was a $5 million client located in our hometown. We landed it with relative ease. No travel would be required and it was five times the income! If we had landed the association of electric cooperatives we would have been precluded from competing for the business. Virginia Power is an investor owned utility. NRECA is an association of user-owned utilities. The philosophies and goals of these two organizations are diametrically opposed. It would have been like having the RC Cola account when Coca-Cola went into review, a bird in the hand when the one in the bush is many times as large.

We are not always as fortunate when we ignore our intuition as I did. What had looked like a disaster turned out to be an act of grace. Even so, if I'd listened to my intuition, I'd have saved my company a great deal of money and the people who worked so hard to win the business a lot of heartache. The message is to follow your intuition even if you don't understand why it's telling you what it is telling you. Trust and persevere. Trust that in the end you will be better off. Persevere until you find the open door.

The question is bound to arise, can your subconscious mind make a mistake? Can it lead you down the metaphorical primrose path? The answer is an emphatic, "No, it cannot make a mistake." You may make a mistake interpreting the answer, but your subconscious mind knows what it's doing. It's plugged into the big dream and has a direct pipeline to the Big Dreamer.

Be cautious. Be cautious until you are one hundred percent confident in your ability to understand what you are being told. Ask for confirmation. Ask for reassurance. Ask and you will receive. But do not ignore your intuition. If you do not pay attention to it, if you do not move at least cautiously in the direction it is pushing you, you'll become blocked. Listening to higher guidance and learning to understand and interpret is like any skill. The more you do it, the better you get at it and the easier it becomes. Like anything, use it or lose it. If you do happen to make a wrong turn, the mistake will not be a disaster — not if you honestly were trying to do the right thing. Intention is what counts. Your subconscious mind, and the grace of God, will come to your aid in situations such as this.

To get on the right path, and to stay on the right path, we each need to realize that we're here for a reason. We also need to buy into the reality that it's up to us to discover what the reason is, and that it's up to us to accomplish it by tapping into the help and support of higher forces. This does not mean we should run out and quit our job. Not today. Not Monday morning. But what we can do is to start working on a plan now, today. The plan begins with a first step. The first step is to look within. Ultimately, that's where the answers to all life's questions reside.

It took a while for you to get into your current situation. So, be patient. It may take a while to get out of it, and onto the path to self actualization and abundance. If nothing else in this book remains with you, I urge you to remember this. You'll never feel the joy of waking up on a Monday morning and bounding out of bed — bounding out — because you can't wait to get going on what you absolutely love to do. You'll never know that joy until you take responsibility for every decision and for the consequences of every action you take. You see, the way you're going to arrive at this joy, this heaven on earth, is to take responsibility for being the one who finds the way. You're going to stop trying to please others, and instead you're to work in concert with the "still, small voice within" in order to please yourself, and in order to please that "still, small voice."

In another place and another time, a man much wiser than I gave people advice about following what was in their hearts, as opposed to chasing the money they thought they needed in order to feed and clothe themselves. He told them to look around at nature, at the birds of the air, for example. Birds don't worry. They don't store up grain for the winter, they don't plant, reap, or sow. They just do what birds do, what nature meant them to do, and they get along just fine.

This wise young man, of course, was Jesus. He probably was standing in a field at the time, and he asked his followers to look around. Then he said,

"See how the lilies of the field grow. They do not labor and spin. Yet I tell you that not even Solomon in all his glory was dressed as one of these."

Luke 12:27

Now, what was he talking about? What he was trying to communicate is that the lilies of the field are doing what they were meant to do, what nature (the Life Force and the Big Dreamer) intended. The lilies aren't working at it. They don't "labor or spin." They're hardly trying, yet they are doing it very well.

The people Jesus was talking to were worried about having enough to eat. They were worried about whether they would have clothes to wear, just as you may be worried about having enough to eat and clothes to wear. Jesus pointed out that these simple lilies of the field, by doing what they were meant to do, were dressed in such glorious outfits that they would put even Solomon to shame.

Who was Solomon?

Solomon had been a king of Israel, king of the Jews, long before the time of Jesus. Solomon's was a glorious period. During his rein, the people of Israel had their most prosperous days. Never before or since had their land been so large, so rich, and so peaceful as it was then. The people Jesus was speaking to instantly would have known who Solomon was because he had been the wisest, wealthiest, and most honored king in their entire history. Yet even Solomon in all his glory was not dressed as magnificently as simple lilies of the field, *doing what nature intended them to do.*

Just like the lilies of the field, you are part of nature. Like the lilies of the field, it was not an accident that you were born. Like the lilies of the field, you have something you were intended to do. You have a calling. You may not know what that calling is, not at this moment, but you *do* have it.

Let me explain why I think this is so. Every one of us is different, just as every snowflake is different. Each person is unique. I believe it follows that each person was born with a special gift, talent, or combination of talents that no one else possesses in precisely the way they do. Our destiny, and your destiny, our duty, and your duty, is to put those talents, or that gift, to work in a way, or ways, that will benefit others.

This is what nature had in mind. Whether or not you now realize it, this is your deep and unwavering desire.

When I talk about desire, I'm talking about motivation that comes from the true and positive self that exists deep down inside each of us, which I've been calling the subconscious mind. I'm *not* referring to kind of desire that wants something to feed an addiction, or another temporary craving such as a bigger house, a new car, or membership in the country club. I'm talking about the desire that exists in your heart to put to work the special talents, gifts, or combination of talents or gifts that only you possess.

In *The Seat of the Soul,* Gary Zukav says that before a soul incarnates, it enters into a contract with the Universe to accomplish certain things. Whatever task your soul has agreed to, the experiences of your life serve to awaken the memory of it and prepare you to accomplish it.

I urge you to spend time every day getting in touch with your innermost desires in order to determine what your calling is.

What can you do better than anyone else? How would you like to spend your time and your life?

You may have a talent for making music, or singing, or writing, that brings enjoyment to others. Maybe you have a special talent for seeing the underlying logic of a complicated system that can lead to a scientific discovery that will help others. Maybe you can bring forth pleasure for others because of a talent you have for putting together just the right combination of spices and ingredients to create a special meal or dish. Or it could be that you have a penchant for order that you can use to bring stability into the lives of others. Whatever your talent may be, believe me, it is there under the surface, waiting for you to discover. Once you think you've found it, begin using it, and if you're correct, you'll experience that intuitive *knowing* that you are on target. You'll become lost in the activity. Time will pass without your realizing it because you're in the *flow*. By following your purpose, you'll help others, and in turn you'll help yourself. This is the natural way. It is nature's way. You, like the lilies of the field, were meant to do your thing, what you do best, what no one else can do quite the same as you. This is why Jesus spoke those words about the lilies of the field 2,000 years ago, and why I now offer them to you.

I realize all this is easier for me to say than it is for you to do. Those fears won't automatically disappear when you snap your fingers. I suggest you write them down. Turn these statements around into positive affirmations. "My needs are being taken care of." "My life is getting better and better." Repeat them to yourself whenever the negative thought reoccurs. And keep in mind what Jesus also said:

> *And do not set your heart on what you will eat or drink; do not worry about it. For the pagan world runs after such things, and your Father knows that you need them. But seek his kingdom, and these things will be given to you as well.*

Luke 12:29-31

It helps to have at least one other person you can talk to about your fears. This should be someone who is also following the path set out for him. It should not be a family member, co-worker, or anyone who is still in the skeptical Stage Three mode. Such people will only reflect your ego fears.

And pray. Pray for guidance. Pray for the best possible outcome in each situation. The power of prayer is very real as we will see in the next chapter.

Chapter Nine: The How and Why of Prayer and Grace

Prayer appears to double the success rate of *in vitro* fertilization procedures that lead to pregnancy, according to a study published in the September, 2001 issue of the *Journal of Reproductive Medicine.* The findings reveal that a group of women who had people praying for them had a 50 percent pregnancy rate compared to a 26 percent rate in the group of women who did not have people praying for them. In the study, led by Rogerio Lobo, chairman of obstetrics and gynecology at Columbia University's College of Physicians & Surgeons, none of the women undergoing the IVF procedures knew about the prayers on their behalf. Nor did their doctors. In fact, the 199 women were in Cha General Hospital in Seoul, Korea, thousands of miles from those praying for them in the U.S., Canada and Australia. According to Dr. Lobo, "The results were so highly significant they weren't even borderline. We spent time deciding if it was even publishable because we couldn't explain it."

The fact is after it was published, skeptics did everything they could to discredit the study, from attempted character assassination of one of the researchers involved to questioning the methodology to do with how the actual praying was carried out. But from what I can determine none of their tactics was more than a thinly veiled attempt to hang on to that erroneous scientific tenet that we now know needs to be expunged.

Besides, this is not the first study to indicate that prayer can have a significant effect on matters of health. Another example comes from Randolph Byrd, a cardiologist, who over a ten-month period used a computer to assign 393 patients admitted to the coronary care unit at San Francisco General Hospital either to a group that was prayed for by home prayer groups (192 patients), or to a group that was not prayed for (201). This was a double blind test. Neither the patients, doctors, nor the nurses knew which group a patient was in. Roman Catholic as well as Protestant groups around the country were given the patients' names, and some information about their conditions. The various groups were not told how to pray, but simply were asked to do so every day.

The patients who were remembered in prayer had remarkably different and better experiences than the others. They were three times less likely to develop pulmonary edema, a condition in which the lungs fill with fluid; they were five times less likely to require antibiotics. None required endotracheal intubation (an artificial airway inserted in the throat), which twelve in the un-prayed-for group required. Also, fewer prayed-for patients died, although the difference between groups was not large enough to be considered statistically significant.

A third study indicating that prayer may have positive health effects is at this writing scheduled to be published in 2002 in the *International Journal for Psychiatry in Medicine*. A team from the University of California at Berkeley found that Christians and Jews who regularly attended services lived longer and were less likely to die from circulatory, digestive and respiratory diseases. Devotees of Eastern religions were not surveyed. The study examined links between religious attendance and cause-specific mortality from 1965 to 1996 in 6,545 residents of Alameda County, California. Even after adjusting for variables like health and frequency of exercise, religious devotees lived longer without succumbing to disease.

"At this point it's a puzzle why there should be this pattern," said the study's author, Doug Oman, Ph.D., a lecturer at Berkeley's School of Public Health. "It's likely a stress-buffering resource. Regular attendance at services can give people an inner peace that is unshakable. That results in less wear and tear on their bodies."

It is not surprising Dr. Lobo of Columbia University and Dr. Oman of Berkeley are puzzled by the results of their own studies. These men were schooled in the erroneous tenet. If you've believed it all your life, it isn't easy to give up the idea that awareness is the result of electrons jumping across synapses and that thought remains inside the skull. We, of course, know why and how prayer works. It does so because all things, including people and their bodies, are products of the universal mind. People's individual subconscious minds are diligent in their efforts to create what the owners' conscious minds believe, and subconscious minds are part of the Universal Mind. The belief of those praying that their prayers will be answered is impressed upon the subconscious, and the subconscious faithfully acts upon the bodies of those being prayed for.

An organization exists that has as its purpose the study of what prayer techniques produce the best results. It's called Spindrift[21] and was founded by Christian Science practitioners who have been at this since 1975. Resting next to my keyboard at this moment is a document an inch thick, printed on both sides of standard letter-size paper called, "The Spindrift Papers." It gives detailed information of prayer experiments conducted under rigorously controlled conditions.

The first question Spindrift researchers sought to answer is, *does prayer work?* The answer as we already know, is yes. In one test, rye seeds were split into groupings of equal number and placed in a shallow container on a soil-like substance called vermiculite. (For city dwellers, this is commonly used by gardeners.) A string was drawn across the middle to indicate that the seeds were divided into side A and side B. Side A was prayed for. Side B was not. A statistically greater number of rye shoots emerged from side A than from side B. Variations of this experiment were devised and conducted, but not until this one was repeated by many different Christian Science prayer practitioners with consistent results.

Next, salt was added to the water supply. Different batches of rye seeds received doses of salt ranging from one teaspoon per eight cups of water to four teaspoons per eight cups. Doses were stepped up in increments of one-half teaspoon per batch.

A total of 2.3 percent more seeds sprouted on the prayed-for

---

[21] See http://www.spindriftresearch.org

side of the first batch (one teaspoon per half-gallon of water) than on the unprayed-for side (800 "prayed-for" seeds sprouted out of 2,000, versus 778 sprouts out of 2000 in the not-prayed-for side). As the dosage of salt was increased the total number of seeds sprouting decreased, but the number of seeds which sprouted on the prayed-for sides compared to the unprayed-for sides increased in proportion to the salt (i.e., stress). In the 1.5 teaspoon batch, the increase was 3.3 percent. In the 2.0 teaspoon batch, 13.8 percent. In the 2.5 batch, 16.5 percent. In the 3.0, 30.8 percent. Five times as many prayed-for seeds in the 3.5 batch sprouted (although the total number which sprouted was small as can be seen from the chart below). Finally, no seeds sprouted in the 4.0 teaspoon per eight cup batch.

Salt	Control	/Grown	Prayed-for	/ Grown	% Increase[22]
1.0	2,000	778	2,000	800	2.3
1.5	3,000	302	3,000	312	3.3
2.0	3,000	217	3,000	247	13.8
2.5	3,000	454	3,000	528	16.3
3.0	3,000	52	3,000	68	30.8
3.5	2,000	2	2,000	10	400.0
4.0	3,000	0	3,000	0	0.0

What this says is what people lying in a ditch with bombs going off around them have always known: the more dire the situation, the more helpful prayer will be. Up to a point. There comes a time when things are so bad that nothing helps.

This experiment was also conducted using mung beans. The solution of salt and water ranged from 7.5 teaspoons per half-gallon of water to 30.0 teaspoons per half-gallon. The increase in the number of sprouts for the prayed-for side ranged from 3.3 percent to 54.2 percent.

Next an experiment was constructed to determine whether the

---

[22] Spindrift Papers, page 1-4.

amount of prayer makes a difference. This involved soy beans in four containers. One container was marked "control" and not prayed for. The other three were marked X, Y, and Z. In each run of the experiment, the X and Y containers were prayed for as a unit, and the Y and Z containers as a unit. So, Y received twice as much prayer as either X or Z. The Y container also had twice as many soy beans germinate. The results were in proportion to the amount of prayer.

Studies similar to this have been and are being carried out by a consortium of scientists put together by Lynne McTaggart, author of the books *THE FIELD: The Quest for the Secret Force of the Universe* and *The INTENTION EXPERIMENT: Using Your Thoughts to Change Your Life and the World.* When she was on my show in early 2008, she described some of these experiments and the terrific success she and her colleagues have had. She said several of these studies were being prepared for publication.

What the Spindrift studies show is reminiscent of a principle set forth by Napoleon Hill in his perennial bestseller, *Think and Grow Rich.* He wrote this granddaddy of all self help books in the 1930s and updated it in 1960. One chapter is devoted to the principle he called "The Master Mind." Hill suggested that whatever project or purpose or goal an individual had, it could be advanced and achieved most readily by bringing together a group of people who could apply their unified brain power to it. Hill never used the word prayer nor did he suggest people sit around and pray. But he did liken a group of minds at work on a project to a group of storage batteries connected together in a series to produce much more power than any single battery possibly could on its own. He wrote, "When a group of individual brains are coordinated and function in harmony, the increased energy created through that alliance becomes available to every individual brain in the group." He cited several examples, including the remarkable successes of Henry Ford and Andrew Carnegie, each of whom had a group of colleagues around him working and pulling together on common goals. Hill wasn't referring only to innovative thinking that leads to marketing and sales results. He was talking about much more, of creating an aura which leads to favorable events taking place, or to what might be considered by Materialists as "good breaks." The Master Mind creates a force with a life of its own, a force I've called grace later in this chapter. This is the force that works much like unseen hands. A case Hill cited was that of Mahatma Gandhi, who led the successful non-violent revolution that freed India from British Colonial rule. Hill wrote, "He came to power through inducing over two hundred million people to coordinate, with mind and body, in a spirit of harmony, for a definite purpose."

If one person can make 54.2 percent more saltwater-soaked mung beans sprout with his mind, imagine what two hundred million can do. They toppled a government which had been in power for more than 150 years, and they did it without firing a shot.

The power of the Master Mind is another good reason to become part of some sort of spiritual brotherhood. You may want to organize a study group as well. I propose that groups range in size from three to ten and that they be dedicated to the expanded consciousness and spiritual growth of each of its members. A group ought to meet a minimum of twice a month, or more frequently if possible. For a period of about five years, I participated in three such groups and experienced quantum leaps in my own development. I continue to participate in one.

The group ought to study a text such as this one, or the Bible, or the Bhagavad-Gita. Share your thoughts, your individual interpretations of what you study, and ideas about how to put what you've learned to use. You'll also want to set aside a time at each meeting to share personal concerns, fears and troubles. Prayer is one of the tools your group can and ought to employ.

For example, you may wish to pray for someone who is trying to get pregnant. As the study cited at the beginning of this chapter demonstrated, prayer can be particularly effective in this regard. This makes perfect sense, since the Life Force's goal is to foster life.

In the Columbia study, the people praying were from Christian denominations and were separated into three groups. One group received pictures of the women and prayed for an increase in their pregnancy rate. Another group prayed to improve the effectiveness of the first group. A third group prayed for the two other groups. According to the authors of the study, anecdotal evidence from other prayer research has found this method to be most effective.

The three groups began to pray within five days of the initial hormone treatment that stimulates egg development, then continued to pray for three weeks.

Besides finding a higher pregnancy rate among the women who had a group praying for them, the researchers found that older women seemed to benefit more from prayer. For women between 30 and 39, the pregnancy rate for the prayer group was 51 percent, compared with 23 percent for the non-prayer group. This would seem to parallel the Spindrift study in that those who needed help the most, up to a point at least, saw the biggest gains from prayer versus no prayer. With Spindrift, it was salt-soaked rye and mung beans. With the Columbia study, it was older women.

Is there anything more the Spindrift researchers learned which would be helpful to know?

The quality of prayer is a factor in how effective it is, as is the quantity or amount of prayer. Like anything, practice makes perfect. More experienced practitioners got better results than less experienced practitioners. Get in the habit of praying. Do not save the practice of it only for the times bullets are flying overhead, or the airplane you're on goes into a tailspin.

The Spindrift research also gives us clues on how to pray. First, you need to know what you're praying for. Some experiments were conducted in which the prayer practitioner was kept in the dark about the nature of the seeds he was praying for. He or she did not know what kind of seeds they were or to what extent they had been stressed. Results showed a drastic reduction in the effect. The researchers concluded that the more the person praying knows about that which is being prayed for, the greater the effect of the prayers.

Another experiment measured the efficacy of "directed" versus "non directed" prayer. Directed prayer was that in which the practitioner had a specific goal, image, or outcome in mind. He attempted to steer the seeds in a particular direction. A parallel in healing might be for blood clots to dissolve or for cancer to isolate itself in a particular place in the body, i.e. where it could be cut out. In the seed germination experiments it was praying for a more rapid germination rate. Non directed prayer used an open-ended approach in which no specific outcome was held in the imagination. The person praying did not attempt to imagine or project a specific result but rather to ask for whatever was best for the seeds in an open-ended spirit of "Thy will be done." Both approaches worked, but the non-directed approach appeared to be more effective, in some cases producing twice the results.

Using the non directed approach is bound to conflict with the beliefs of many who hold that one must visualize a specific result and hold it in his mind. No doubt in some cases this works well. The problem is that we humans often do not know what the best outcome of any given situation might be. The theory put forth by Spindrift researchers is that prayer reinforces the tendency of an out-of-balance organism to return to balance. It enhances the Life Force, which as we both know by now is the opposite of entropy. In other words, the goals of nature are harmony and growth, and prayer supports this. To quote the Spindrift research document, "If the power of holy prayer does, indeed, heal, then such a power will be manifest as movement of a system toward its norms since healing can be defined as movement toward the optimal or 'best' conditions of form and function."[23] The Spindrift researchers did not try experiments in which prayer was used to try to prevent seeds from germinating. If they had, and if what they say here is true, this would not have worked.

Chances are, we don't know the best way for an organism to

[23] The Spindrift Papers, page 1-51.

achieve balance. Likewise, the subconscious mind and the Big Dreamer are interested in growth and evolution. The best outcome of a situation will have growth of some kind as a result. In this way, nature achieves harmony and balance, or the healing of a splintered soul.

This may be bad news for anyone who picked up this book thinking it would provide a formula for conjuring riches without the conjurer having first to change. If a new Mercedes will not help foster your spiritual development or someone else's in some way, you're wasting your time praying for it no matter how clearly you can picture just such a shiny new auto in your mind.

Here's what Jesus's brother James had to say about this: "You do not have, because you do not ask God. When you ask, you do not receive, because you ask with wrong motives, that you may spend what you get on your pleasures." (James 4:2-3.) Our motives need to be in line with the goals of the universe. God is not in the business of satisfying our selfish whims. He wants something much more valuable. He wants us to evolve.

Finally, here is what Thomas Troward has to say about creating mentally, or prayer. The text below is taken from the modern English version of his *Edinburgh Lectures on Mental Science* as they appear in *How to Master Life*, published in 2007 by the Oaklea Press:

> *Some people possess the power of visualization, or making mental pictures of things, to a greater degree than others. This faculty may be employed advantageously to facilitate the working of the Law. But those who do not possess this faculty in any marked degree, need not be discouraged by their lack of it. Visualization is not the only way to put the law to work on the invisible plane. . . .*
>
> *We must (simply) regard our mental creations as spiritual realities and then implicitly trust the Laws of Growth to do the rest. . . .*

Our subconscious mind is in touch with the Big Dreamer and the big dream. It has access to, is immersed in, all the information needed in any situation. The way to the best result may be exactly the opposite of what we expect, which means that in many cases it is best to put things in God's hands and pray for the best possible outcome. Visualize the outcome you want. Consider this outcome already accomplished. Do not attempt to explain to the universal subconscious what course it should take to arrive at the desired destination. Let the universal subconscious find the best way.

The readings of Edgar Cayce have something to say about all this. Suppose, for example, someone you love is suffering from an addiction such as alcoholism. You want to help, but how? Prayer is certainly one action you can take. But if this loved one is not yet interested in changing, what form of prayer is best? Cayce described two kinds: direct and protective. In direct prayer, you ask for a specific healing to take place. Such a prayer is appropriate, he said, only if the target of your prayer has asked for such efforts. In this case, you are adding energy to a process of change that he or she has already willed. If the person you are praying for is not in sympathy with your efforts, your prayers may actually aggravate the problem. In such a case protective prayer is best. With this type of prayer, ask that the person be surrounded and protected by the forces of love and healing, while at the same time allowing that individual his or her own free will in choosing whether or not to change.

You recall my prayer to have events take place that would wipe out the bad karma I felt was hanging over me. This was a direct prayer, and I got just what I asked for — although it was perhaps *more* than I bargained for. Nevertheless, the experience caused me to grow. Even my wife divorcing me turned out for the best. I suspect that neither of us had been happy for quite some time. Today, both of us are remarried and more content than we had ever been before.

I've often seen direct prayers answered. They always seem to result in growth, and sometimes in unexpected ways. A friend in one of my study groups, for example, recounted a story recently about how we should be careful what we ask for because we just might get it. Her son had spent a miserable autumn and winter, first on the bench of his high school football team and then on the bench of the basketball squad. Lacrosse season was getting underway and the first game was scheduled for that afternoon. Her son was in the starting lineup. At last he would have a chance to show his prowess. "Please, Lord, have him score a lot of goals," she prayed. "Let him be the star of the team today."

She was thrilled and amazed as she watched the game. Not only did his team win, her son scored all the goals for his side. He was all over the place; seemed to be everywhere at once. She patted herself on the back and praised the Lord all the way home.

But her joy was short-lived. When her son came home he was depressed.

"What's wrong?" she asked. "You should be feeling good. You were sensational."

"Aw, Mom. No I wasn't. I was a ball hog. It was like I never gave anyone else on my team a chance. It didn't even feel like it was me out there playing. It was as though I was possessed, or something. Like someone else scored those goals — not me."

My friend had wanted a feel-good experience for her son and herself. What was received was a growth experience for her son, and a learning experience for herself.

Next time you pray, think about what you are really asking. Will it help you or someone else grow? Think, too, about what is happening in the unseen world as a result. Here is what Betty Eadie experienced when out of her body while clinically dead. In *Embraced by the Light* she wrote:

> I saw many lights shooting up from the earth like beacons. Some were very broad and charged into heaven like broad laser beams. Others resembled the illumination of small pen lights, and some were mere sparks. I was surprised as I was told that these beams of power were the prayers of people on earth.
>
> I saw angels rushing to answer the prayers. They were organized to give as much help as possible. As they worked within

this organization, they literally flew from person to person, from prayer to prayer, and were filled with love and joy by their work.

I imagine what Betty saw was a metaphor constructed by her mind. It seems logical to me that mental constructions are how we experience the spirit realm. Heaven and hell are what we imagine and believe them to be. Nonetheless, her vision is one of beauty.

Let's sum up what we need to keep in mind about prayer:

1. Belief is a key. Believe that what you pray for already exists in spirit.
2. Practice makes perfect, or in other words, experienced prayer practitioners receive the best results.
3. Quantity is a factor. More prayer brings more result.
4. The more a person or group knows about the subject of their prayers, the better.
5. If the desired outcome is clear, visualize it, and pray for it. Consider it an accomplished fact. But do not tell the universal subconscious how to arrive at this outcome. Let it find the way.
6. If the best outcome is not clear, prayers should be kept general in nature. Pray for the best outcome. The universal subconscious knows.
7. For good results, the purposes of the universe need to be served by our prayers. This includes spiritual growth and development, the healing of the soul and life, or in the case of physical healing, the bringing of a stressed body or physical system into harmony or balance.

If you truly want to find your purpose, if you want a fulfilling life and the buoyant feeling of following the path laid out for you, if you want to make progress in this lifetime, and if you want to enter the Kingdom of God, ask for help. Pray for guidance and assistance in bringing this about. Ask to be shown the way. You will be led into the most exciting adventure you will ever take.

A word of caution may be in order. Once you ask, be prepared to experience events you never would have chosen for yourself. At first it may seem like a roller coaster ride, and you may wish you could get off. What seems to be a disaster may happen. You may get transferred. Your wife may ask for a divorce. Your apartment building might burn down. Of course, you might get a promotion, win the lottery, be offered a dream job out of the blue. But I predict that whatever happens, the path won't be easy. Growth takes effort and means change. A transformation must take place in you.

Most people resist change. This is their ego fighting for what it thinks is survival. Even if you want to transform, it won't be easy. So you might as well anticipate a number of character-building challenges. A friend in one of my study groups relates a story which illustrates my point. One day, feeling frustrated with a situation he had to deal with, he prayed, "Lord, give me more patience." Soon, he found himself in a situation that took every ounce he could muster.

Later, it came to him that we have to learn by doing — that "practice makes perfect." He was sent what he needed, an opportunity to exercise patience. He'd thought God would hand him more patience as a gift but more patience came to him in the only way it could — he had to learn and eventually earn it.

When you ask for change, don't be surprised if some of the change that occurs is unrelated to the central issue. For example, when I was making the transition from advertising agency president to full time writer, my car started falling apart. It wasn't a particularly old car, but nevertheless, one thing after another went wrong. I believe now this was an outward sign of inward change taking place in my life. Since everyone and everything is connected, and part of the whole, I guess we need to expect this sort of thing. Trust. Continue asking for guidance. If you think you have an answer but aren't positive, don't do anything precipitous. Ask for further guidance, confirmation, or some form of reassurance.

And expect to be helped by the invisible hands of grace. What is Grace? Grace is what happens when the universal subconscious is working in people's lives to insure or further growth and development. To the untrained eye, grace appears to be a set of mysterious or unexplainable conditions, events and phenomena that support, nurture, protect or enhance human life and spiritual growth. Grace works in all sorts of ways. The forms of grace seem to be universal. Our immune systems, for example, are tied to it. Modern medicine has only a vague idea why one person exposed to an infectious disease will come down with it and another experiencing the same level of exposure will not. On any given day, in practically every public environment, potentially lethal microbes and viruses on surfaces or floating in the air are too numerous to estimate. Yet, most people do not get sick. Why? Doctors would say it is because most people's resistance is fairly high. But what do they really mean? That most people are not rundown or depressed? Perhaps. Not everyone who is rundown and depressed contracts an infectious disease. Yet many do who are perfectly healthy and in good shape.

In some cases, however, getting sick may be an act of grace. At one point after leaving the ad business, I got discouraged. I very nearly threw in the towel with respect to my dream of writing full-time. I concluded it was time to return to the rat race and took several steps in that direction. I actually had promotional materials printed and was putting together a mailing list. It wasn't what I wanted to do, but I was worried that I'd never make it as a writer. I was afraid my money would run out. So I stood on the brakes and was in the process of making a U-turn. Then grace stepped in. I got sick. I caught the flu. It was a bad case that lasted almost two weeks, and it gave me plenty of time to think.

Whenever I get sick I always ask myself, "Why?" Sometimes the answer is that I'm pushing myself too hard and need to slow down. This time, my system was telling me I'd be making a big mistake to reverse course. I was as certain of the message then as I am of it now.

For me, the viola twanged its low-pitched note.

Most people do not get sick or die each day because their illness or death are not in the interest of their own spiritual evolution, or the evolution of humankind as a whole. It doesn't happen because it will not advance their growth. In my case, catching the flu was just what needed to happen. It was my wake up call, and it worked. I decided to stay the course.

I'm sure this sort of thing happens every day. I didn't need a really big, life-threatening illness to get my attention because I'm on the lookout for such things. But think about those who have stalled in terms of personal growth and have no idea how these things work. A serious illness can be the wake-up call needed to snap them out of it and get them back on track. ("My God, if I die I won't be able to accomplish X, Y, and Z, and I really want to do that. Please, God, let me have another chance!")

Or, it may be that nothing is going to do the trick. They've truly reached a dead end. ("Doggone it. Wouldn't you know? Life's a bitch. Then you die. It looks like this is the end.")

This individual's subconscious mind and the Big Dreamer may come to the conclusion that the usefulness of the present incarnation has come to an end and that it's time for the individual to move on. This person will not pull through. Those who are left behind may grieve and wonder why, but this course will allow the subconscious mind to assimilate what has been gained in this lifetime. The individual is now free to be born again into a new body and begin a new life cycle of growth. In the big scheme of things, getting on with a new incarnation and moving ahead will be preferable to figuratively treading water until the individual has lived out his or her allotted three score years and ten.

By the way, the grace of resistance is not limited to infectious disease. Have a chat with a state trooper who has been on the scene of a number of motor vehicle accidents. Ask the trooper what percentage of crashes appeared fatal when he first arrived, and how many actually turned out to be. You're likely to hear some amazing stories of cars or trucks smashed beyond recognition, metal so collapsed, twisted or squashed the trooper will say, "I don't see how anyone could have survived. And yet the person walked away without a scratch," or with only minor injuries. How is it scientifically possible for metal to collapse in such a way as to conform perfectly to the shape of the human body contained inside? Nevertheless, I'm willing to bet the trooper will tell you that this happens more often than not.

When she was about a year old, my now five-year-old daughter body-surfed down the steep flight of stairs from our kitchen to our basement playroom—not just once, but twice. Another time, a babysitter turned her back while changing a diaper, and the same daughter rolled off the counter top and fell straight to the bare kitchen floor. Any of these three falls easily could have been fatal. None caused so much as a bruise.

Almost everyone has experienced a close call that could have killed him. One day when I was fourteen, I darted across Jefferson Davis Highway without looking properly. At the time, this was the main north-south highway on the East Coast. This particular stretch had six lanes (three north and three south) with a grass median. A car struck me in mid-stride. Maybe it was the way the car's bumper caught my foot that lifted me into the air, but I should have been pushed down and run over. Instead, I was lifted up, seemed to fly through the air, and landed on the grass median. The driver was certain I was dead—until I stood up and dusted myself off. I didn't have a scratch. The only evidence of the accident was the stain on my trousers where I'd slid on the grass as I came to a stop. Also, both my shoes were missing. I found them eighty or a hundred feet away where the car had screeched to a halt. If the laws of Newtonian physics had been working that day, I wouldn't be here to put this down on paper.

How, physically, was I lifted into the air? Were angels responsible? It certainly seems possible. But whatever happened, the phenomenon called grace came to my aid, and I lived to be an adult.

As a result, I grew and studied and learned enough to enable me to write this book. And you know what? If this book didn't exist, at least some who would have read it, perhaps including you, would die before it was necessary for them to do so. They'd check out of this life before accomplishing the objectives set out before they were born. So the angels that lifted me up did them a favor as well as me.

The role of grace is to help advance the evolution of souls. This fits with the forms of communication with your subconscious mind discussed in the last chapter: The voice telling you to wake up and take note because the mother of your children is approaching, the clairvoyant message that says someone you love is in trouble, a dream that brings the answer to a question. Or grace may manifest as the answer to a prayer.

If you want to take advantage of the higher intelligence available to you, it makes sense to align yourself with grace. Make the evolution of your soul, and the souls of others, your number-one and number-two priorities. The forces of the universe will fall in behind you to help make this happen. I know, because I experience this daily.

Let me give another example. A few years ago, a friend in one of my study groups and his wife quit their full time jobs in order to attend seminary together. They both had to work part-time and even then were only able to bring in enough to just get by. Unexpected bills arrived, as they always do. They totaled $578, money they simply didn't have. The couple's bank balance registered zero. They had no place to turn. Creditors were calling. Our group prayed that the money they needed would come to them. My friend and his wife prayed, too, as did others.

Two days later, the couple received an envelope in the mail from the IRS saying that their petition had been reviewed. Their tax return from two years prior had been found to be in error. Along with this notice, was a check to them for $588.

Good timing? True. But the amazing thing was, the couple had not filed a petition. Nor had they filed an amended return. Somehow or other, the IRS had done this recalculation on their own. The couple rummaged in their files and pulled out their return from two years prior. The IRS was correct. They found the error which had been referenced.

In my experience, the IRS is not in the mode of helping people out this way. It was grace that brought them that check because they needed the money to stay in school. Seminary was helping them grow, and their growth and the degrees they would receive would someday allow them to help others grow as well.

Why was the check for ten dollars more than they needed? Maybe, since our group met at a restaurant over breakfast on Thursday mornings, grace wanted to pick up the tab.

You may also be familiar with the story of psychiatric pioneer Carl Jung that he related in an article called "On Synchronicity." Jung had a patient, a young woman, who was the type who thought she knew everything. She was well educated and used highly polished rationalism as a weapon to defend herself against Jung's attempts to give her a deeper, spirit-based understanding of reality. Jung was at a loss as to how to proceed and found himself hoping something unexpected and irrational would happen in order to burst the intellectual bubble she'd sealed herself inside.

One day, they were in his office. He had his back to the window, and she was talking. She was telling him about a dream she'd had the night before in which she'd been given a golden scarab — an expensive piece of jewelry. Jung heard something behind him tapping at the window. He turned and saw a large flying insect knocking against the pane on the outside, trying to get in. He opened the window and caught the insect. It was a scarabaeid beetle, or rose-chafer (Cetonia aurata), whose golden-green color resembles a gold scarab.

Jung handed the beetle to his patient with the words, "Here is your scarab." This poked the desired hole in her rationalism, exactly as Jung had hoped.[24] She had dreamed about the gift of a scarab and now it had happened. What she received, however, was a much bigger gift. She was shown through grace that everything is One Mind — that she was but one dreamer in the dream of life. Grace worked, as always, to aid in her spiritual development.

Perhaps you are now saying to yourself, these sorts of things never happen to me. This Martin fellow is living in a fantasy world. To this I will ask, are you making an effort to advance and grow spiritually? If so, are you on the lookout for acts of grace? Do you expect synchronicities? You must be open to them and permit them to happen. You must *expect* them. If Jung hadn't been looking for an unusual, irrational occurrence, if he hadn't been *expecting* it, he might not have bothered to open the window. If I didn't expect to find the quotation I need or the answer to a question when I walk into a library or bookstore, I doubt I ever would. If I did happen to find what I need, I'd chalk it up to coincidence, wouldn't I? I'd tell myself it probably wouldn't happen again. And I probably wouldn't see it when it did. As I've said a number of times in this book, you usually get, or don't get, what you expect.

Expect grace to happen. Then be on the lookout.

Let's suppose you have decided to strike out on the path of spiritual growth. One way to insure you'll be helped along by grace is to cut off avenues of retreat. This is what the couple in seminary had done. Both had quit their jobs. It seems possible they received help partly because there was no other alternative. I'm reminded of the general of ancient times who took his army across a sea to fight a distant enemy. As soon as he and his men landed, he ordered the ships that had brought them burned, cutting off all means of retreat. This created a big incentive — his men had no choice but to win or die. Of course, they won. But the question is, was it purely the will to live that led to victory? Isn't it also possible they got some breaks because of the desperate situation they were in? If you cut off all

---

[24] Campbell, Joseph (1971), *The Portable Jung*, Viking Press, New York, pages 511-12.

means of retreat, your subconscious mind, or perhaps your guides aor guardian angels will be left with no other alternative but to help you. I believe this is precisely what they want to do. They want you to make progress. They want you to wake up and live. If they do allow you to stumble and fall, it will be because this is necessary before you can climb to new heights.

Making the effort to grow spiritually is difficult, and it takes courage. Perhaps most difficult is being totally honest with yourself about yourself and your surroundings. You may not like what you see, and this can be painful. Just keep in mind that growth means change. Your goal is to become the best you can be. The problem is, most of us think we are just fine the way we are. Our ego self does not want to change for fear that change will wipe it out of existence. Of course, this isn't true. The new you will be happier, stronger, more vital, alive, awake and aware. But this transformation will take effort. There will be hardships to overcome. Pursuing spiritual growth is not an undertaking for the faint of heart or the lazy.

It's human nature to be lazy. Everyone is at least lazy part of the time. Unfortunately, a lot of us are lazy a lot of the time. We think the world owes us a living. We think we can get by without trying all that hard. What we need to get through our heads that life will be difficult whether we chose to stay put and "play it safe," or to strike out on the wondrous adventure of growth. It can be "life's a bitch, and then you die," or "life's a bitch, but at least you know why."

Laziness is dangerous. Most Christians believe hell is permanent separation from God or Christ. I would say that hell also involves separation from one's own soul. (This is the source of the expression, "lost soul.") If you are lazy and look only for the easy way, you will end up doing a lot of evil. Not only will you pile up a great deal of negative karma, but you run the risk of becoming so separated from your subconscious mind, or soul, that it will be impossible to find your way back. People who are evil have "sold out" to the easy way. They have lost touch with their souls and may never reunite. They may spend eternity looking. Surely, this is the worst kind of hell. In life, they will end up spending a good deal of effort desperately trying to hold themselves together. In death, they will spend eternity searching. Finally, if they do decide to expend the effort to improve their existence, they may invest their energy in the pursuit of money or material success, because they think this will bring the maximum return. But the fear of falling apart cannot be overcome by money or fame. If anything, being way up on top with a big fat mortgage and a lot of "responsibilities" only makes the prospect of falling more intimidating. Such a life becomes unbearable. Invariably the person who pursues only financial gain will find himself in a situation he thinks he must manage through the sheer effort of will. But all the will power a human can muster will not keep his life together. The subconscious mind and the Big Dreamer will knock out the supports in an effort to wake up this individual. A financial crisis, a serious illness or accident, the loss of a job — something like this will happen. I've come to the realization that it's better to let go and submit to one's subconscious mind. Stepping forward in an effort to live your destiny is the best course, even with the difficulties that must surely come. In the end, this will turn out to be the easier way. When you and I differentiated to become separate and unique entities, we cut off any avenue of retreat as surely as the general who burned his ships. If we make no progress in this lifetime, we will have to come back and try it again. And again. And again. In between tries, we will have to suffer the sorrow that an understanding of the full impact of each of our transgressions will bring, plus the frustration of knowing what might have been if we hadn't been so lazy or fearful.

Getting on the right path is what each of us needs to do, and what I hope for you. Remember. You exist to evolve, and this means going the direction of the flow. Your subconscious mind and the Big Dreamer want you to join them. They want a relationship that will eventually lead to a merger. But don't kid yourself, you will have tomake major adjustments in your life, and these take strength and courage. But as you get to know your subconscious mind, and form a

Seven Steps to Growth

1. *Recognize that a force exists that's not yet acknowledged by science. The opposite of entropy, it fosters evolution and growth.*

2. *Form an alliance with it through your subconscious mind. Ask for direction and guidance.*

3. *Expect a "call to adventure," which is the Life Force beckoning for you to follow your destiny to a higher level of understanding.*

4. *Look for communication and guidance, which will come through intuition, the Scriptures, the written word, others, and your circumstances.*

5. *After answering the call, expect a crisis. Resist the temptation to abandon the quest. Press ahead. Watch grace come to your aid.*

6. *Major adjustments in your life will probably be required. Make them.*

7. *Self-actualization will flow to you as you obey your inner voice and accomplish the work assigned. Abundance, joy, and fulfillment will be yours.*

relationship, you will grow to the point where you would not trade the relationship or the growth for anything. Love, abundance, and a sense of fulfillment will begin flowing into your life. You will be on your way to self-actualization.

In the next chapter we will assemble what we have learned and lay out the map.

*"Every journey of a thousand miles
begins with the first step."*

—Chinese proverb

Chapter Ten: Putting It All Together to Make the Shift

Now having taken most of the journey of this book together, what can we be fairly certain that we know? Perhaps we should begin with what we don't know. We don't know how the universe began, when it will end, or why it exists. We can't be certain why life exists but one thing seems to make sense. Because the universe consists of subjective mind, life may exist so that the universe can step outside itself — and know itself. Life for the universe may simply be a form of amusement, but intuitively, it seems highly possible that life is an effort by the universe to replicate itself. One thing we know is that the subjective mind underlying everything is an organizing intelligence. It is the opposite of entropy, and as such fosters growth and evolution. It is a force we have called spirit or Life Force. It is mind, the medium of thought. It helps to conceptualize thoughts as things that exist in this medium. Once formed on the spirit plane, thoughts are ready and seemingly eager to manifest themselves on the physical plane. Thoughts are non-local. They are everywhere at once just as spirit, or the Life Force, is everywhere.

While we may think in terms of thought forms, Rupert Sheldrake writes of fields. Morphic fields. These might be compared to gravitational or electromagnetic fields — except that these fields are comprised of thoughts. Life on earth has a field. Within this are the fields of families of plants and animals. Within these family fields are the fields of species. You and I and each other human being have our own morphic fields that contain the memories of bodies, experiences and lessons learned since we first began incarnating into physical form.

The universal mind, this underlying organizing intelligence we have been considering, is not God in the sense God is normally conceived of by Western theologians. The universal mind does not make decisions or grant wishes arbitrarily, but rather, the universal mind matches things up that may benefit from being matched up — which is called synchronicity — and it pushes toward growth and evolution. Life, health and harmony within an organism are supported perforce. When it comes to praying, the more help needed the more help given. In all matters, whatever outcome will result in evolution will receive top priority. Moreover, the universal mind will make events work in such a way that even the most horrific tragedy will produce the maximum good possible in the form of growth and evolution. This may be the meaning behind the Apostle Paul's words in Romans 8:28, "And we know that in all things God works for the good of those who love him." That they love him means they are striving to evolve in order to become more like him. Difficulties often cause us to evolve and to become better people.

Though it is powerful, purposeful and all-knowing, the universal mind reasons deductively. It cannot step outside itself to analyze a situation. Therefore, it does not play favorites or hold grudges. According to Jesus, "[God] causes his sun to rise on the evil and the good, and sends rain on the righteous and the unrighteous." (Matthew 5:45)

Inductive reasoning is progressing from result to cause, step by step, logically. For example, a detective called in to solve the mystery of a crime would look upon the result, the finished deed, and by reasoning backward attempt to tell how the crime was committed and by whom. Deductive reasoning, on the other hand, is done from the cause forward to its ultimate end instead of backward to the cause. Deductive reasoning embraces no question, no analysis, no examination, but is a mere chain of subsequent actions, each a logical result of the former. It is the kind of reasoning that a criminal might use in committing a crime.

It consequently follows that an individual's subjective mind — which is in fact a portion of the universal subjective mind — is entirely under the control of its owner's objective mind. The subjective mind works be bring about whatever the objective mind impresses upon it. Hypnotism shows, for example, how ideas can be impressed on a subjective mind by an objective mind.

The subjective mind is the builder of the body. For example, the experience of Edgar Cayce and other psychics indicates that a patient's subjective mind is able to diagnose the character of the disease from which he is suffering and to point out suitable remedies. In addition, the subjective mind can bring about spontaneous healing, as was the case with Nancy in Chapter One who suffered from a lump in her breast. Through prayer, the subjective mind of an individual or individuals can work in concert with the universal subjective mind to bring about healing like Nancy's, lessen the severity of an illness like San Francisco General Hospital's heart patients', or bring about successful *in vitro* fertilization as in the case of the Columbia University Study. Indeed, the beliefs held by the individual's objective mind are impressed upon his or her subjective mind with the result that the very circumstances of an individual's life are adjusted accordingly.

Katie's subjective mind produces brass foil pursuant to her thought of getting back at her husband.

That the subjective mind is impersonal in and of itself is shown by its readiness to assume any personality a hypnotist chooses to impress upon it. The unavoidable inference of this is that any personality the subjective mind may appear to possess comes about as the direct result of an association with the particular objective mind of its owner. In other words, the personality the objective mind impresses upon it is the personality it assumes. Since the subjective mind is the builder of the body, it will build up a body in correspondence with the personality thus impressed upon it. Moreover, the personality of the God our objective mind assumes will be the personality of the God we have to deal with. The subjective mind simply plays back to us whatever we impress upon it. If we assume a loving and forgiving father God as Jesus said to do, this indeed will be our God. (If you happen to prefer a loving

What we know

- Behind and giving form and existence to physical reality is subjective mind or organizing intelligence, i.e. Universal Mind. Everything, including ourselves, evolved from this.

- Sub fields exist within this field. Life has a field. Each species has a field. Each person has a field we call a "soul." Sub fields are individual and yet at one with the whole just as television transmissions represent a single bandwidth and separate channels simultaneously.

- The field and sub fields evolve. Universal Mind and its component Life Force push us and all nature to grow. It is the opposite of entropy.

- Universal Mind is subjective. It cannot step outside itself and does not play favorites.

- The field supports and fosters life and harmony of body, mind and spirit. Prayer (thought) can add energy to this. More and higher-quality prayer will bring greater results.

- Human beings are highly-evolved sub fields which have manifested in physical form that can think objectively. They can step outside themselves and consider their own existence. In this way, the universe experiences itself.

- Because our minds are objective, we have the power of choice or "free will." This gives us the ability to attune our thoughts and actions with the directional force (toward growth, evolution, and harmony) of the Universal Mind. By aligning ourselves and subjugating our wills to that of the Universal Mind, we "go with the flow" and life works better for us.

- It may be that through human evolution the universe is creating co-creators or perhaps even new universes.

- No predetermined plan is being followed. (Recall the Panda's thumb.)

- Thoughts are sub fields within the field and can be compared to things. Formed and left alone, they eventually will manifest in physical form.

- Thoughts are non-local and timeless. They exist everywhere at once. Distance is not a factor.

- Univeral Mind brings into being what we create and hold in our objective (conscious and unconscious) minds. In effect, our experiences are reflections of our thoughts, feeling, beliefs and attitudes. In this way, what we hold inside becomes our reality, i.e. love begets love, hate begets hate. This is why, "What we give, we receive and what we keep we lose."

- The personality of the God an objective mind assumes exists will be the personality of that person's God.

mother God, instead, that sounds just fine to me. Go for it.) But if one believes in an unforgiving, wrathful and capricious God who hates Westerners as some Islamic extremists apparently assume, this will be their God. All I can say is, too bad for them. And us Westerners, too, when they unleash their hatred on us.

If we believe that God favors us and showers us with abundance and opportunities for fulfillment and joy, then this will be our experience. If we believe that God will punish us for our transgressions, we will indeed be punished. Our beliefs become our reality. What we need to do to change our reality, then, is to change our beliefs. The same is true in matters of health. If our fixed belief is that the body is subject to all sorts of influences beyond our control, and that this, that, or the other symptom shows that such and such an uncontrollable influence is at work on us, then this belief impresses itself on the subjective mind, and the subjective mind accepts it without question and proceeds to fashion bodily conditions in accordance with the belief. Once we fully grasp this realization, we shall see that it is just as easy to externalize healthy conditions as it is the contrary.

What else do we believe we now know?

Our current incarnation is one of a long line than may date back to the first life on earth or another planet. Our physical bodies are projections of our morphic fields in combination with those of our parents and their genes, and the morphic field of our species. Some would say Earth is a kind of theme park for the Universal Mind, where it can play hide-and-seek with itself and experience the distraction of being in physical form. Because the Universal Mind is the opposite of entropy and does not play favorites, however, it seems more likely that Earth is a school where lessons are learned that help us to advance in evolution. When we die, our morphic fields — which are also our individual subconscious minds, or souls — will return to the spirit, or mental, realm. There, it is likely that we are members of a group on a similar level of evolution. These souls cooperate to help one another advance. Some souls on Earth in physical form, and others in the realm of spirit, work as teachers and guides to help others advance. Still others, such as Jesus, Moses or Buddha may be ascended masters who have returned to earth from time to time to help others find the way. It appears that Jesus was one such *bodhisattva* and the embodiment of the Christ Consciousness. This consciousness exists in spirit and is the likely end goal of earthly evolution. Jesus gave us the teachings we need and set the example. He showed us the way. No matter what path you follow, however, I think it's important to work toward the end goal in a systematic way.

Each lifetime on Earth usually has a particular purpose. It may be to learn a particular lesson. It may be to help others in some way. Some have missions they agreed to before an incarnation. When this is the case, the circumstances of one's life support the accomplishment of that mission.

A reader of the Akashic records at the School of Metaphysics told me that I have a mission and that it is one of leadership. In striving to learn just what this mission of leadership entails, I've earnestly tried to think back as far as I can to the very first thing I can remember. Occasionally, I've had glimpses of what may be my most recent previous life. One that recurs is being in an airplane, a World War II fighter. I'm the pilot. I'm in a tight bank desperately trying to outmaneuver an enemy aircraft diving from two o'clock with cannons blazing. (I'm not sure which side I'm on, but I'm either German or American. Not Italian, French, British or Japanese.) My plane is hit. I go into a spin.

To tell the truth, I don't know if this is actually a memory or a scene from some long-forgotten movie that I saw as a child. I was born in 1944, so the timing is right for either.

Once, when I was in France, I took a flight in a small plane piloted by an old man, a friend of my father-in-law, who offered to turn the controls over to me. He asked if I'd ever flown a plane.

"Never," I said.

"Here. Give it a try."

I did, and as I'd expected, it wasn't difficult. From the moment that I took the controls I was able to bank and turn.

The old man was amazed. "Go on," he said. "Keep going."

I circled the field we'd taken off from.

"Take her down," he said. "You can do it. Land the plane."

I continued to circle until the runway was directly ahead, then started down. A few hundred feet from touchdown, I lost my nerve, and returned the controls to him. But I'm almost certain I could have landed that plane.

He said he'd been flying more than fifty years and had never seen someone who hadn't flown a plane handle one as I'd just done. The vision flashed in my mind of being in the cockpit of that World War II fighter. I could almost feel my hands on the joystick.

I've had other experiences that seem to bring back memories of former lives. There is, for example, a castle in France that gives me a strong sense of déjá vu each time I approach. It's as though I'm returning from the Crusades.

Other places in France give off a similar sense of familiarity, but they are not from the same life. They are ancient sites where Druids lived, worked, and worshiped.

I was a Druid. I can feel it as surely as I feel eyes on my back. Even though I was born in America, my life unfolded in such a way that I was led to spend a good deal of time in France so I'd remember. Writing this book is the culmination of a process that began with a life or set of lives in pre-Christian Europe. My guides are friends from that epoch. The last time I saw their faces was the moment before I left the causal plane and grew this physical body. They were dressed in long purple-gray robes and were gathered close around me, laughing and joking. It was a kind of farewell party. They were kidding, jostling me, saying, "Don't worry, we'll be with you. Only you won't be able to see us. Not until you return." I haven't experienced anything close to that scene in this lifetime. I was bathed in a delightful aura of love so strong that it cannot be described. And joy. Such joy. Nothing comes close.

I do not remember being born, but I do remember looking up from my crib. Even then, I did not have the sensation of being the center of the universe that logic says an infant would. I knew I was separate and unique. I recall wondering where my friends were. I possessed no memory, but their faces flashed before me, and I felt snippets of the love and joy they had for me. I missed them. Where had they gone? I longed to be in the glow of their presence.

At last faces did appear and disappointment settled in. They were not my friends. I did not know these people whom I later came to realize were my mother and father, brother and sister.

And so began this incarnation. As I grew, I had the feeling it was in my power to work magic. I tried my hand at magic in small ways and it worked. But as I grew, I repeatedly was told that magic did not exist. Nothing that I couldn't see existed. Only matter was real. In time, I came to doubt myself and to believe what I was told. As my doubts and false beliefs increased, I lost it. Only now, after more than half a century, am I regaining the power bit by bit — as at last I pursue the mission I came to carry out.

I now have come to understand my mission is threefold: To be a guide to my sons and daughter until they no longer need me. To continue my own evolution. To help lead others to a clearer understanding of who and what we are. This is the purpose of this book. Up to this point in my life, this book represents the crux of my effort at leadership to a better and more complete understanding.

In other lives, you too knew why you were here. Not so long ago, when we Druids worshiped nature gods and cut mistletoe from the sacred oak tree with a golden knife, you looked up at the great arch of night sky and saw a million stars. This filled you with a sense of mystery. In the mornings, the sun miraculously rose in the east. Its rays shot across the heavens and lit the underbellies of clouds, pink and orange. In such moments, you understood that you were one tiny facet of a wondrous creation more astounding than words could convey. You felt communion with all that surrounded you. But unlike all that surrounded you, in some ways you felt separate and distinct. Even so, the owl, the deer, and other woodland creatures were your cousins, and you recognized them as such. You worshiped them, and their spirits, and they returned the favor by providing you with the food you ate and the clothes you wore and the covering for your dwelling that kept out rain and snow. The membrane that separated your mind and thoughts from the mind and thoughts of all creation was very thin — so thin that at times when you lay on your back and gazed at the stars, you felt yourself merge with your surroundings. At such times, you knew all. You knew your purpose. Creation and you were one single being. And this was ecstasy.

In time, though, you came to understand that you were different. Other creatures were driven by instincts, which were predictable. The course and timing of their migrations, their habits of reproduction and birth could be plotted like the seasons. These events were as sure to happen on schedule as the Summer and Winter Solstices. The animals had no choice. But you could behave as you pleased. You could stay another day, take a different route. Have your babies in the fall or winter.

Even so, you lived your life in accordance with the spirit that guided you with a higher understanding than your own. To do otherwise would have been foolhardy. And if you lost touch, if you were unable to contact the spirit on you own, the shaman or the Druid could be counted on to help you regain it.

Unconsciously, you knew your purpose. It was built into the cycles of time, of spring and summer and fall and winter, of birth and life and death and sleep. And rebirth. It was to grow and to evolve. It was to evolve and expand, to join with creation and eventually to become what you had come from. You would be a new creation. You would become so by remaining conscious of your separateness but rejoining and absorbing the all into yourself. It was the way of nature and could be seen in the deer and the rabbit and the bear. You had become separated from the mother of your soul as the woodland creatures had become separated from the mother of their birth. This was the way, the wheel of life, as surely as the seed that fell to earth would someday grow into a giant oak.

But time went by, incarnations came and went, and you lost sight. You lost the sense of sacredness of all-that-is, and you lost touch with your purpose. This was as it had to be. For your destiny was to grow and evolve to a state that encompasses all, while at the same time retaining your own identity. For this to be possible, it was essential that your sense of separation become strong and indelible. So you began to view the world not as one whole, but as separate pieces. It no longer seemed unified, but rather a collection of rocks, trees, individual plants and animals. Even the animals became to you as though they were constructed of distinct parts, such as hearts, eyes, kidneys and bones. You lost touch with the invisible. You ignored your intuition and the call of the spirit and came to believe the senses of the physical world provided what was needed for you to know and understand. Your separation was now utter and complete. You were lost and fell into deep despair. A sense of hopelessness descended upon you.

This was necessary. You had to lose your soul before you could find and reclaim it. But the state of being lost is dangerous. Now, you and others are in jeopardy of eternal separation. If you continue on a path away from your soul, you may wander much too far. When you next cross to the nonphysical plane, you may find that the way is not clear. You may be misled by entities you mistakenly believe to be benevolent, and they may gain power over you.

Humankind has reached this point on the spiritual journey. Like W. E. Butler's flock of sheep, we are slowly climbing the mountain. Not all will make it. The oak produces many acorns but only a small number reach self-actualization in the form of full grown trees. This is not difficult to understand. The way is hard. It requires courage, perseverance and a willingness to change. Man and woman hang onto their self-centeredness. It is not easy to let go. To grow requires sacrifice. And we are lazy. And often weak.

But laziness is not the only difficulty that must be overcome. We are surrounded by a culture that pushes us in the wrong direction.

The one constant message is to pursue success and happiness through what seems on the surface to be the most direct route. Grab all the gusto you can get. Get your fair share. Or more. Go for the gold. These are the battle cries.

But like Katie's brass, it is fool's gold.

Not until our intuition and our experience communicate the error of this thinking are we free to follow the correct path. Indeed, there is hope; one branch of science, quantum physics, denies the very existence of what society tells us we should pursue — materialism. Quantum physics says there is no material as such, but rather that matter is energy when we look beyond surface illusion.

Moreover, all creation is one connected whole, with no separate pieces. We are the whole, and the whole is us. What happens here influences what happens there, even if it is halfway across the galaxy. Energy takes time to travel, but information is transmitted instantaneously because only one mind exists. A slit that is opened changes the field, provided someone knows that it is open. The act of observing changes the outcome because the known cannot be separated from the knower.

We are creatures of the mental realm, the dimension that supports and informs physical reality. Without this realm, nothing on the physical plane would exist. The nonphysical comprises morphic fields which contain the history of each species. Someday these fields' existence will be demonstrated scientifically. They contain information which shapes our noses, our feet, and our world. The overall field is composed of fields within fields within fields.

Your soul is a field that has been built to its present state over many incarnations. You came out of it and will return to it. Your present physical body is a projection of this field. Your destiny is to keep your identity, this field, intact, but eventually to encompass all.

For many millennia, you existed in the mineral world. You evolved into human form from the first one-celled animal that lived in the sea. You were part of the field and at one with the whole until you realized yourself to be separate.

Then, as now, you created your own reality. You are who you believe yourself to be in your heart. Just as a tree is known by its fruit, you can know yourself by where you are today. You arrived here through your own actions, whether you took them consciously or unconsciously. You must accept and take responsibility for yourself if you are to advance. If you do not like yourself, you must forgive yourself and resolve to begin anew, remembering that you get back what you give. Give kindness. Receive kindness. Pay respect, receive it. Bestow wealth, be wealthy. Hold love in your heart for yourself and others, and love will come back to you. Hold hate or bitterness, and your life will be filled with bitterness and hate.

To change, you must forgive. You must forgive yourself as well as others.

You came into the physical world to learn this because you needed the thickness of matter to slow down the process of creating your world. In this way, you learn lessons that remain with you.

Love is what you must learn. Once you have learned to love perfectly, without selfishness or hesitation, the time for a new creation will be at hand. You will become part of that and will continue to evolve. Or you may not. The choice is yours. Until you learn to love unselfishly, you will continue on the wheel of life and death and rebirth.

Remember, too, that your fears block you as surely as bitterness and hate do. Therefore you must learn to trust. Put yourself and your fate in the hands of the Divine. Once you learn to trust rather than to fear, and once you learn to love instead of to hate, the channel between your ego self and your subconscious mind will open wide. This will lead to a new Self.

Life is the dream of God, and you are a dreamer in that dream. You have a role or roles to play. Before you arrived, you took them on and made a solemn vow to carry them out. You can either make good on your promise, or you can welsh. If you welsh, you will view the consequences when the time comes for your life to be replayed before you, your judges and your guides. You may or may not be given another go at getting it right.

But getting it right won't be easy. To get started, you must clear the junk from your mental attic. You must forgive yourself and others. You must get past your fears and replace them with positive belief. You must learn to trust. You must commit to change. You must be willing to suffer hardships. You must give up the "certainties" of the world you have created.

You can begin by devoting a half-hour once, perhaps twice each day to meditation. In between, keep listening to the still small voice. When you review your life, you will think about the decisions that brought you here. Were they the right decisions? Did you feel good after you made them?

Do you like where you are?

You will try to discover why your subconscious mind chose the circumstances of your birth. You will think back to what you loved to do as a child. You will ask for guidance, and you will receive it. You will follow your bliss.

First, you will follow the direction you receive in making small decisions. Eventually you will follow the gentle voice you come to know inside as you make the big ones. This will be frightening at first. It will be frightening because you will not know your destination, and you will not know how you will get there, wherever there may be. But after a while, after you have learned how to trust, not knowing will become part of the fun, like opening packages at Christmas. You will be on an adventure as thrilling as any attempted by Indiana Jones. You will be the director of your own lucid dream.

Or you may finish this book, put it down and forget about it. No doubt this is what many will do. They've spent their lives doing what others told them. They've carved out a place for themselves. It isn't all that exciting or fulfilling, and it can be difficult. But they've become comfortable with who and what they are. Why change? There's no proof they're in danger of getting so far away from their subconscious mind that they may never find the way back. No conclusive proof can be produced that a nonphysical realm exists.

No scientific experiment shows that any part of a human being survives death. Those who died and were resuscitated? Some scientists say it was all in their heads. A trick of the brain; a lack of oxygen. Besides, it's so much trouble to change. And what would people think? Things are comfortable the way they are. Life isn't so bad. Why rock the boat? And this Martin fellow says that once a person gets started, he or she won't want to stop, and may end up changing completely, as though all they wanted was to remodel the kitchen and ended up rebuilding the entire house.

Sun room done? Now how about the den? Oh, and you need a wing off to the side. And a second-level master bedroom with sky lights and a fireplace.

All the while this renovation is going on, dust and debris are piling up, and the person occupying the house has to live in the middle of it.

"Wait a minute, I had a nice little bungalow," you may be tempted to say. "All I wanted was a new kitchen. You're turning this into a mansion. When will the job be complete?"

The architect, your subconscious mind, will shake his head and say, "Not for a very long time, I'm afraid. You'd best get used to it."

Maybe you don't want a mansion. If this is the way you feel, I doubt there's anything I can say now to change your mind. You might as well stick with the bungalow.

I'll tell you something from personal experience, though. There is no greater joy in life than doing what you are here to do. Getting there may be difficult, it's true. But if you listen and persevere, if you earnestly follow the path laid down, you will receive help. After a while you will begin to sense unseen hands guiding you and the way will become less difficult to find. The trials won't be as hard to bear. There will be blind alleys, of course. There will be disappointments. There will be tough lessons to learn, but gradually you will come to a gut level understanding of what your existence as a human being is about. You will come to a gut level understanding of how you fit into the scheme. You will feel at one with it all and yet maintain your sense of self. You will come to know what you are doing. You will see outcomes materializing well before they arrive. You will choose what to pursue and what to avoid.

When you arrive at this point, you will realize that you have come to power, spiritual power, and with this realization will come joy. Can you imagine the buoyancy you'll feel? Whether it's mastery of a sport such as tennis, mastery of the card game of bridge, a musical instrument or a foreign language, the arrival at the state of really knowing what you are doing always brings joy.

The riches of the universe, which are in fact non material, will flow effortlessly to you because you are working with the universe, instead of rowing against the current.

And health. Your body will respond to the new life you've found. No longer will there be any reason for aches and pains. No longer will there be any thought of or reason to contemplate the possibility of death, for you are on the path to Eternal Life. You will be a vibrant, living cell in the larger body of humankind, fulfilling your purpose and your promise. You will grow every day and help others do the same.

Yet with all this will come a sense of deep humility because you will know that it is not you who brought you here. It is your subconscious mind and the mind of God. Perhaps there will be some small pride in knowing that you finally have learned how to listen. But you will be careful to guard against feeling a sense of pride in any form. One of the lessons you will have learned on the way is that support is withdrawn from those who believe they are accomplishing great things on their own. The saying, "Pride goes before a fall," is true. The prideful soon learn how little they can accomplish on their own.

There will also come a sense of aloneness. Not loneliness, because you will have friends, you will have family, you will have others on the path. But few, if any, will have arrived where you have arrived. Few will be the number with whom you can share your feelings and insights. Few will understand them completely. If you want a sense of what this is like, read the Gospels. Time and again you will witness the frustration Jesus experienced. Often, even his closest Apostles could not grasp the truth of his words.

Despite all this, there will be a new, deep understanding of your true worth. It will be impossible to continue to think of yourself as meaningless or insignificant once you understand that grace exists for you, that guides are constantly with you, that you and the universal subconsicous mind are one, and that in reality you are the very Force of Life itself seeking expression and self awareness.

In closing, let me say that my wish, my prayer, my hope is that you will put to work the special talents and gifts that only you possess for the benefit of the greater whole and for creation. My wish is that you will answer the call to adventure when it comes, and in so doing enter with me into what Jesus called God's Kingdom.

Until now, perhaps, fear and doubt have been holding you back. Now you know you have much more to fear by rejecting the call. You know that by answering the call you choose life over death. You now know that the forces of the universe will fold in behind you and give you their support. You will be pulled forward and be pushed along by the hands of grace. Each step will be guided. All you need do is be aware, be watchful, and *expect* things to break your way. Stay the course. Believe. As you grow more and more attuned, as you put your talents to work in the service of others, abundance will begin to flow. You will find new joy and be led to Eternal Life, now and forever.

I feel sadness for Scientific Materialists and nihilists, whom I suppose are inevitably one and the same. If they hold on to the belief that the purpose of life is the mindless duplication of DNA, how meaningless and insignificant they must believe themselves and others to be. How hopeless and yawning must be the gulf of separation of their ego minds from their souls. Surely, the anguish and anxiety they experience daily is intense.

And to what end?

They'll be in for a surprise at death. And perhaps not a happy one. Instead of the end of their consciousness, their consciousness will leave their bodies. And where will it go? A friend of mine, a psychic, won't go near graveyards because of all the confused souls who hang around the plots of ground where their bodies are planted. These lost souls don't know what to do or where to go. And if by chance they somehow enter the tunnel that leads to the next plane of existence, they may find it completely dark—indeed according to Betty Eadie's experience recounted in *Embrace by the Light* they may be unable to see the light at the end of it. Imagine their desperation when, contrary to their expectations, there's no end to the end of their lives.

I feel gladness for you and joy that I might have been a conduit in bringing a deeper understanding of yourself. Now you know who you are, where you are going, and what the possiblities are. My sincere wish is that my efforts have helped you make that vital shift. Thanks for spending this time with me.

Keep moving ahead, keep expanding your awareness. Remember always to look for the light. Expect it to be there, and it will. Go for it.

Remember always: As you believe, so will it be for you.

And don't worry about December 21, 2012. Just remember, no matter what happens, you are eternal. Nothing can change that.

And, please, whatever you do, *share* what you have learned. Share with those you love, share with your neighbors, share with coworkers. This, more than anything, will be what fulfills the prophecy of the end of the world as we know it and the beginning of a new and better reality.

There's another way you can help the world move closer to that reality, today. Don't put this book on the shelf to gather dust. Give it to someone and ask them to read it.

And tell them, please, to pass it on.

Bibliography

Alexander, David and Pat, *Eerdmans Handbook to the Bible*, William B. Eerdmans Publishing Company, Grand Rapids, 1973 and 1983

Allen, James, *As a Man Thinketh*, Peter Pauper Press, Mount Vernon, New York, circa 1904

Anderson, U. S., *The Secret of Secrets*, Thomas Nelson, & Son, New York, 1958

Armstrong, Karen, *A History of God*, Alfred A. Knopf, Inc., New York, 1993

Backster, Cleve, *Primary Perception: Bio Communication with Plants, Living Foods, and Human Cells*, White Rose Millennium Press, 2003

Bohm, David, *Wholeness and the Implicate Order*, Rutledge & Kegan, London, 1980

Braude, Stephen E., *THE GOLD LEAF LADY AND OTHER PARAPSYCHOLOGICAL INVESTIGATIONS*, Chicago University Press, 2007

Braude, Stephen E., *Immortal Remains: The Evidence for Life After Death*, Rowman & Littlefield Publishers, Inc., 2003

Butler, W. E., *Lords of Light*, Destiny books, Rochester, Vermont, 1990

Campbell, Joseph with Bill Moyers, *The Power of Myth*, Doubleday, New York, 1988

Campbell, Joseph, *The Portable Jung*, Viking Press, New York, 1971

Carter, Chris, *PARAPSYCHOLOGY AND THE SKEPTICS: A Scientific Argument for the Existence of ESP*, SterlingHouse Books, 2007

Chopra, Deepak, *Ageless Body, Timeless Mind*, Harmony Books, Crown, New York, 1993

Conner, Sibella, "The Dark Side of Near Death," *Richmond Times-Dispatch*, September 4, 1994, pages G1 and G4.

Dass, Ram, *Journey of Awakening*, Bantam New Age Books, New York, 1978

Eadie, Betty J., *Embraced By The Light*, Gold Leaf Press, Placerville, California, 1992

Gibran, Kahlil, *The Prophet*, Knopf, New York, 1993

Goldberg, Philip, *The Intuitive Edge*, Jeremy P. Tarcher, Inc., Los Angeles, 1983

Gould, Stephen Jay, *The Panda's Thumb*, W. W. Norton & Company, New York, 1980

Herrigel, Eugen, *Zen in the Art of Archery*, Panteon Books, Random House, New York, 1953

Hill, Napoleon, *Think and Grow Rich*, Fawcett Crest, New York, 1960

Howe, Quincy, Jr., *Reincarnation for the Christian*, The Westminster Press, Philadelphia, 1974

Johnston, William, *The Inner Eye of Love*, Harper & Row, New York, 1978

Karpinski, Gloria D., *Where Two Worlds Touch*, Ballantine, New York, 1990

Keyes, Ken Jr., *Handbook to Higher Consciousness*, Fifth Edition, Love Line Books, Coos Bay, Oregon, 1975

Kubler-Ross, Elisabeth, *On Life After Death*, Celestial Arts, Berkeley, California. 1991

McTaggart, Lynne, *THE FIELD: The Quest for the Secret Force of the Universe*, Harper Paperbacks, 2008

McTaggart, Lynne, *The INTENTION EXPERIMENT: Using Your Thoughts to Change Your Life and the World*, Free Press , 2007

Monroe, Robert A., *Far Journeys*, Souvenir Press, Ltd., London, 1985

Moody, Raymond A., M. D., *The Light Beyond*, Bantam, New York, 1988

Morse, Melvin, M.D. (with Paul Perry), *Closer to the Light*, Ballantine Books, New York, 1990

Newton, Michael. Ph.D., *Journey of Souls*, Llewellyn, St. Paul, Minnesota,1994

Parker, DeWitt H., *Schopenhauer Selections*, Charles Scribners Sons, New York, 1928

Peck, M. Scott, *The Road Less Traveled*, Simon and Schuster, New York, 1978

Peck, M. Scott, *Further Along The Road Less Traveled*, Simon and Schuster, New York, 1993

Peat, F. David, *The Philosopher's Stone*, Bantam, New York, 1991

Reid, James A., *BORN AGAIN AND AGAIN AND AGAIN: A Bible-Based View of Reincarnation, getpulished.com*, 2001

Schwartz, Stephan A., *OPENING TO THE INFINITE: The Art and Science of Nonlocal Awareness*, Nemoseen Media, 2007

Sheehy, Gail, *Passages: Predictable Crises of Adult Life*, Dutton, New York, 1976

Sheldrake, Rupert, *The Rebirth of Nature, The Greening of Science and God*, Bantam, New York, 1991

Smith, Huston, *The Religions of Man*, HarperCollins, New York, 1986

Smith, E. Lester, *Intelligence Came First*, Theosophical Publishing House, Wheaton, Illinois, 1975

Spindrift Papers, *Exploring Prayer and Healing Through the Experimental Test*, Volume I 1975-1993, Spindrift, Inc., Ft. Lauderdale, Florida

Strapp, Henry P. *MINDFUL UNIVERSE: Quantum Mechanics and the Participating Observer*, Springer, 2007

Stevenson, Ian, *Where Reincarnation and Biology Intersect*, Praeger Publishing, 1997

Stevenson, Ian, *Twenty Cases Suggestive of Reincarnation*, University Press of Virginia, Charlottesville, 1974

Troward, Thoma; Allen, James; Martin, Stephen Hawley, *How to Master Life: The Science Behind The Secret,* "The Edinburgh Lectures on Mental Science" and "As a Man Thinketh," Oaklea Press, 2007

Wade, Nicholas, "Double Helixes, Chickens and Eggs," *New York Times Magazine,* January 29, 1995

Watts, Alan, *The Book,* Vintage Books, Random House, New York, 1966

Weiss, Brian L., M.D., *Many Lives, Many Masters,* Simon & Schuster, New York, 1988

Zukav, Gary, *The Dancing Wu Li Masters,* Bantam, New York, 1979

Zukav, Gary, *The Seat of the Soul,* Simon & Schuster, New York, 1989

INDEX

Stephen Hawley Martin *is a cofounder and former principal of a major advertising firm, The Martin Agency, now boasting such clients as Wal-Mart, UPS, and GEICO. His books have won a total of six national awards for excellence. His weekly radio show, THE TRUTH ABOUT LIFE, can be heard on demand by visiting* **SHMartin.com** *and clicking on "Listen to Steve on the Radio" in the left-hand column.*